ECONOMIC POLICY and STABILIZATION in LATIN AMERICA

ECONOMIC POLICY and STABILIZATION in LATIN AMERICA

NADER NAZMI

Routledge
Taylor & Francis Group

LONDON AND NEW YORK

First published 1996 by M.E. Sharpe

Published 2015 by Routledge
2 Park Square, Milton Park, Abingdon, Oxon OX14 4RN
711 Third Avenue, New York, NY 10017, USA

Routledge is an imprint of the Taylor & Francis Group, an informa business

Library of Congress Cataloging-in-Publication Data

Nazmi, Nader, 1960–
Economic policy and stabilization in Latin America / Nader Nazmi.
p. cm.
Includes bibliographical references and index.
ISBN 1-56324-583-3 (hc : alk. paper).—ISBN 1-56324-584-1 (pbk. : alk. paper)
1. Economic stabilization—Latin America—Case studies.
2. Inflation (Finance)—Latin America—Case studies.
3. Monetary policy—Latin America—Case studies.
4. Latin America—Economic policy—Case studies.
I. title.
HC125.N39   1995
339.5′098—dc20
95-30476
CIP

ISBN 13: 9781563245848 (pbk)
ISBN 13: 9781563245831 (hbk)

To
Corinna

Contents

Tables and Figures   ix
Acknowledgments   xiii
Introduction   3

1. Causes and Consequences of Inflation in Latin America   13
   Introduction   13
   The Monetarist and the New Classical Models   16
   The Neostructuralist Theory of Inflation   23
   Empirical Evidence   28
   The Costs of Inflation   30
   Conclusion   36

2. The Brazilian Experience with Inflation: 1964–94   38
   Introduction   38
   Inflation under Military Regimes: 1964–85   39
   The Cruzado Plan   47
   The Bresser Plan and the Summer Plan   52
   The Collor Plan   55
   The Real Plan   64
   Conclusion   68

3. Chile: Economic Reform, Transformation, and Progress   71
   Introduction   71
   Damage Control and Economic Stabilization: 1973–78   72
   The Exchange Rate Stabilization Anchor and the
      Mini-Miracle: 1978–81   75
   Economic Crises: 1981–84   77
   A Decade of Reform and Growth: 1985–94   79
   Conclusion   85

4. **Mexico: Reform and Stability**   **87**
   Introduction   87
   From Stabilizing Development to Economic Instability   88
   The 1982–87 Economic Crises   92
   The Long Road to Stabilization   100
   Economic Stability for Whom?   108
   Conclusion   111

5. **Argentina and Bolivia: The Road from Inflation to**
   Stabilization   **112**
   Introduction   112
   Modern Stabilization Policies in Argentina   113
   The Bolivian Experience: From Hyperinflation to
       Stabilization   126
   Conclusion   132

6. **Empirical Analysis of Inflation: Evidence from**
   Error-Correction Modeling and VAR Models   **135**
   Introduction   135
   The Model   136
   The Data and Testing for Stationarity   141
   Cointegration and Error-Correction Modeling   142
   Empirical Analysis of the Inertial Component of Inflation   151
   Conclusion   162

7. **Conclusions**   **165**
   Why Fight Inflation?   165
   How to Fight Inflation?   166
   Restoring Fiscal Balance   167
   The Choice of Nominal Anchors   169
   From Stabilization to Growth   170

Notes   172
Bibliography   183
Index   199
About the Author   207

Tables and Figures

Tables

I.1   Basic Economic Indicators: Argentina, Bolivia, Brazil, and
      Mexico   4
I.2   Economic Growth and Inflation in Selected Countries   10
2.1   Annual Rate of Inflation (December to December) and Rate
      of Money Expansion (Fourth Quarter to Fourth Quarter),
      1960–70   40
2.2   Government Expenditure and Inflation Rates, 1974–85   43
2.3   Balance of Payments, 1978–86   45
2.4   Monthly Inflation Rate, Exchange Rate, and Trade Balance:
      1986–87   54
2.5   Key Domestic Variables and the Collor Plan, 1990:1–1991:4   55
2.6   The Rate of Inflation and Liquidity, 1970–89   57
2.7   Revenues, Expenditure, and Surplus/Deficit, 1986:1–1991:12   60
2.8   Average Capacity Utilization for Various Industries, 1988–90 63
2.9   Capital Inflow, 1992–94   66
3.1   Major Macroeconomic Variables for Chile, 1970–94   73
3.2   Total External Debt, 1970–87   77
3.3   The Performance of the Chilean Export Sector: 1986 and 1991 80
3.4   Exports of Mining Products, 1988–94   81
3.5   Chilean Forestry Production and Exports, 1980–93   82
3.6   Chile's Exports of Livestock and Agricultural Products,
      1983–94   82
3.7   Chile's Imports Breakdown, 1988–94   84
4.1   Nominal GDP, Real GDP, GDP Growth Rates, and Inflation
      Rate, 1970–93   93
4.2   External Sector Performance: Current Account, Merchandise
      Exports and Imports, Trade Balance, and Balance of
      Payments, 1960–90   94

4.3	Mexican Oil Price, Export Volume, and Revenues, 1980–89	95
4.4	Public Sector Indicators As a Percentage of GDP, 1983–92	101
4.5	Foreign Debt Indicators, 1970–89	106
4.6	Income Distribution in Mexico, 1984–92	
4.7	Public Sector Expenditure on Social Programs As a	109
	Percentage of Total Budgeted Expenditure	110
4.8	Government Expenditure in 1980 Pesos by Category,	
	1983–90	110
5.1	Argentina: GDP Per Capita Annual Growth Rates and	
	Annual Inflation Rates, 1976–1985	114
5.2	Prices, Inflation, and Government Deficit in Argentina,	
	1985:1–1990:12	120
5.3	Monthly Inflation Rate in Argentina, 1990:1–1991:12	124
5.4	Money, Exchange Rate, Prices, and Industrial Production for	
	Bolivia, 1974:1–1990:4	128
5.5	Real GDP, Population, GDP Per Capita, and Change in GDP	
	Per Capita for Bolivia, 1985–92	133
6.1	Perron-Phillips Tests for Unit Root with No Trend and Lag = 4	142
6.2	Eigenvalues, Maximal Eigenvalue Statistics, and Eigenvalue	
	Trace Statistics for Cointegration Analysis of Inflation	
	Equation	144
6.3	General Autoregressive Distributed Lag Model for Prices,	
	Agricultural Prices, Money, Wages, Interest Rate, Exchange	
	Rate, and Imports Prices	147
6.4	Eigenvalues, Maximal Eigenvalue Statistics, and Eigenvalue	
	Trace Statistics for Cointegration Analysis of Money	
	Demand Function	147
6.5	General Autoregressive Distributed Lag Model for Real	
	Money, Income, Expected Inflation, Interest Rate, and	
	Inflation	149
6.6	Eigenvalues, Maximal Eigenvalue Statistics, and Eigenvalue	
	Trace Statistics for Cointegration Analysis of Exchange Rate	
	Equation	149
6.7	General Autoregressive Distributed Lag Model for Exchange	
	Rate, Price Differential, Money Differential, Income	
	Differential, and Interest Rate Differential	150
6.8	The Final Error-Correction Model for Inflation	153
6.9	Composition of Forecast Error Variance for Inflation	162
6.10	Historical Decomposition of Brazilian Inflation,	
	1978:1–1985:4	163

Figures

1.1	Welfare Cost of Anticipated Inflation	31
2.1	Quarterly Rates of Inflation, 1975–90	39
2.2	Trade Balance and Balance of Payments, 1986:1–1987:4	50
2.3	Monthly Budget Deficit (Nominal Government Revenues—Nominal Government Expenditures): 1986:3–1986:12	51
2.4	Monthly Government Revenues, Expenditures, and Surplus (Deficit), 1989:1–1990:12	59
2.5	Brazilian International Reserves, 1987–94	67
2.6	Monthly Rates of Inflation, 1992:6–1994:12	67
3.1	High-Powered Money, 1977:1–1982:4	76
3.2	Public Investment in Infrastructure, 1987–90	83
3.3	Real Urban Minimum Wage: Annual Index	83
4.1	Peso Devaluations and Mexico–U.S. Inflation Gap, 1981:1–1989:12	96
4.2	Inflation and Percentage Change in Nominal Minimum Salary	104
4.3	Real Wages (Annual Average and December-December), 1983–93	104
4.4	Monetary Aggregates and Inflation, 1984–93	107
5.1	Argentine Inflation Rate, 1978:1–1985:12	119
5.2	Quarterly Inflation Rates in Bolivia: 1984:1–1986:4	131
6.1	Actual and Estimated Rates of Inflation in Brazil: Long-Term Dynamics of Inflation	146
6.2	Actual and Estimated Changes in the Brazilian Inflation Rate: Short-Term Dynamics of Inflation	152
6.3	Inflation Response to Price Innovation Based on VAR	155
6.4	Inflation Response to Money Innovation Based on VAR	155
6.5	Inflation Response to Wage Innovation Based on VAR	156
6.6	Inflation Response to Exchange Rate Innovation Based on VAR	156
6.7	Inflation Response to Own Innovation with Only I(0) Variables and VAR Model	157
6.8	Inflation Response to Money Innovation with Only I(0) Variables and VAR Model	157
6.9	Inflation Response to Wage Innovation with Only I(0) Variables	158
6.10	Inflation Response to Exchange Rate Innovation with Only I(0) Variables	158

6.11 Inflation Response to Own Innovation with Only I(0)
      Variables and SVAR Model   160
6.12 Inflation Response to Money Innovation with Only I(0)
      Variables and SVAR Model   160
6.13 Inflation Response to Wage Innovation with Only I(0)
      Variables and SVAR Model   161
6.14 Inflation Response to Exchange Rate Innovation with
      Only I(0) Variables and SVAR Model   161

Acknowledgments

A book such as this naturally brings its author many debts. The research for this book began four years ago with generous funding provided by a CICALS grant from Michigan State University. A Fulbright–Hayes Research Grant supported my in-country study in Brazil. Parts of this book were written while I was a visiting scholar at the Center for Research on Economic Development at the University of Michigan. Various research grants from Lake Forest College made my travels to Argentina and Mexico possible. The University of São Paulo and El Colegio de México made their research and library facilities available to me with great courtesy. To all these institutions I remain indebted.

My debts to individuals, too, are considerable. I am especially grateful to Bruno and Hilda Gut for their exceptional hospitality. Many individuals have read various parts of this book and have given me helpful comments and suggestions. While thanking all these individuals, without implicating, I am particularly grateful to William Moskoff, William Gruben, Eliana Cardoso, Werner Baer, Albert Fishlow, Miguel Ramírez, Paul Newbold, and Lydia Paulini for their input. Very special thanks should go to Corinna, for everything.

ECONOMIC POLICY and STABILIZATION in LATIN AMERICA

Introduction

The 1980s were years of unusual hardship for the people and economies of Latin America. Repeated external shocks and domestic economic mismanagement combined to bring about the most devastating decade in modern Latin American history. During this decade, living standards fell sharply as real per capita income dropped considerably, the debt problem assumed unforgiving magnitudes, and inflation reigned triumphant (see Table I.1).

In response to these conditions, Latin American countries have employed a wide variety of stabilization blueprints in an effort to restore economic balance and control inflation. In addition to stabilization attempts, some countries introduced unprecedented reform programs aimed at revitalizing their economies. The short-term stabilization efforts, together with the longer-term structural reforms, comprise the so-called adjustment programs. While these programs have generally resulted in stabilization, in most cases they have failed to restore economic growth.

The profound economic crisis that engulfed Latin American countries during the 1980s and early 1990s, and policy responses to it, offer important lessons for understanding the causes of macroeconomic instability and for choosing policies that restore economic equilibrium and growth. First, the Latin American experience allows us to explore the intricate relationship between economic stability and economic growth. Second, it helps us identify the origins of high inflation. Third, it provides broad guidelines for ending chronic inflation and hyperinflation. Fourth, from the Latin American vantage point we can draw general conclusions about the impact of inflation and stabilization on income distribution and poverty. Finally, the Latin American experience can help us choose pro-growth policies.

The 1980s witnessed an important controversy between the orthodox and heterodox (nonmainstream) camps regarding what types of economic pro-

Table I.1

Basic Economic Indicators: Argentina, Bolivia, Brazil, and Mexico

Country	Human development rank	GDP (1990 US$—bil.)	GNP/ capita annual rate of growth (1980—90)	Average annual inflation rate (1980—90)	Percentage of GDP (1990) in government expenditure as % of GDP	Agriculture	Industry	Services
Argentina	46	93.3	−1.8	395.1	13	41	46	16
Bolivia	122	4.5	−2.6	318.4	24	32	44	19
Brazil	70	414.1	0.6	284.4	10	39	51	36
Mexico	53	237.8	−0.9	70.4	9	30	61	18

grams were more suitable for fighting the perils of inflation, instability, and low economic growth. In chapter 1, we shall see how each of these schools diagnosed the root causes of inflation differently and prescribed fundamentally different policies for fighting inflation. Here, we give a brief overview of the orthodox approach and sketch possible alternatives to it.

During the 1960s and 1970s, the International Monetary Fund (IMF) and conservative think tanks recommended an orthodox approach to economic management to Latin American countries based on the Chicago school monetarist framework.[1] Inflation was considered to be a strictly monetary phenomenon, and long-term economic growth could not be engineered through fiscal or monetary policies. At a time when even President Richard Nixon adhered to Keynesian economics, the monetarist view did not enjoy consensus support in Washington. But as the Keynesian paradigm collapsed,[2] the monetarist view as set forth by Milton Friedman and Arnold Harberger found its way from Chicago to Washington. There it found common ground with (1) a powerful position in favor of free trade developed by, *inter alia*, Ballasa, Kruger, and Bhagwati, (2) the rational expectation/new classical model pioneered by Lucas and Sargent, and (3) the public-choice school of James Buchanan, to form the contemporary orthodox approach to economics.[3] Today the support pillars of the orthodox view in Washington include the United States government, the Federal Reserve Board, and the IMF and its sister institution, the World Bank—a combination of heavyweights that give the neoliberal perspective unparalleled political and financial clout.

While support for the orthodox view spreads far beyond the Washington Beltway, here we use Williamson's (1990b) "Washington consensus" to identify the neoliberal perspective. The ten ingredients for an economic management recipe that is to Washington's liking, as set forth by Williamson (1990), combine to create a policy mix that is decidedly in favor of relying on the market system, opening the economy to foreign competition and foreign investment, securing property rights, and maintaining fiscal balance.

The Washington consensus requires the government to adhere to fiscal discipline through keeping its spending low and by introducing a broad-based taxation system with low marginal rates. In achieving fiscal balance, the government is expected to redirect its spending priorities from subsidies to education and human capital development. Washington also strongly supports privatization programs that reduce the role of the state in the economy.

Measures designed to strengthen the market system include the introduction of well-defined, secure property rights, widespread deregulation aimed at promoting competition, and the implementation of reform programs that enable market forces to determine interest rates, exchange rates, and wages. Finally, Washington insists on opening the economy to the world marketplace and encouraging foreign capital inflow.[4]

To these guidelines, others have added new principles such as: (1) the implementation of the "right" macroeconomic policy, which includes market-based incentives for increasing saving and investment and the introduction of a social safety net;[5] (2) an allowance for market-friendly, open, and reluctant government intervention in education, infrastructure, population control, environmental protection, and poverty relief;[6] (3) the proper "sequencing" of policies, such that stabilization is followed by adjustment and growth;[7] and (4) devaluation of the domestic currency together with the elimination of multiple exchange rates.[8]

According to the orthodox or neoliberal perspective, adherence to the basic "ten commandments" put forth by the Washington consensus brings about economic stability and growth. Policymakers and economists who do not believe in the orthodox view, because of repeated failures of neoliberals to deliver the promised state of the economy, have long played an important role in shaping Latin American economies policy. The structuralist approach, which found its origins in the United Nations Economic Commission for Latin America (ECLA), was the most influential alternative to orthodox prescriptions.

Prior to the 1980s, for decades the structuralist view of Latin American economies played a prominent role in designing policy.[9] The structuralist perspective, as pioneered by Raul Prebisch and his associates,[10] espoused a vision of Latin America very different from the orthodox view. From the observation that the terms of trade (price of exports relative to the price of imports) for Latin American countries were deteriorating, the structuralists concluded that free trade was detrimental to the economies of Latin America and recommended inward-looking industrialization policies. Because they detected widespread market imperfections such as oligopolistic competition and production bottlenecks, the structuralists discounted exclusive reliance on market forces. They identified institutional factors, production bottlenecks, and market imperfections as causes of underdevelopment, inflation, and instability. They assigned a significant role to the state by requiring it to have a well-defined policy aimed at rapid industrialization.[11] This industrialization was to be achieved through the domestic production of previously imported products.

Structuralism, as an intellectual and policy force, lost much of its luster with the crises of import-substitution industrialization and development economics. The economic protectionism that ruled during the 1960s, 1970s, and 1980s in the form of import-substitution industrialization yielded during the 1980s to policies that favored free trade. This transition occurred for three reasons: (1) import-substitution industrialization, which was supposed to protect Latin American countries from the negative impact of external shocks, made these countries especially vulnerable to such shocks by relying on inward-looking policies that undermined external competitiveness; (2) empirical evidence, both from substantial analysis of data and from country studies, spelled a strong preference for free trade; and (3) policymakers, especially in Washington, made a firm commitment to the ideals of free trade and made trade liberalization a prerequisite for new funding.

Economic Commission for Latin America (ECLA), once a structuralist stronghold and a strong proponent of import substitution, became a free-trade advocate in the 1990s as it became clear that countries with more liberal trade policies outperformed more closed economies. Even the vocabulary pioneered by the structuralists was seized by Washington. Whereas for structuralists "structural bottlenecks" signified market failures that needed to be corrected through government intervention and through "structural change," to Washington "structural flaws" were caused by government intervention in the marketplace, and "structural change" meant market reforms that drastically reduce government's role in the economy.[12]

Despite the demise of structuralism as a dominant paradigm in Latin America, opposition to the orthodox approach has not disappeared. Taylor (1993) suggests nine points on which a "non-Washington consensus" can be built:

1. Fiscal equilibrium is desirable but the links between fiscal, foreign, and savings gaps should be recognized. This recognition implies that foreign resources may be needed for attaining equilibrium. Moreover, distributional and political aspects of fiscal equilibrium need a closer scrutiny.
2. Getting the prices (exchange rate, interest rates, wages) right is neither easy nor without cost.
3. Wage reductions that result from economic reforms may have adverse effects on socioeconomic and human-capital development of developing nations.
4. The orthodox interpretation of sound macroeconomic policy—that is, austerity—may result in an anemic state and economic stagnation.
5. Privatization is not in itself desirable.
6. External liberalization is not always superior to intelligent use of quotas and controls.
7. While a better-educated, better-paid, and healthier labor force is

needed for long-term economic growth, human-capital development does not bring about short-run economic expansion.

8. Stabilization prior to adjustment may not always be the correct sequencing.

9. Preset blueprints for macroeconomic policymaking do not apply to all cases. Each country has its own set of historical circumstances and institutional norms that need to be taken into consideration when designing policy.

Along the same lines, Bresser Pereira (1993) sets forth a "social-democratic" or "pragmatic" approach to economic reform. According to this approach, stabilization and structural adjustment policies should restore the health of the state, which can then actively pursue development policies. Moreover, reform packages should institute a social protection system for those who are likely to suffer from the consequences of reform. Finally, reform measures should be arrived at through open and democratic dialogue in the society.

Most alternatives to the neoliberal perspective share the philosophy that exclusive reliance on markets does not result in optimum social outcomes. Markets may fail to allocate resources effectively. Moreover, the social return to certain crucial investments such as infrastructure and education may exceed the private return to such investments. The resulting free-rider (externality) problem translates into a reluctance on the part of the private sector to make the needed investments.

For these reasons, the state, if freed from its fiscal crises, can and should play an important role in shaping the economic destiny of Latin American and Third World countries. The state should serve as a coordinator, not necessarily an engine, of development. It should invest in projects that complement private investments, fight the poverty problem, and find solutions to the problem of income and wealth distribution. In order to secure long-run economic growth, the state should aggressively invest in human-capital development. Finally, alternatives to the Washington consensus question the premise that free trade is always superior to managed trade where, for example, the domestic market is protected while exports are promoted.[13]

In spite of differences that persist between neoliberals and supporters of alternatives to the Washington consensus, during the past few years a general agreement has emerged that the *sine qua non* of stabilization is fiscal balance. Moreover, a consensus regarding the need for secondary stabilization tools in the presence of inflation inertia has developed. In particular, it is now widely recognized that nonorthodox measures of exchange-rate and price-and-wage freezes may be necessary to bring inflation under control immediately. Some economists, especially neostructuralists (see chapter 1), believe that this need arises from structural idiosyncrasies, such as indexation of nominal wages that perpetuate today's inflation into the future; others believe that the inflationary inertia is caused by the expectations mechanism. Fiscal deficit is another factor that can give rise to inflationary inertia. Financing the budget through money growth brings about an inflationary process that propagates into the future. The initial money expansion, intended for financing the budget, reduces the real value of tax revenues which, in turn, accentuates the deficit problem and results in more money creation and higher inflation. Whatever the cause of inertia may be, some form of nominal anchor or a combination of nominal anchors is needed for eliminating the persistence of inflation.

Despite the success of fiscal restraint *cum* exchange-rate anchor in fighting inflation (see chapters 2, 3, 4, and 5), a number of caveats apply. First, in the presence of strong inflationary inertia, the combination of fiscal discipline and exchange-rate nominal anchor may not be sufficient for restoring stability. In such cases, additional support from income policies that deindex the economy may be needed.[14] But the use of multiple anchors introduces rigidities that disrupt markets and diminish economic efficiency. Second, the use of the exchange rate as the nominal anchor has the built-in danger of bringing about balance-of-payments difficulties that undermine stabilization.[15] Such difficulties could emerge for two reasons: (1) the balance of trade may come under pressure as the overvalued exchange rate reduces competitiveness; and (2) substantial capital flight may occur because of the overvalued currency and in anticipation of devaluation. In chapters 2, 3, 4, and 5, we examine how the exchange-rate variable has been a source of both instability and stability in Latin America.

The relationship between stabilization and economic growth is both delicate and elusive. The consensus view holds that economic stability is needed for sustainable growth, but stabilization is not a sufficient condition for renewed growth. Because stabilization is often achieved through reductions in aggregate demand, economic slowdown and recession are its usual by-products. Economic stabilization has often brought about a decline in living standards and has been achieved at the cost of jobs and social and welfare programs.

An important question regarding stabilization and growth asks at what time a victory over inflation should be declared and pro-growth policies adopted. While there is no consensus as to what the magic number for the inflation variable is, the increasingly popular view that lower inflation is always better does not have much theoretical or empirical support (see

Table I.2

Economic Growth and Inflation in Selected Countries

Country	Average inflation rate 1965–80	Average growth rate 1965–80	Average inflation rate 1980–89	Average growth rate 1980–89
Brazil	31.3	9.0	227.8	3.0
Columbia	17.5	5.7	24.3	3.5
England	10.7	2.0	6.1	2.6
Finland	10.6	4.1	7.0	3.6
Germany	5.2	3.3	2.7	1.9
Hong Kong	8.1	8.6	7.1	7.1
Italy	11.4	3.3	10.3	2.4
Japan	7.6	6.6	1.3	4.0
Norway	7.7	4.4	5.6	3.6
Singapore	5.1	10.0	1.5	6.1
South Korea	18.4	9.9	5.0	9.7
Spain	12.3	4.6	9.4	3.1

Source: World Bank: Informe sobre el desarrollo mundial, 1991.

chapter 1). Nor is this view supported by recent Latin American experience. Cases-in-point are the Mexican and the Chilean experiences. Chile, often the subject of unbridled praise by the majority of economists because of its success in achieving stabilization *cum* growth, lived with relatively high inflation rates for many years while registering impressive rates of growth. Mexico, on the other hand, has religiously sought single-digit inflation rates at heavy cost to output and living standards (see chapters 3 and 4). Moreover, as suggested by Table I.2, the calculus of economic growth and stabilization is much more complicated than assuming that lower inflation brings about faster growth. The experiences of the countries that appear in the table with inflation and growth are so varied that no overall generalization is possible.

I argue in this book that fiscal balance is the essential component of a successful stabilization program. Moreover, when inflation has an inertial component, the use of an exchange-rate anchor is prudent policy because it speeds up the stabilization process and reduces the cost associated with stabilization. Finally, I show that while stabilization and economic growth are not intertwined phenomena—it is possible to have one independent of the other, but the Latin American experience makes it clear that long-term economic growth is not likely in an environment characterized by high inflation and instability.

In this book we consider the experiences of Brazil, Chile, Mexico, Argentina, and Bolivia with macroeconomic policymaking, in search of universally valid lessons and conclusions that can be applied in countries that face the problems of stabilization and growth. These five countries cover the gamut of economic policy while providing the diversification needed for drawing reasonable conclusions. They include the largest and most-industrialized country (Brazil) and one of the smallest and least-industrialized countries (Bolivia) in Latin America. They cover experiences of chronic inflation (Brazil, Chile, Argentina, Mexico) and hyperinflation (Brazil, Argentina, Bolivia). They also give us varieties of orthodox (Chile, Brazil, Mexico, Argentina, Bolivia), heterodox (Brazil and Argentina), and mixed policies (Argentina and Mexico).

Despite the obvious and significant differences that exist among the economies of Brazil, Chile, Mexico, Argentina, and Bolivia, these countries have a number of key features in common with each other and with other Latin American and developing countries. First, all five countries erected protectionist walls in the 1950s and relied on import-substitution policies for expanding their industrial bases. Second, while the state has historically played a prominent role in the economy of each of these countries, over the last two decades the perceived usefulness of state intervention in the economy has been gradually challenged and a general tendency toward privatization has emerged. Third, after having relied on foreign resources in the 1970s to finance their chronic fiscal and current account deficits, in the 1980s all five countries experienced a substantial reduction in the inflow of foreign capital. Finally, also during the 1980s, these countries faced economic instability and paralyzing inflation rates.

While these countries faced similar problems in the 1980s, they differed in how they dealt with their economic difficulties. Chile continued with bold, pro-market structural adjustment programs based on neoliberal prescriptions. By the mid-1980s, Brazilian and Argentine policymakers had concluded that structural idiosyncrasies of their economies made IMF-style orthodox stabilization programs ineffective (see chapters 1, 2, and 5).[16] During the 1985–90 period, turning away from orthodox policies, Argentina and Brazil opted for nonorthodox (heterodox) stabilization prescriptions. In 1985, Bolivia attacked its inflation through decidedly orthodox tactics, while in 1987 Mexico launched an orthodox stabilization plan with heterodox elements. The Mexican and Bolivian programs resulted in stabilization, while heterodox plans employed in Brazil and Argentina invariably failed to tame inflation. By the end of the 1980s, five years of failed attempts made it clear to Argentine policymakers that heterodox policies were counterproductive. Argentina thus abandoned neostructuralist tactics in favor of orthodox reforms, which soon proved successful. In chapters 2, 3, 4, and 5, we shall see that while inflation in each of these countries was contaminated with inertia, the stabilization plans that failed in the 1980s attached more importance to fighting the inertial component of inflation at the expense of a meaningful assault on the deficit problem.

Over the last fifteen years, Latin America has been trapped in the vicious cycle of low investment, low growth, low savings, and low investment. As the resource inflow of the 1960s and 1970s played an important role in helping Latin American countries register impressive rates of economic expansion, the savings outflow of the 1980s retarded economic growth significantly.[17] For countries that achieved stabilization, economic recovery has proved elusive. Thus, a thorny issue for Latin America is how to resume long-term economic growth in the aftermath of stability. Lack of savings and investment, together with a significant cut in government expenditures and foreign capital inflow, have translated into slow growth rates. In surveying the difficult road from economic stabilization to economic growth, Taylor (1993) adds the third factor of fiscal constraint to the traditional two gap models of macroeconomic performance. Taylor argues that the interconnection between these constraints needs to be recognized and he assigns an active role to the state in the process of economic development and income and wealth distributions. In this book, we shall see how these constraints have shaped the economic destinies of Brazil, Chile, Mexico, Argentina, and Bolivia.

The organization of the book is as follows. In chapter 1, we ask what the causes and costs of inflation are, paying special attention to the Latin American case. We show how differences in the orthodox and heterodox views on root causes of inflation translated into different policies for fighting price instability. We also consider the important but overlooked question of inflation costs and ask whether these costs have been overestimated.

In chapter 2, we consider Brazil's difficult experience with inflation and macroeconomic (in)stability over the last three decades. Chapter 3 analyzes the Chilean experience with neoliberal reforms. Chapter 4 describes Mexico's recent experience with inflation and stabilization. Chapter 5 gives a general summary of stabilization policies adopted in Argentina in the period 1976–90, in addition to examining Bolivia's 1985 New Economic Policy. Using the Brazilian case and econometric analysis, in chapter 6 we show that the inertial component of inflation is weaker than claimed by the proponents of the heterodox approach to stabilization. Moreover, by employing recently developed cointegration analysis and error-correction modeling, we identify the variables that determine the behavior of the inflation variable. In chapter 7, we draw general conclusions from our analysis of the Latin American experience with economic management, stabilization, and adjustment.

1

Causes and Consequences of Inflation in Latin America

Introduction

The purpose of this chapter is to offer a broad analytical overview of the existing literature on the causes and consequences of inflation, paying special attention to the Latin American experience in general and the Brazilian case in particular. In an attempt to analyze the genesis of the inflation problem in Latin America, we begin with a brief survey of inflation theories. Theories of inflation constitute such a voluminous literature that a complete treatment of the subject matter is beyond the scope of this book. Our analysis will thus be limited to aspects of these theories that are needed for understanding the Latin American experience with inflation and stabilization over the past two decades.

Inflation refers to a general rise in prices and is usually measured as the percentage increase in some aggregate price index, such as the consumer or the producer price indexes, over a specific period of time. Alternatively, today's inflation can be defined as an increase in the relative price of goods today and goods yesterday. In order to expedite our discussion, we distinguish between four different types of inflation: "moderate," "high," "chronic" and "hyper." While different societies have different notions of moderate inflation, here we define it as very low to low annual rates not exceeding single digits. The United States' roughly 4 percent annual inflation and Ireland's 1.5 percent inflation are considered as moderate. High inflation usually refers to double-digit annual inflation rates, as has been the case in Chile (roughly 14.5 percent per year for the period 1990–93). Chronic inflation is associated with the bulk of the Latin American experience, where inflation rates are very high (double-digit monthly rates that do not exceed 50 percent) but do not reach hyperinflation levels. Following Pazos (1972), we distinguish between hyperinflation and chronic inflation by noting that the latter is usually of longer duration and lower intensity. Following Cagan (1956), hyperinflation is conventionally defined as monthly inflation rates in excess of 50 percent. It should be emphasized that these labels are adopted merely for descriptive convenience and are not meant to be universally acceptable or applicable.

Latin American countries with chronic inflation have often introduced institutional devices such as formal indexation of wages and nominal contracts to reduce inflation-induced distortions in wages and other nominal variables. The introduction of these indexing mechanisms has made inflation in these countries highly vulnerable to major shocks to the budget, terms of trade, or the exchange rate, as each shock can potentially result in a substantial or even an explosive rise in prices.[1] During the 1980s, stabilization in countries that suffered from chronic inflation took the form of policies that temporarily stopped the inflation ascent followed by vengeful returns of inflation. Brazil and Argentina provide instructive examples of the nature and causes of chronic inflation and the difficulties inherent in achieving stabilization in such environments (see chapters 2 and 3).

During the last decade, Latin America also experienced hyperinflationary episodes in Brazil, Bolivia, Argentina, Peru, and Nicaragua. Because in hyperinflationary environments prices move extremely rapidly and nominal contracts adjust very frequently, the inertial component of inflation weakens or disappears. In such circumstances, a sudden and sharp decline in inflation can be accomplished through effective policy. But what are effective polices for combating inflation? Do different types of inflation require different stabilization tools? To answer these questions one needs to consider theoretical frameworks that explore the causes of inflation.

In general, theoretical models that have dominated the analyses of the inflation problem in Latin America can be separated based on their assumptions regarding the speed of adjustment of prices and wages to changes in nominal aggregate demand. The proponents of the new classical model envision a world with instantaneous and equiproportionate price adjustments where anticipated changes in policy do not affect real output.[2] The monetarist alternative, on the other hand, allows for gradual price adjustments and short-term output deviations from the natural rate levels. From this perspective, movements in the money stock manifest themselves in short-term variations in both output and prices and long-term changes in prices alone. The neostructuralist framework assumes a much stronger inertia in price adjustments, concluding that changes in the money stock will have a more pronounced impact on the output level than on prices. As a result, output and employment losses caused by constraining aggregate demand persist and the return path to the full employment output level would be costly in terms of lost output and employment. Finally, in a similar fashion to neostructuralists, the neo-Keynesians emphasize the stickiness of wages and prices in the short run, but like the monetarists, believe in the long-run neutrality of money and the existence of a short-term trade-off between employment and output.

Despite their disagreement regarding the speed of adjustment of nominal variables to a monetary shock, the new classical and the monetarist frameworks agree that in the long run inflation is caused by a rate of monetary growth that outpaces output growth. Through demand channels, the discrepancy between money and output growths manifests itself in higher prices. The neostructuralists and the neo-Keynesians, in contrast, discount the excess demand factor as the primary cause of inflation and consider supply shocks and structural idiosyncrasies of the economy as the principal determinants.

The policy implications of these widely divergent views are naturally strikingly different. The new classical and the monetarist perspectives regard income policies as inherently counterproductive and consider prudent fiscal and monetary policies to be sufficient for controlling inflation. In contrast, the neostructuralists favor stabilization prescriptions based on income policies and assign an active stabilizing role to the government. While the monetarists consider a short-term output sacrifice necessary for achieving stabilization, the new classical and the neostructuralist economists hold that stabilization can be achieved with a very low or even zero output cost.

We examine the monetarist and the new classical models of inflation in "The Monetarist and the New Classical Models" (see page 16), and consider the neostructuralist alternative in "The Neostructuralist Theory of Inflation" (see page 23). Of these three frameworks, the monetarist and the neostructuralist paradigms have been most influential in shaping the policies of various Latin American governments and as such the bulk of our discussion will focus on these two models. The neo-Keynesian paradigm, on the other hand, has not been influential in policy and academic circles in Latin America and as a result we refrain from a detailed analysis of this model.[3]

The second goal of this chapter is to provide a critical analysis of the available econometric studies of Brazilian inflation. This is done in the section "Empirical Evidence" (see page 28), where the causes of Brazilian inflation are examined and econometric problems associated with reported results are investigated. This section also motivates chapter 6, where an alternative approach for analyzing Brazilian inflation based on newly developed econometric techniques is explored.

The third and the final goal of the current chapter is to address the important but often overlooked question of the costs of inflation. One can reasonably argue that inflation costs are negligible and thus inflation is primarily a political issue with few or no economic ramifications. This argument is worthy of serious consideration if inflation is fully anticipated and if society has developed well-established and effective frameworks such as perfect indexation mechanisms to adjust to inflation. In such ideal circumstances, the economic costs of inflation are negligible. More generally, the costs of inflation are determined to a great extent by (a) the source of inflation; (b) the structural characteristics of the economy; (c) the accuracy of inflation expectations; and (d) the intensity and the length of inflation. We consider the costs of inflation under various scenarios below (see page 30), paying special attention to the peculiarities of Brazilian inflation and the institutional settings of that country, which were designed to make living with inflation less costly.

Economists have long argued that confronting inflation is prudent only when the cost of inflation is higher than the cost associated with implementing stabilization programs. In the light of this general observation and our analysis of the costs of inflation, we ask if implementing various stabilization plans in the 1986–90 period was beneficial to the Brazilian economy.

The Monetarist and the New Classical Models

The monetarist view on the causes of inflation is perhaps the oldest. It is highly likely that not long after the advent of money as a medium of exchange, it occurred to someone somewhere that a sudden increase in the amount of money in circulation translated into higher prices without having any lasting output effect. David Hume put this observation into succinct perspective by noting that an overnight doubling of all citizens' money would result only in a doubling of prices the next day. Less than a century later, Irving Fisher formalized the basic monetarist relationship in his equation of exchange:

$$MV = PT \qquad (1.1)$$

where M is the nominal money supply, V is the velocity of money, P is the general price level, and T is the number of transactions or the index of the volume of trade. The Cambridge version of the quantity theory is given by

$$\frac{M}{P} = kY \qquad (1.2)$$

where Y is the gross domestic product (GDP), which is assumed to have a fixed relationship with T. The constant k captures the implicit relationship between T and Y. In addition, k also reflects the relationship between the payment and the transaction period: the more they coincide, the smaller the value of k would be because of smaller cash balance requirements.[4]

Friedman (1956) reinterpreted Fisher's equation as a money demand function that related the demand for real balances to the income level. Using a two-sector model of the economy, Friedman obtained the equilibrium price level by setting the money demand equal to the exogenous money supply. To make his model of six equations and seven unknowns identified, Friedman relied on the natural rate hypothesis to assume the exogeneity of the real income variable through a long-run output constraint. By doing so, he incorporated the assumption of a long-term unemployment rate constrained at the natural level and ruled out money illusion.[5] In the long run, the output level is determined exogenously by the supply side; as a result, increases in the money supply are manifested in inflation alone. Friedman's important conclusion was that

> short-run changes in both particular prices and in the general level of prices may have many sources. But long, continued inflation is always and everywhere a monetary phenomenon that arises from a more rapid expansion in the quantity of money than in total output—though Iq hasten to add that the exact rate of inflation is not precisely or mechanically linked to the exact rate of monetary growth.[6]

In other words, while short-term price increases may be caused by factors such as oil shocks or droughts, continuous and persistent inflation can be caused only by excess money creation.

Central to the monetarist view of inflation and stabilization is the assumed ineffectiveness of changes in the money supply on the real-sector demand functions. This "homogeneity postulate," as first used by Leontief (1936) in analyzing Keynes's monetary theory and later employed by Patinkin (1965) in studying the neoclassical monetary theory, holds that excess demand functions are homogeneous of degree zero with respect to all nominal variables in the system, implying the absence of money illusion. In the long run, a k-fold increase (decrease) in the quantity of money would bring about a k-fold increase (decrease) in prices, leaving real variables in the economy unchanged.

The monetarist perspective also rests on the assumption that prices and wages adjust quickly to a money shock, an assumption that needs to be relaxed in an economy where contracts introduce wage rigidity. In such an economy, changing the money supply may have a prolonged effect on real variables because while wages adjust slowly to the change in the quantity of money, prices adjust quickly. The resulting change in the price–cost ratio that lasts as long as the full adjustment in wages is not materialized, provides producers with incentives for altering the production levels. This effect is more pronounced in Latin American countries, where labor is relatively cheaper and the wage bill constitutes a larger share of the production cost. Thus, while the monetarists' neutrality hypothesis rules out the existence of a *long-term* relationship between a nominal variable (money or prices) and a real variable (employment), a *short-term* Phillips curve that inversely relates unemployment to inflation can exist.

Even in an environment of smooth and speedy price and wage adjustments, a relationship between nominal and real variables can develop under two circumstances: information asymmetry, and aggregate/relative price-change confusion.[7] In response to ample empirical evidence that emerged in support of the existence of a trade-off between the unemployment rate and the inflation rate during the 1960s, Friedman (1968) argued that this observed relationship was merely a short-term phenomenon caused by information asymmetry. When prices increase in response to increased money supply, employers recognize the overall inflationary environment before their workers do. This enables employers to increase output by offering higher nominal wages but unchanged real wages. The workers, on the other hand, will be willing to work more as they mistake the rise in nominal wages for increased real wages. The asymmetric nature of information available to employers and workers results in a short-term increase in output that lasts only as long as workers do not recognize the overall inflationary environment. This explanation is somewhat ambiguous since it is not clear why employers recognize a general price increase before workers do.[8]

A more formal explanation of the observed Phillips curve relationship was offered by Lucas (1972b, 1977). In Lucas's model, firms mistake individual price changes for changes in aggregate prices and make production decisions that create a short-term Phillips relationship. An inverse relationship between employment and inflation can also develop if labor suppliers perceive the increase in wages as temporary and thus postpone current leisure until the future, when it has a smaller opportunity cost.

It is worth emphasizing that there is a unifying thread to Friedman's and Lucas's versions, since in both cases a short-term Phillips curve relationship can arise only if the change in money supply is unanticipated. To see this, consider an expectations-adjusted Phillips relationship:

$$\dot{P}_t = \alpha(Y_t - Y_t^*) + \beta\, E(\dot{P}_t) \qquad (1.3)$$

where Y^* is the full employment output and E denotes the expectation operator. Because of information asymmetry (Friedman) and/or aggregate-individual price distortion (Lucas), in the short run the expected rate of inflation may deviate from the actual rate, resulting in a short-run Phillips curve relationship. A necessary condition for this to occur is that the change in the quantity of money that causes a change in the inflation rate be unanticipated. In the long run ($\beta = 1$), changes in the money supply and the inflation rate are fully anticipated [$\dot{P}_t = E(\dot{P}_t)$], output will be at the full employment level ($Y_t = Y_t^*$) and the Phillips curve's nominal-real relationship disappears.

It is at once clear from the above discussion that the assumption about the formation of inflation expectations has significant implications for the monetarist and new classical views on inflation–output trade-off. The monetarists' assumption about how expectations are formed dates back to Cagan's (1956) adaptive expectation model. According to this view, economic agents form their inflation expectations by relying on their forecasting experience. In particular,

$$E(\dot{P}_t) = \dot{P}_{t-1} + \lambda[\dot{P}_{t-1} - E(\dot{P}_{t-1})] \qquad 0 < \lambda \le 1 \qquad (1.4)$$

where [.] is the forecast error made in the preceding period. This type of expectations formation results in a continuous and gradual adjustment of forecasts that is strictly backward-looking and does not necessarily use all available information. Moreover, this type of inflation forecasting can lead to systematic errors since serial correlation of forecast errors is an inherent feature of expectation formation based on Equation 1.4. If forecasts are based on adaptive expectations, economic agents may be perpetually wrong about their expectations and they will never learn from their mistakes by adjusting their forecasts accordingly in future. As long as a discrepancy between the forecast and the actual inflation rates exists, monetary policy will be non-neutral, as suggested by Equation 1.3. The monetarists assume that in the long run economic agents have enough experience to make accurate forecasts.

Unimpressed by the adaptive expectation model utilized by the monetarists, the new classical economists relied on Muth's (1960) rational expectations hypothesis as the cornerstone of their theoretical model. In contrast to the adaptive expectation model, the rational expectation hypothesis assumes that economic agents are forward-looking in forming their expectations. Furthermore, these agents are expected to utilize all information available to them in making their forecasts as long as the marginal benefit of obtaining and using the additional unit of information exceeds its marginal cost. Thus in a rational expectation framework,

$$E(\dot{P}_t/I_t) - \dot{P}_t = E_t \qquad (1.5)$$

where I_t denotes the pool of relevant information available at time t, and ε is a white-noise forecast error term with a zero mean. The assumption that $E(\varepsilon_i\varepsilon_j) = 0$ for $i \neq j$ rules out the possibility of a systematic forecasting error. As a result, even a short-run output–inflation trade-off is ruled out unless changes in the money supply surprise economic agents. The new classicists, relying on the rational expectations hypothesis and assuming efficient market clearing, derived the important postulate of policy ineffectiveness: regardless of the time horizon involved, monetary policy has no *systematic* effect on real variables.

According to this perspective, to eliminate inflation the government needs to be credible and announce a set of policy measures that are aimed at ending or controlling inflation. If the public believes the government, inflation can be brought under control without any significant output cost since anticipated policy changes have no impact on output. But as Barro and Fischer (1976) point out, even in a world where expectations are formed rationally, stabilization policy may be ineffective because of short-term stickiness of wages and prices or because of incomplete information about inflation.

In the 1980s, some proponents of the nonorthodox approaches to stabilization in Latin America pointed out that in Latin America tight monetary policies did not result in lower inflation. From this observation, it was concluded that in Latin American countries, where structural peculiarities were different from industrialized nations and where political factors in the form of fights for shares of national income were particularly pronounced, a tight monetary policy was hopelessly ineffective and unacceptably costly. These proponents of the nonorthodox prescriptions assumed that tight monetary policy and inflation could coexist only because of wage and price inertia and the structural characteristics such as wage indexation. But even in the absence of an inflationary monetary policy, inflation can still result in two situations: (1) in the presence of a dominating and inflationary fiscal policy; (2) the presence of rational bubbles. In the first situation, as analyzed in detail by Sargent and Wallace (1981), a tight monetary policy and inflation can coexist in the presence of an imposing inflationary fiscal policy. Sargent and Wallace pushed the policy ineffectiveness hypothesis one step further by arguing that if the fiscal policy is inflationary, monetary policy cannot control prices. In light of the significance of fiscal policy and its impact on monetary policy, the new classicals introduced government bonds in the model. Once bonds are introduced, the government budget constraint is given by:

$$B_t + M_t - D_t = B_{t-1}(1 + r) + M_{t-1} \qquad (1.6)$$

where B is the stock of government bonds, M is the money supply, D is the government deficit, and r is the interest rate. Equation 1.6 makes the interdependence of fiscal and monetary policies quite clear and it shows that fighting inflation can be successful only if fiscal and monetary authorities coordinate their stabilization efforts. Sargent and Wallace considered two situations. In one case, the monetary policy dominates; in the other case, the fiscal authorities dominate. Monetary authorities cannot control the inflation problem if fiscal authorities do not cooperate or cannot be forced to cooperate. Once fiscal authorities determine the deficit level, monetary policy is automatically determined. The monetary authorities may choose a tight monetary policy or a relaxed monetary policy. It does not matter; in both cases inflation will be the outcome. The degree of tightness of monetary policy only affects the timing of inflation: a loose monetary policy implies a higher inflation in the present period. A tight monetary policy at the present time, on the other hand, requires a larger bond issue today and results in higher inflation rates in the future.

In the face of persistent deficits, over time the government will face a larger deficit burden because of higher interest rates. If the government attempts to pay for its interest expense on the old debt by contracting new debt, the debt–GNP ratio will rise, making it difficult for the government to rely on continued domestic borrowing; the public will become reluctant to lend to a less-creditworthy government.

In the special and dangerous case where the real interest rate paid by the government on its debt exceeds the real GNP growth rate, the debt–GNP ratio will grow without bound. Once the expectations of these higher future inflation rates are written into today's nominal contracts, inflation is introduced even in the absence of excess money. The important question here is whether monetary policy can impose discipline on fiscal policy or vice versa. Sargent and Wallace focus on a situation in which fiscal policy dominates.[9] This latter case is very close to most Latin American experiences, including the Brazilian situation where, by and large, independent monetary authorities do not exist and the same political entities usually control both the monetary and the fiscal arms.

In the period prior to the outburst of the debt crises in 1982, the Latin American countries in general and the Brazilian government in particular could avoid the "unpleasant monetarist arithmetic"[10] explicit in the Sargent and Wallace analysis by relying on foreign resources for financing their deficits. Since during most of the 1970s and early 1980s foreign capital was an important source of financing the government deficit, we extend Equation 1.6 by incorporating a variable for changes in foreign-exchange reserves at the Central Bank:

$$B_t + M_t - eR_t - D_t = B_{t-1}(1+r) + M_{t-1} - eR_{t-1} \qquad (1.7)$$

where R is the stock of foreign reserves and e is the exchange rate measuring the value of domestic currency in terms of foreign currency. Equation 1.7 shows that the government can finance its deficit in three ways: by contracting debt internally through issuing bonds, by increasing the money supply, or by contracting foreign debt. Assuming that the government cannot finance its deficit through domestic borrowing because of the immaturity of financial markets for government bonds and because of the lack of citizens' confidence in their government, Equation 1.7 can be rewritten as:

$$D_t = (M_t - M_{t-1}) - e(R_t - R_{t-1}) . \qquad (1.8)$$

By assuming purchasing power parity:

$$P_t = eP_t^* \qquad (1.9)$$

where P^* is the foreign price variable, by assuming a fixed exchange rate, and by using Equation 1.2, we can rewrite Equation 1.8 as

$$D_t = (keP_t^* Y_t - keP_{t-1}^* Y_{t-1}) - e(R_t - R_{t-1}) . \qquad (1.10)$$

Under a fixed exchange-rate regime, and constant foreign prices, Equation 1.10 is reduced to:

$$D_t = \lambda(Y_t - Y_{t-1}) - e(R_t - R_{t-1}) \qquad (1.11)$$

where λ is a constant. This equation has two fundamental implications. First, if the economy operates at the full employment level ($Y_t = Y_{t-1}$), the government can finance its deficit in a noninflationary way by relying on foreign reserves. Once the reserves are depleted, a balance of payments crisis is the likely outcome, as the fixed exchange rate can no longer be maintained and the value of the domestic currency collapses. Second, tight monetary policies that reduce output (Y_t) in an attempt to reduce inflation will initially increase the deficit. This once again shows the importance of having coordinated fiscal and monetary policies for fighting inflation.

This interdependence of monetary and fiscal policies also helps us solve the Brazilian riddle as to why over the last two decades prices increased as the real money supply (M/P) declined. This implies that in the absence of excessive money growth, inflation has persisted. What then are the causes of Brazilian inflation if the money supply is not a factor? The fact that the government deficit has never been brought under control (see chapter 2) partly explains why inflation has persisted despite a noninflationary monetary policy. A second way in which the absence of inflationary monetary growth inflation could result is inflation through rational bubbles. In general, the empirical evidence about the existence or nonexistence of rational bubbles is not compelling[11] and no generally accepted procedure for testing rational inflation bubbles has been developed. Yet the bulk of empirical evidence suggests that rational bubbles did not exist during the European and Latin American episodes of hyper- and chronic inflation. Studies of the German hyperinflation of 1920–23 concluded that an inflationary bubble did not exist,[12] and for the recent inflationary episodes of Brazil and Argentina, Welch (1991) offers strong evidence against the existence of inflation bubbles.

The Neostructuralist Theory of Inflation

While in the monetarist and neoclassical frameworks inflation is determined in the monetary sector, the neostructuralists trace the origins of inflation in the labor and goods sectors and give a passive, accommodating role to money supply.

At the heart of the neostructuralist view of the economic world lies the assumption that Latin American economies are fundamentally different from the economies of the advanced industrialized nations. While in the industrialized world competition reigns, in Latin America production is dominated by oligopolistic firms, or so the neostructuralists contend. This domination, caused by the uncompetitive nature of production across many markets, results in prices that are not sensitive to changes in aggregate demand but rise quickly and fully in response to increased production costs. Unlike their price-taker counterparts in the industrialized world, Latin American firms are assumed to act as price-makers and supply their products at a markup above their cost. Formally, for such firms with a homogeneous production function and three inputs of labor, capital, and imported intermediate goods, the price is determined by

$$P_1 = (1+m)[\beta_1 W + \beta_2 r + (1-\beta_1-\beta_2)eP_f] \qquad 0 < \ < 1] \qquad (1.12)$$

where m is the markup factor, W and r correspond to labor and capital costs, respectively, e is the exchange rate, and P_f is the price of imported goods. Assuming that the economy is divided into producers that set their prices (price-maker firm) and firms whose prices are dictated by the market (price-taker firms), the general price level in the economy is given by

$$P_t = \alpha P_{1,t} + (1-\alpha)P_{2,t} + s_t \qquad 0 \le \alpha \le 1 \qquad (1.13)$$

where P_1 and P_2 correspond to price-maker and price-taker prices, respectively, and s_t is a shock variable. The parameter α shows the extent to which price-maker firms determine the overall price level in the economy: the larger this parameter, the more influential are the price-maker firms in determining the general price level. In this context, the neostructuralists assert, without offering any solid empirical evidence, that the value of α is much higher in Latin American countries than it is in the industrialized nations. Adding a wage-setting equation such as

$$w_t = f(W_t, P_t, g_t) \qquad f_1 > 0; f_2 < 0; f_3 < 0 \qquad (1.14)$$

where w is the real wage and g is the output gap completes a simple model for inflation with a wage-price spiral. In this model, an initial increase in prices (P) initially reduces real wages, thus causing an offsetting increase in nominal wages (W). The increase in nominal wages (W) results in an increase in P_1 in Equation 1.12, which, in turn, increases the general price level (P) in Equation 1.13. This causes a reduction in real wage, w, which encourages the unions to press for increased nominal wages, thus completing the circle.

It is worth noting that in this model, the impact of a restrictive monetary policy that increases the output gap is ambiguous. A reduction in wages caused by a recessionary monetary policy may be offset by higher interest rates (the cost of capital). This result is consistent with studies by Cavallo (1977), Bruno (1979), Taylor (1980), and van Wijnbergen (1982, 1983) that placed the stagflationary impact of restrictive monetary policies in the structure of the financial system. In particular, because of the relative immaturity of equity markets in developing nations, working capital is mostly financed through bank borrowing. As a result, while a restrictive monetary policy has an impact on real wages only gradually because of the strong presence of inertia, it increases production costs immediately. This, in turn, translates into higher prices and, over time, higher unemployment rates. In such an environment, aggregate demand management through a restrictive monetary regime only leads to lower output without damping the inflation rate. Finally, it should be noted that the phenomenon of stagflation is also consistent with the monetarist view once uncertainty regarding the permanence of shocks to the economy is introduced into the model. If the public misperceives a permanent reduction in output as being a transitory shock, stagflation can appear.[13]

In the Brazilian context, Lopes (1984), Lara Resende and Lopes (1981), Arida and Lara Resende (1985), and Modiano (1983, 1985) showed that decreases in output did not bring about corresponding declines in the inflation rate. These findings reinforced the general conclusion that orthodox policies that constrained the output level in hopes of controlling inflation through aggregate demand management were generally ineffective and that a different framework for analyzing the nature of Brazilian inflation was needed. This different framework was developed based on the view that widespread indexation of nominal contracts in the economy was the source of price increases. In an economy where staggered contracts are indexed to prices and money is accommodating, inertial inflation appears even in the absence of fiscal deficit. In such an economy, a supply shock will be especially inflationary and attempting to achieve price stability through monetary policy would only result in output and employment losses.

Two versions of the inertial theory of inflation emerged from the works of Brazilian economists in the early 1980s. In one version, advanced by Lopes, inertial inflation exists independent of inflationary expectations. In Lopes's model, the source of continued inflation is to be found in a labor market where economic agents constantly seek to readjust their nominal incomes to reach the previous peak of their real incomes. Lopes and others hypothesized that individuals faced with a decline in their real wages would focus their efforts on reestablishing the previous peaks of their real wages. This results in an ongoing distributive conflict that propagates past inflation into the future and gives inflation its inertial nature. Lopes remains highly unconvincing as to why economic agents whose well-being depends on their real *average* wages seek to reestablish the previous *peak* of their real wages. Lopes (1986, 126) compares the behavior of economic agents in his model to the worker in Keynes's model: "The worker in the *General Theory* attempts to defend his nominal wage while his well-being is dependent upon his real wage. Our economic agent attempts to defend the peak of his real wage instead of his real average wage" (my translation). Thus Lopes himself is aware of the problem but he does not offer any convincing explanation of the puzzle since the fact that Keynesian workers suffer from money illusion does not tell us why economic agents in Lopes's model defend the peak of their wage and not their real average wage.

A more credible explanation for the emergence of price inertia is provided by Tobin (1981), who argued that in an inflationary environment every economic agent adopts a risk-minimizing strategy by assuming the continuation of the inertial pattern and by assuming that everyone will make the same assumption about the future behavior of inflation. This explanation is based on Keynes's (1936) notion that social groups will not accept reductions in their nominal wages unless their *relative* real wages remain intact. In an inflationary environment this is possible only through coordination and government intervention. This conflict over maintaining the relative real wage can result in inertia, and "rigidities in the path of money wage rates can be explained by workers' preoccupation with relative wages and the absence of any central economy-wide mechanism for altering all money wages together."[14] An analogous explanation that also offers some theoretical grounds for the behavior of Lopes's economic agents is provided by Simonsen (1988) and Simonsen and Cysne (1989, 534), who view the economy as a noncooperative game where a Nash equilibrium would be the demand for average real incomes by agents. But if one economic agent claimed the previous peak of his or her real income, other agents would follow suit. Thus, as a defensive strategy, economic agents attempt to maintain the previous peak of their real income. This type of analysis also provides an important role for the government. The government is given the task of leading the economy back to the Nash position by intervening in the market and adopting incomes policies, thereby essentially setting the rules of the game.

The use of the conflict variable to explain the emergence of inflation was not original to neostructuralists or Lopes. Jackson et al. (1972) described the dynamics of price rises as strato-inflation where past inflation persists because social groups organize and form mechanisms whereby they recover the loss in their relative income. In Jackson et al. past inflation also propagates due to staggered wage contract settings. Recently, de Carvalho (1993) argued that what separates the Jackson et al. model from the neostructuralist framework of a decade later is that strato-inflation is a disequilibrium condition while in the neostructuralist framework inertia inflation is an equilibrium condition. But once institutional factors that adapt to inflation and institutionalize conflicts are introduced, self-generating inflation results. Also in an important work, Otto Eckstein (1981) diagnosed inflation as having an inertial component or a core rate that persists over time regardless of demand shocks. By the end of the seventies the conflict-core explanations of inflation were so popular that in 1978 the then president of the United States, Jimmy Carter, summarized the causes of inflation in a manner not very different from the neostructuralist explanations of a few years later:

> Inflation has now become embedded in the very tissue of our economy. It has resisted the most severe recession in a generation. It persists because all of us—business, labor, farmers, consumers—are caught on a treadmill which none can stop alone. Each group tries to raise its income to keep up with present and anticipated rising costs and eventually we all lose the inflationary battle together.[15]

Perry (1980) developed the notion of inertia to argue that wages and thus prices rise independent of demand factors. While wages and prices may rise because of outside shocks, their upward evolution could persist over time because of inertia.

In a more analytical version of the neostructuralist approach, put forth by Arida and Lara Resende (hereafter denoted AL), inflation assumes an inertial characteristic because of the behavior of rational economic agents who in an economy with widespread formal and informal indexation form their best forecast of the future rate of inflation by using the lagged rate of inflation. The AL model is in a way similar to the model developed by John Taylor (1979), in which rational expectations in the presence of staggered contracts results in weak inertia. In AL's view, inflation assumes an inertial characteristic whenever indexation of wages is widespread.

Just as Lopes and AL differed on their views about what gives Brazilian inflation its inertial characteristic, they also differed on how to bring inflation under control. Lopes proposed a heterodox shock that consisted of freezing prices and wages. This amounted to changing the rules of the game by having the government forbid a return to the peak of real wages by freezing all wages and simultaneously guaranteeing a stable real wage by freezing prices. The temporary price and wage freeze was designed to provide what Dornbusch and Simonsen (1988) have called a "breathing spell." This "breathing spell" comes at the expense of efficiency and post-freeze inflation. Because of the staggered nature of contracts, freezing prices at any point in time results in disequilibrium relative prices and market inefficiencies. In the post-freeze period some inflation will return as relative prices adjust toward the equilibrium conditions. In the post-shock economy, the government was to follow a "passive" monetary policy and a non-expansionary fiscal policy. The "passive" monetary policy would be dictated by first choosing an optimal interest rate and then having the monetary authorities adopt policies consistent with this interest rate.

AL's remedy to the Brazilian inflation problem relied more heavily on the market mechanism. It explicitly recognized the importance of demand management by emphasizing the need to control the public deficit and to bring the money supply under control such that no pressure on prices resulted from excess demand.[16] But it also argued that demand management in itself was not sufficient for eliminating the inflation problem since the ghosts of inflations past were present in people's memories and economic agents' behavior through indexed contracts. To eliminate this link to past inflation and to erase the inertial nature of inflation, AL argued in favor of the introduction of a new indexed money. This monetary reform was designed to remove the inertial component of inflation in two ways: first, by using the domestic money instead of the exchange rate as the nominal anchor for stabilization,[17] and second, by changing the indexation structure of the economy to avoid the staggered contracts problem highlighted by John Taylor. The monetary reform was to be performed by the introduction of a new monetary unit (cruzeiro novo), which would replace the cruzeiros in circulation. The value of the new currency was to be pegged to the Treasury's Readjustable Obligations (ORTN) to be fully indexed for inflation. In addition to monetary reform, AL's proposal sought to attack the root causes of inflation through fiscal discipline and tight monetary policy. In chapter 2, we investigate in detail how neostructuralists' prescriptions were put in practice in Brazil during the 1986–90 period and why they failed.

Empirical Evidence

The paramount issue in empirical studies of Latin American inflation has been that of the sensitivity of the inflation rate to changes in aggregate demand. As discussed before, the proponents of the heterodox approach to stabilization widely believe that because of structural idiosyncrasies, the aggregate supply curve is relatively flat in Latin American countries, rendering anti-inflation policies based on demand management ineffective. The supporters of implementing stabilization programs based on incomes policies have relied on the empirical evidence that shows the absence of a significant relationship between the output gap and the inflation rate to conclude that fiscal and monetary policies that constrained output are ineffective in combating inflation. The monetarists, on the other hand, have countered by showing that a significant short-term trade-off between the output gap and inflation exists, and hence restrictive monetary policies that first constrict output eventually bring down the rate of inflation.

In the Brazilian case, for the last fifteen years the primary focus of empirical studies of inflation has been analysis of the Phillips curve. During the 1980s the empirical findings that showed the absence of a trade-off between output and employment was used to support anti-inflation policies that relied more on price and wage controls and less on orthodox tools.

An early contributor to the empirical examination of the relationship between the inflation rate and the level of economic activity is Lemgruber (1978), who used ordinary and three-stage least-squares procedures to estimate a simultaneous equation system. His results indicated that an accelerationist version Phillips curve captured well the Brazilian experience with inflation for the period 1954–72.[18] Lemgruber (1984) and Contador (1977, 1982) also found a significant and inverse relationship between the output gap and the rate of inflation and added support for the existence of an accelerationist type Phillips curve in Brazil. Similar results were reported by Bomberger and Makinen (1976).

Lara Resende and Lopes (1981) criticized the previous estimates of the Phillips curve for Brazil by noting that these studies had ignored the external supply shocks and the compulsory wage indexing mechanism that dominated the Brazilian labor market. By formally introducing these two elements in their model, Lopes and Lara Resende concluded that there was no significant relationship between the output gap and the inflation rate. Lopes (1984) introduced unsynchronized wage indexation into the model and found a significant but small impact of the output gap variable on the inflation rate. In particular, Lopes showed that if the output gap were to increase by 27 percent in 1982, the inflation rate in that year would decrease only modestly from 99 percent to 92 percent. A similar conclusion was drawn by Modiano (1985), who concluded that a 10 percent increase in output gap resulted in only a 9 point reduction in the inflation rate—not an encouraging result for a country facing three-digit inflation rates.

Bomberger and Makinen (1976) used a dynamic version of a wage Phillips curve and allowed for time-varying coefficients to conclude that the excess demand variable did not significantly enter the Phillips curve relationship but had a stable impact on the wage variable. Barbosa and McNelis (1990) also employed transfer functions and Kalman filter estimation of time-varying coefficients to show that while indexation slowed the response of inflation to changes in monetary policy, monetary correction retained its effectiveness in controlling inflation. Finally, Parkin (1991) took on the heroic task of estimating a fifty-two-equation simultaneous system for studying the dynamics of inflation. Using annual data for the 1966–83 period, Parkin concluded that the structuralist explanation of Brazilian inflation was closer to the mark.

Most of these studies, however, suffer from serious econometric problems, which makes their conclusions highly suspect. For example, Lemgruber (1984) used a simultaneous equation system to motivate his empirical study, but at the estimation stage used the least-squares method, making his results subject to serious simultaneity bias.[19] Barbosa and McNelis (1990) introduced important variables of output, productivity, and average wage in their model, but at the estimation stage dropped all these variables due to unavailability of data, thus introducing omitted variable bias. Parkin's results (1991) are to be considered especially cautiously since they are drawn from the unenviable exercise of estimating a model with forty exogenous variables and sixteen lagged exogenous variables by using only eighteen observations.[20]

Moreover, these studies have, by and large, overlooked the nonstationary nature of the inflation rate variable and its determinants. As discussed in greater detail in chapter 6, estimation results from models with nonstationary variables are usually suspect because of the spurious relations problem.

Mechanical differencing of nonstationary data is also not advisable because valuable long-term information may be lost in the process. Furthermore, while some variables in the model may be nonstationary individually, it may be possible to find linear combinations of them that are stationary. If such a combination exists, cointegration analysis and error-correction modeling can be used to investigate the nature of long-term equilibrium relations among model variables and to analyze the nature of short-term adjustments toward the long-term equilibrium. A full discussion of these concepts and their application to the analysis of Brazilian inflation can be found in chapter 6.

The Costs of Inflation

While different rates of money growth result in different rates of inflation, the important "superneutrality" question asks if these variations in nominal variables have any long-run real effects.[21] The answer to this question is not always straightforward and, in the case of inflation, depends on a variety of factors, including the source of inflation, the size and significance of the surprise component of inflation, the structural characteristics of the economy, and the government's reaction to inflation. Inflation may have a negative impact on the economy by reducing social welfare, causing income and wealth redistribution, and disrupting the workings of the economic system.

In a seminal paper, Martin Bailey (1956) measured the welfare cost of anticipated inflation by the area of a triangle under the demand for real high-powered money. In Figure 1.1, this triangle is marked by EB_0B_1. An increase in the inflation rate from π_0 to π_1 brings about a consumer surplus loss of $A_1B_1B_0A_0$. The windfall from this increased inflation to the government is measured by $m_1X(\pi_1\!-\!\pi_0)$. Assuming that taxes are reduced by the same amount as the increase in government revenues, and assuming that money is superneutral—that is, inflation does not affect real wealth and real interest rate variables—the net loss of anticipated inflation to consumers is computed by EB_0B_1. This welfare loss is in the form of "shoe leather" cost to consumers because at higher inflation rates they are forced to economize on their holding of cash balances and spend more resources for conducting the same number of transactions as before. Figure 1.1 can also be used to derive the optimal quantity of money (Friedman 1969) rule. It can be seen that by reducing the nominal interest rate from $r + \pi_0$ to zero, consumers' surplus can be increased without incurring any additional costs. As a result, given the real interest rate, the optimal inflation rate is identified as that rate which makes the nominal interest rate zero: $\pi = -r$.

For seven hyperinflation episodes studied by Cagan (1956), Bailey

Figure 1.1 **Welfare Cost of Anticipated Inflation**

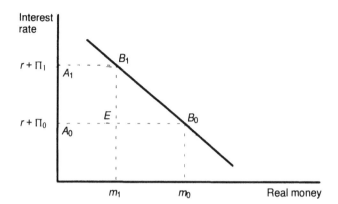

(1956) computed the maximum welfare cost of inflation as a fraction of income. His estimates ranged from 2 percent (Russia) to 48 percent (Hungary) with the median value of 30 percent (Greece) of income. Bailey also calculated the maximum fraction of income the government could obtain through an inflation tax that ranged between about 1 and 16 percent, consistently considerably lower than the welfare cost of inflation. In a more formal analysis of the same data set, Barro (1972) obtained a welfare cost for inflation that was more than double the increase in government revenues brought about by seigniorage.

Many of the conclusions regarding the inconsequential costs of moderate inflation are drawn by economists influenced by Bailey's (1956) original contribution. But it is important to remember that Bailey assigned very high costs to high inflation and relatively low costs to moderate inflation by using a formula that increased the welfare cost of inflation with the square of the nominal interest rate. A recent study by Lucas (1993) shows that if a square-root cost function is adopted, the welfare cost of moderate inflation is much higher than previously estimated. By contrast, the welfare cost of very high inflation is much smaller than Bailey's estimates. From a theoretical perspective, Lucas's results are more attractive since they are developed in a general equilibrium framework based on Sidrauski (1967a, b) as opposed to the partial equilibrium approach adopted by Bailey. Nevertheless, Bailey's general conclusion seems to hold: even fully anticipated moderate inflation does not make society immune from incurring "shoe leather" costs. But these costs, measured by the size of the triangle under money demand function, are usually negligible for very low inflation rates and may or may not increase drastically at higher inflation rates, depending on what

cost function is chosen. Yoshino (1991) added to Bailey's traditional rectangular a credit market rectangular by adding a banking sector that col-
lected an economic rent. He then calculated the cost of Brazilian inflation
for the period 1963–87, finding a striking difference between his cost estimates and the estimates obtained from applying the Bailey method for high
rates of inflation.[22] For example, for 1987, Yoshino calculated a cost of 53
percent of GDP as opposed to 15 percent found from Bailey's method.

Inflation can also be costly to the society by disrupting the economic
system in three ways. First, as suggested by Okun (1975) and Friedman
(1977b), higher inflation may undermine the allocative efficiency of the
price system by increasing the variability in relative prices. There are several generally accepted theoretical models that link the variability in relative
prices to both anticipated and unanticipated inflation. Among others,
Cukierman (1979, 1982, 1984) provides models that relate inflation to increased relative price variability by using Lucas's (1973) relative-aggregate
and transitory-permanent confusion. Models developed by Sheshinski and
Weiss (1977), Mussa (1977), and Rotemberg (1983) link both anticipated
and unanticipated inflation to relative price variability.[23] The empirical evidence for the U.S. and Latin American data shows that a direct relationship
between inflation and relative price variability exists such that both expected and unexpected inflation are positively associated with variability in
relative prices.[24] Fischer (1981b) offered evidence of a positive relationship
between inflation and relative price variability but found no (Granger) causality relationship between these two variables. Fischer concluded that the
observed relationship between relative prices and inflation may have been
induced by outside shocks and policy responses to these shocks. In analyzing the Argentine data, Blejer (1983) offers evidence in favor of (1) a direct
link between higher relative price variability and increases in the unexpected component of inflation; and (2) the "menu cost" explanation of
the relationship between relative price variability and inflation. In general, the link between unexpected inflation and relative price variability
seems to be stronger than the link between expected inflation and variability in relative prices.[25]

Second, higher inflations are suspected of causing more price uncertainty.
Higher inflation uncertainty, in turn, translates into higher economic costs in
terms of lost output and employment, as economic efficiency is lowered.

In his Nobel lecture, Milton Friedman (1977b) sought to explain the
phenomenon of a positively sloped Phillips curve by arguing that inflation
and its variability are positively correlated. Taking variability in the inflation rate to be the same as inflation uncertainty, Friedman argued that,
ceteris paribus, higher inflation rates would have real consequences in the

economy as they would result in higher unemployment and lower output levels through diminishing economic efficiency. Since then a number of important empirical studies have investigated the link between higher inflation rates and higher inflation uncertainty.

In the empirical investigation of the relationship between inflation and its uncertainty, one thorny issue has been how to measure "uncertainty." One common practice has been to use inflation rate variability as a proxy for inflation uncertainty. This pragmatic approach is somewhat worrisome since it identifies inflation uncertainty with inflation variability. These two, of course, are not necessarily the same thing, and higher inflation variability does not always translate into higher uncertainty. It should also be noted that using the variance of inflation as a proxy for price unpredictability requires a stochastic process for prices with a constant mean plus a shock term.

An early empirical study in support of the hypothesis that increased inflation uncertainty in the United States resulted in higher unemployment and lower output (industrial production) was given by Mullineaux (1980). Engle (1982, 1983) used an autoregressive conditional heteroscedasity (ARCH) model to show that while conditional variance of inflation was time-variant, the evidence did not show a relationship between the inflation rate and its variance. Using a generalized ARCH (GARCH) model, Bollerslev (1986) offered additional evidence in support of the hypothesis that a strong relationship between inflation and uncertainty does not exist. Ball and Cecchetti (1990) and Evans (1991) provided evidence in support of the long-term inflation-uncertainty hypothesis but concluded that no relationship exists in the short term. Brunner and Hess (1993) used conditional moment state-dependent models (SDMs) to find a link between higher inflation and higher price uncertainty. John Welch (1989) applied Engle's ARCH estimation procedure to the Brazilian data and concluded that for the period 1974–82 the inflation variance was positively related to the inflation rate.

Employing a general equilibrium model and using inflation forecast errors as a proxy for uncertainty, Miller (1992) demonstrated that as inflation uncertainty increases, the length of contracts for financial instruments shrinks. In general, higher inflation rates lead to higher inflation uncertainty in the long run. This increased price uncertainty leads to a reduction in economic efficiency as the society is forced to switch from nominal to real assets, adopt widespread indexation mechanisms that work imperfectly at best, and shorten the length of contracts.[26]

Third, in response to high and politically unacceptable inflation rates, the government may decide to intervene in the economy by introducing stabilization plans and initiating wage and price controls. These plans are typically counterproductive and cost society by increasing uncertainty about future prices and introducing inefficiencies. Studies by Fischer and Modigliani (1975) and Driffil et al. (1990) concluded that the cost of inflation in terms of welfare loss is not caused by inflation itself but by government's quest to control or reduce the inflation rate.

In addition to direct welfare and disruptive costs, inflation can also have redistributive consequences. In the presence of nominal contracts for debt instruments, labor and goods, or imperfect indexation, inflation can result in income and wealth redistribution. But the direction of these redistributions (from labor to capital, and so forth) cannot a priori be known since it is largely determined by the source of unanticipated inflation[27] and the relative degree by which the owners of productive resources (workers, capitalists, etc.) can protect themselves from inflation. The evidence from post–World War II United States data shows that inflation has resulted in a small, negligible redistribution of income toward wage earners.[28] This could simply imply that wages were the source of unanticipated inflation in post-war U.S. economy.

In the Brazilian case, the resurgence of inflation in the 1970s and 1980s coincided with a worsening income distribution. In 1970 the richest 10 percent of Brazilians earned forty times more than the poorest 10 percent; this ratio increased to forty-one in 1980 and 80 in 1989.[29] While this fact does not necessarily imply a causality link from inflation to income redistribution, Cardoso, Paes de Barros, and Urani (1992) offered some reasons for suspecting the existence of such a relationship. Cardoso et al. (1992) examined the impact of inflation on inequality for the six largest metropolitan areas of Brazil for the period 1982–91 and concluded that inflation increased inequality by making the middle-income groups worse off. They offered three reasons why inflation may have resulted in a worsening of income distribution. First, inflation redistributes assets toward upper-income groups who are better prepared to participate in and benefit from financial markets. Second, an inflation tax especially hurts the middle-income groups whose cash holdings are likely to be higher than other groups. Third, higher-income groups usually benefit from more perfect wage indexation clauses than lower income groups. At the present time, however, these findings do not stand on solid empirical or theoretical grounds and lack formal analyses. More detailed work on the relationship between high inflation and income distribution is needed and, as mentioned above, Brazil, by the virtue of having had both the most unequal distribution of income and the highest rate of inflation among newly industrialized countries, provides a fertile environment for examining this relationship.

In addition to income redistribution from one social class to another, unanticipated inflation can also result in intersectoral and intergenerational redistribution of income. Fischer and Modigliani (1975) note that in the absence of indexation, older people with retirement claims witness a decrease in their outstanding claims against the government. This implies a decline in future tax payments resulting in income transfers from the older generation to the younger generation.

The wealth redistribution effect is more easily understood since it is always from nominal lenders to nominal borrowers. Increased unanticipated inflation translates into a transfer of financial resources from net lenders (the banking sector) to net borrowers (borrowing firms). This resource transfer will leave the net wealth of corporate debt unaffected by simply transferring resources from risk-averse to less risk-averse households.[30] For the United States it is estimated that 1 percent unanticipated inflation results in a redistribution of wealth of about 1 percent of GNP. In countries such as Brazil, where interest rates are artificially set and the market mechanism for determining the equilibrium interest rate is handicapped, the repercussions of unanticipated inflation on the real economy are more pronounced. In Brazil, inflation uncertainties have repeatedly resulted in a credit crunch by the banking system's defensive strategies that hold the real rate of interest artificially high as a hedge against inflation-induced creditors' loss. It is not surprising that Brazilian presidents have repeatedly attacked the banking system for setting interest rates too high.

A much discussed remedy to the negative impacts of inflation is the introduction of widespread indexation mechanisms that automatically adjust nominal variables to inflation. Indexation is commonly perceived as being able to lessen the redistributive impact of inflation and reduce the welfare, output, and efficiency losses brought about by it. Commenting on indexation, Friedman (1974) echoed the widely held view that "no other (mechanism) . . . holds out as much promise of both reducing harm done by inflation and facilitating the ending of inflation." Despite such enthusiasm among some economists, policymakers have traditionally been reluctant to implement widespread indexations. The problem with the view echoed by Friedman is that the second half of the statement is true only conditionally: indexation makes fighting inflation easier and less costly *if* there are no shocks to the economy. Simonsen (1983) shows that if shocks are absent and widespread indexation is adopted, the output–inflation trade-off disappears even in the short run, thus facilitating ending inflation. But once shocks are introduced, the conclusion is dramatically different. Gray (1976), Fischer (1977), and Simonsen (1983) show that wage indexation can accentuate the inflation problem by protecting output and employment from shocks and transmitting the entire shock effect into prices, resulting in even more price instability. Ball (1990) shows that quick disinflation is possible if indexation is absent. In staggered price–wage change models disinflation is more difficult (Taylor 1983, Ball 1990) and disinflation becomes even more challenging and costly once indexation replaces staggered contracts (Bonomo and Garcia 1992).

As discussed in chapter 2, indexation has long been an important feature of the Brazilian economy. First introduced to reduce the welfare cost of inflation, indexation later became a troubling element in propagating inflation and undermining the effectiveness of stabilization programs in Brazil. As a result, four heterodox disinflation plans that were implemented in the 1986–90 period sought to rid the economy of formal indexation. In each case, despite the temporary removal of indexation, inflation returned because its underlying causes (read disequilibrium in internal and external accounts) were largely intact.

Conclusion

In this chapter we have examined the current theoretical frameworks for identifying the causes of and the remedies for inflation in Latin America. We have also addressed the question of costs of inflation.

From a theoretical perspective, the neostructuralist framework lacks the secure micro foundations upon which the new classical approach is constructed and is devoid of the sophisticated formal analysis and rich empirical support associated with monetarism. Nevertheless, neostructuralism has had a lasting and influential, albeit not always productive, impact in Latin America. Following the prescriptions offered by the neostructuralists, in the second half of the 1980s Argentina and Brazil adopted various heterodox stabilization programs. These programs are examined in detail in chapters 2 and 5. Here it suffices to mention that these programs uniformly failed in their quest to bring inflation under control.

The inertialists assume that the practice of markup pricing, caused by the oligopolistic nature of production in Brazil, is one of institutional factors responsible for the inertial nature of Brazilian inflation. In the environment of high inflation, it is easy to misconstrue markup pricing, which is a symptom of high inflation, as a cause of inflation. As discussed above, higher inflation is suspected of causing increased relative price variability and price uncertainty. To protect themselves from losses from inflation, producers may resort to markup pricing that adjusts their prices for previous-period inflation as well as expected inflation. This can happen even in highly competitive markets because for consumers the cost of obtaining information about various vendors' prices becomes very high.

We concluded that inflation can have welfare, redistributive and disruptive impacts on the economy. Recent studies indicate that the welfare cost of high inflation is perhaps much higher than indicated by earlier studies. For Brazil, some estimates of the welfare cost of inflation exceed 50 percent of GDP. The redistributive effect of inflation works at income and wealth levels. The redistribution effect on the income level depends greatly on the source of inflation. For the Brazilian case, a recent study concluded that inflation worsened income inequality by redistributing income in favor of upper-income groups, mostly by squeezing middle-income groups. The wealth effect of inflation is more straightforward, as it always benefits net borrowers at the expense of net lenders. Finally, the disruptive impact of inflation results from efficiency losses. Higher inflation rates result in more general price and relative price variability and thus make it more difficult to make decisions based on prices. As the role of prices as a signaling mechanism for economic decision making is hindered, economic efficiency is reduced.

Some authors have argued convincingly that the evils of inflation are often brought about by governments eager to eradicate them. In other words, deflation policies introduced by governments are likely to prove more costly to the society than inflation itself. In these situations, inflation costs the economy indirectly through government policies. As we examine in chapter 2, the Collor Plan in Brazil, which attacked the inflation problem aggressively through a combination of incomes, fiscal, and monetary policies, provides a sobering example of this possibility. The Collor Plan brought about the most severe recession in the history of Brazil without solving the inflation riddle. Governments anxious to provide overnight remedies to the inflation problem are more dangerous to the economy than high inflation.

2

The Brazilian Experience with Inflation: 1964–94

Introduction

High inflation rates have long been a prominent feature of the Brazilian economy (see Figure 2.1). With the exception of 1953, the Brazilian annual inflation rate has fluctuated in the two- to four-digit range since 1947. Yet Brazilian policymakers have rarely confronted the inflation problem forcefully.

Until the 1980s, the primary goal of Brazilian administrations was achieving high economic growth rates. Inflation was considered threatening only when it interfered with official development objectives. As a result, various governments tolerated "moderate" inflation and devised defensive mechanisms such as wage indexation to make living with inflation easier. This pattern of downplaying the adverse effects of inflation—partly reinforced by the popular structuralist approach that viewed inflation as a natural by-product of growth—was seriously challenged in the 1980s and 1990s as the economy repeatedly reached the brink of hyperinflation and experienced severe slowdowns. Since the mid-1980s, controlling inflation has been the highest priority of Brazilian governments.

Between 1986 and 1990 Brazil introduced four comprehensive heterodox stabilization plans: the Cruzado Plan (1986), the Bresser Plan (1987), the Summer Plan (1988), and the Collor Plan (1990). These stabilization programs imposed comprehensive wage, price, and exchange rate freezes, implemented or promised monetary and fiscal reforms, and introduced new currencies. However, these plans, as well as other less ambitious miniplans (Cruzado Plan II and Collor Plan II), failed to remedy the inflation problem

Figure 2.1 **Quarterly Rates of Inflation, 1975–90**

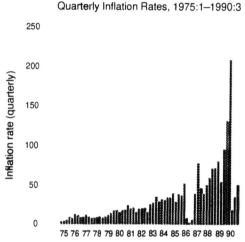

Quarterly Inflation Rates, 1975:1–1990:3

and cost the economy dearly in terms of lost employment and output. The unspectacular performance of heterodox policies of 1986–90 persuaded the Brazilian policymakers to abandon the heterodox approach and return to more orthodox measures.

This chapter analyzes the Brazilian experience with inflation during the period 1964–94. The main focus is the stabilization plans that were adopted after the return of democracy in 1985. The chapter is divided into six sections. The following section provides an overview of inflation and stabilization during the years of military rule (1964–85). Other sections offer a comprehensive study of the Cruzado Plan, consider the Bresser and Summer plans, and provide an in-depth study of the Collor Plan. In the final section, we briefly examine the recent Real Plan; this is followed by the conclusion.

Inflation under Military Regimes: 1964–85

When President João Goulart's government was overthrown by a military takeover on March 31, 1964, the Brazilian economy was in dire need of a comprehensive stabilization program. During the preceding two years, Goulart's goal of bringing about income redistribution through haphazard but substantial increases in nominal wages had placed considerable upward pressure on prices.[1] Despite rampant inflation, the government refused to adjust public utility and transportation prices and continued its expensive

Table 2.1

Annual Rate of Inflation (December to December) and Rate of Money Expansion (Fourth Quarter to Fourth Quarter), 1960–70

Year	Inflation rate	Money growth rate
1960	30.4	33.3
1961	47.8	52.3
1962	51.6	62.1
1963	79.9	74.6
1964	92.1	66.9
1965	34.2	46.5
1966	39.1	30.6
1967	25.0	26.7
1968	25.4	41.7
1969	19.3	25.5
1970	19.2	23.4

Source: Conjuntura Economica, various issues.

subsidy programs.[2] To support its populist agenda, the Goulart administration resorted to deficit spending and inflationary monetary expansion. As a result, between 1961 and 1963, the money supply increased at an average annual rate of 63 percent and prices rose by about 575 percent. (See Table 2.1.)

Goulart's approach to macroeconomic management had its roots in traditional populism as evidenced by economic policies that "emphasize[d] economic growth and income distribution and de-emphasize[d] the risk of inflation and deficit finance, external constraint and the reaction of economic agents to aggressive non-market policies."[3] This approach ignored much-needed stabilization measures and led to the political and economic instability that helped pave the way for the military takeover.[4] The experience of Goulart's administration[5] offers two important lessons that are extensively discussed elsewhere in the literature: (1) the implementation of harsh and unpopular stabilization measures are difficult, especially for democratic governments of countries in which pronounced strife among various socioeconomic classes exists;[6] and (2) macroeconomic populism, despite its good intentions, is counterproductive in the long run and results in deficit problems, inflation, and instability.[7]

After the *coup d'état* of 1964, the administration of Castelo Branco (1964–67) immediately launched a stabilization program (Programa de Ação Econômica do Governo—PAEG) to bring inflation under control. Octavio Bulhões and Roberto Campos, the architects of the plan, employed a combination of fiscal, monetary, and incomes measures to stabilize the economy. They decided to pursue an anti-inflationary policy that (1) avoided a deep recession, and (2) restored the allocative function of the free market. The commitment to the first goal signified the government's decision to follow a "gradualist" approach rather than "shock" treatment, while the second criterion meant that the government would tolerate "corrective inflation" as previously distorted prices were allowed to rise toward their market equilibrium levels.[8]

The new government's long-term goal was to stabilize prices through a drastic reduction in its budget deficit. This deficit reduction was to be accomplished through expenditure containment and revenue enhancement. The government was determined to increase its revenues through *long-term* restructuring of the tax system. In the immediate aftermath of the coup, however, the deficit problem was to be tolerated because cutting expenditures and abolishing subsidies to popular programs seemed politically risky. Instead of bringing public sector expenditure under control, the government granted substantial salary increases to military personnel and public sector employees in order to consolidate its base of popular support.

To neutralize the inflationary impact of the deficit, the government attempted to attract investors to the bond market, which was especially depressed because of a "usury law" that limited annual nominal interest rates to 12 percent. In the inflationary environment of Brazil, this "12 percent rule" translated into very low or even negative real interest rates. To remedy this problem, the government promptly introduced National Readjustable Treasury Bonds (ORTN), which pegged bond prices and interest rates to the inflation rate.[9]

Given the government's decision to tolerate moderate inflation, the Brazilian authorities decided to institutionalize widespread indexation of mortgage payments, rents, exchange rates, and time deposits in order to bring about "inflation without tears."[10] While nonwage adjustments were designed to remedy the distortionary impact of inflation, the purpose of wage policy was to reduce the inflation rate through real wage compression.[11] Until 1968, wages were adjusted according to the formula:[12]

$$W_{t+1} = W_a(1 + \beta^e_{t+1})(1 + \tfrac{1}{2} \Pi^e_{t+1})P_t$$

where W_a was the two-year average real wage, β^e was the expected rate of productivity growth, and Π^e stood for the expected inflation rate. The government succeeded in reducing inflationary wage pressures by systematically underestimating both the anticipated rate of productivity growth and the expected rate of inflation.[13] Between 1964 and 1967 this policy of wage squeeze resulted in a 25 percent decline in the average real wage in the industrial sector.[14]

During the "Brazilian Miracle" years (1968–73), the government reduced its deficit to 750 million cruzeiros, compared to a deficit of 2 billion cruzeiros, in 1964. Furthermore, the government adopted a tight monetary policy, actively sought foreign investors, continued administrative control of prices, and followed a repressive wage policy.[15] Such actions resulted in stable prices along with impressive rates of economic growth. During the "miracle years," the annual inflation rate averaged 19.5 percent while real GDP per capita rose at an average yearly rate of 11.3 percent.

In March 1974, Ernesto Geisel replaced Emilio Medici as the new Brazilian president. The breakdown of the Bretton Woods system during the last two years of Medici's government contributed to a substantial inflow of foreign capital. As a result, Brazil's foreign reserves increased to $6.4 billion in 1973 from $1.74 billion in 1971. In 1972, Brazil acted decisively to sterilize the increased reserves by reducing domestic credit, but in 1973 the monetary authorities did not neutralize augmented reserves.[16] As a result, Geisel's government inherited the previous administration's sterling record of economic performance and faced pronounced inflationary pressures.

To further complicate matters, the oil shock of 1973–74 increased the price of imported oil by 400 percent and caused a $4.7 billion trade deficit. Brazil, no longer able to rely on its strong current account for financing its growth, faced a difficult policy quandary. In response to the balance-of-payments disequilibrium caused by the oil price revolution, the Brazilian government could choose from three alternatives: (1) do nothing and simply accept a lower income level with relatively higher prices; (2) adopt contractionary fiscal and monetary policies that would control inflation at the cost of lower growth rates; or (3) continue with high-growth policies by relying on foreign capital at the risk of higher inflation rates.

The Geisel administration favored the last option. It decided that a continuation of the high-growth policies of the Medici government was the only politically feasible alternative, for three reasons. First, the impressive economic record of the previous administration was still fresh in people's minds. Second, continued economic growth was necessary for alleviating the poverty problem and addressing the lingering question of inequity in the distribution of income, which was attracting damaging negative attention abroad.[17] Third, Geisel's goal of political decompression required a robust economy.[18]

Having opted for high growth *cum* inflation, the Brazilian government relied on extensive foreign borrowing to pay for its ambitious economic growth blueprint, dubbed the Second National Development Plan. On the supply side, the abundance of petrodollars and the perceived safety of investing in developing countries[19] made foreign capital readily available to Brazil. As can be seen in Table 2.2, between 1974 and 1985 real govern-

Table 2.2

Government Expenditure and Inflation Rates, 1974–85

Year	Government expenditure (cruzeiro$ Bil.)	Inflation rate (%)	Change in government expenditure (nominal)	Change in government expenditure (real)
1974	72.9	33.2	38.6	29.0
1975	95.4	30.1	30.9	23.7
1976	165.8	48.2	73.8	49.8
1977	241.8	38.6	45.8	33.1
1978	344.3	40.5	42.4	30.2
1979	507.8	76.8	47.5	26.9
1980	1,271.4	110.2	150.4	71.5
1981	2,258.9	95.2	77.7	39.8
1982	4,611.2	99.7	104.1	52.1
1983	11,301.9	211.0	145.1	46.7
1984	33,766.0	223.8	198.8	61.4
1985	121,209.0	235.1	259.0	77.3

Source: *Conjuntura Economica*, various issues.

ment expenditure increased by an average of 60 percent. Thus, after the oil shock of 1973, the Brazilian military remained committed to an active and expansionary fiscal policy.

On March 15, 1979, President João Baptista Figueiredo took office. As the government continued to steer the economy along a high growth–high inflation path by borrowing and spending, dangerous winds were gathering momentum on the horizon. Interest rates on the Brazilian $70 billion foreign debt[20] began to increase, and a worldwide recession spread among Brazil's major trading partners. As Brazil increased its dependence on foreign capital, other newly industrialized countries such as South Korea reacted to warning signs by adopting adjustment programs that substantially reduced their exposure to foreign debt. In Brazil, Planning Minister Mário Simonsen favored a mix of orthodox fiscal and monetary policies aimed at controlling the government deficit, the inflation rate, and the mounting foreign debt, but political arithmetic made his recommendations unattractive to the military government. President Figueiredo, intending to be the man credited for bringing back democracy to Brazil, did not want a recession to interfere with his plans for a gradual transition from a military to a civilian government. Figueiredo thus preferred to pursue what Bresser Pereira has termed "populist-developmentist" economic policies.[21] Figueiredo's influential agriculture minister Delfim Neto openly criticized the adjustment plan set forth by Simonsen. Architect of the economic growth of the miracle years, Delfim loomed larger than life in the eyes of the Brazilian business community, and believed miracles could happen twice. Conveniently overlooking the balance-of-payments and deficit problems, Delfim stressed that adjustment could be achieved without a recession and promised more years of prosperity and high economic growth.

Through the introduction of the Third National Development Plan (1980–86) Delfim hoped to mastermind a repeat of the Miracle Years performance. But relative to 1968, in 1979 the Brazilian economy was much more anemic: the balance-of-payments difficulties had made the country dangerously vulnerable to unfavorable external shocks. Furthermore, unlike a decade earlier, the wage squeeze card was no longer available to the government as it sought to open up the political process. Having opted for an inflationary fiscal and monetary mix, in November 1979 the government replaced the practice of annual wage negotiations with automatic biannual wage adjustments in order to compensate workers more rapidly for the loss in real wages caused by inflation. Meanwhile, inflationary pressures were also mounting on a different front as the second oil shock of the 1970s doubled the price of oil-derivative products in four months.

Under Figueiredo's leadership, Brazil continued its reliance on foreign capital for financing high rates of growth—an 8 percent average annual GDP growth rate between 1979 and 1981—and postponed the needed adjustment. Between 1979 and 1982, the public foreign debt increased from $35.5 billion to $47.6 billion. In the meanwhile the price of oil continued to increase from $12.4 per barrel in 1978 to $17.1 and $29.6 in 1979 and 1980, respectively. As increased oil prices resulted in a substantial rise in the import bill and a worldwide recession reduced demand for Brazilian exports, the trade balance turned from a surplus of $1 billion in 1978 into a deficit of $2.8 billion in 1979 and 1980.[22] In response to a continued deterioration in the balance of payments, the government devalued the cruzeiro and promoted exports through subsidies. Although these measures helped create current account surpluses, balance-of-payments difficulties continued because of the heavy burden of foreign debt (see Table 2.3).

During the 1979–80 period, for political reasons surrounding both the question of sovereignty and strained relations with the United States regarding human rights violations in Brazil, as well as Brazil's *abertura*, the Brazilian government was hesitant to subject the country to policy dictates of the International Monetary Fund and thus introduced its own orthodox austerity measures. A drastic reduction in real public sector spending was the hallmark of the plan. In 1981, despite a 95 percent inflation rate, government expenditures increased by only 77 percent. Government subsidies dropped from 3.6 percent of the GDP in 1980 to 2.7 percent in 1981, and government's real expenditure on wages and salaries declined by 4 per-

Table 2.3

Balance of Payments, 1978–86 (in millions of U.S.$)

	1978	1979	1980	1981	1982	1983	1984	1985	1986
A. Trade balance	1,024	-2,839	-2,830	1,213	780	6,470	13,089	12,471	8,249
B. Services	-6,037	-7,920	-10,212	-13,127	-17,082	-13,415	-13,215	-12,893	-12,912
C. Goods and services (A+B)	-5,013	-10,759	-13,041	-11,914	-16,302	-6,945	-126	-627	-876
D. Unrequited transfers	71	18	115	197	42	107	170	155	86
E. Current transactions (C+D)	-6,990	-10,741	-12,886	-11,717	-16,260	-6,837	-45	-268	-4,476
F. Capital	11,891	7,656	9,804	12,917	7,851	1,742	-1,245	-2,729	-7,340
G. Errors and omissions	-638	-130	16	-77	-195	-574	402	-529	-540
The sums of rows E, F, and G: Surplus(+) or Deficit(-)	4,262	-3,214	408	-578	-8,605	-5,670	-798	-3,526	-12,356

Source: Banco Central do Brasil, *Boletim Mensal*, September 1994.

cent.[23] But as the government reduced its expenditure on subsidies and wages, it faced a growing financial burden because of increased indebtedness of public enterprises and larger debt-servicing requirements due to substantial exchange rate devaluation and higher interest rates.[24] The drastic decline in government expenditure in the real sector of the economy, together with a tight monetary policy (an 82 percent increase in the money supply), resulted in a severe contraction that reduced the level of industrial production by about 12 percent. Despite considerable output cost, the inflation rate dropped only modestly—from 110 percent in 1980 to 95 percent in 1981 (see Table 2.2).

The pronounced reversal of external financing flows in the aftermath of the Mexican moratorium of August 1982 exerted enormous pressure on the balance of payments of Brazil. As can be seen from Table 2.3, the balance-of-payments positions of the country deteriorated substantially from a deficit of about $800 million in 1984 to a punishing deficit of more than $12 billion in 1986. The dangerous external imbalance that manifested itself in the balance-of-payments position of the country forced Brazil to turn to the IMF for help. The IMF prescribed its usual package, which included elimination of the public sector deficit together with overly optimistic nominal targets for money expansion. The public deficit was expected to be eliminated in two years. But the persistence of stagflation made the IMF's targets highly unrealistic. Partly because of a severe recession and partly because of an inflation that reduced the real value of tax receipts, real government revenues declined by about 21 percent between 1980 and 1983. In the face of persistent three-digit annual inflation rates, the IMF belatedly accepted the need for revising its preset nominal targets. As the Brazilian policymakers and an inept IMF staff team continued missing a moving target, they negotiated seven letters of intent in twelve months.[25]

In February 1983, the Brazilian government again devalued the cruzeiro by 30 percent and decreased the real quantity of money (M_1) by about 14 percent.[26] On the fiscal side, government spending was reduced substantially and the public deficit was cut from 7.3 percent of GDP to 3.1 percent of GDP. These contractionary policies caused a more than 3 percent reduction in the GDP but failed to bring inflation under control. The annual inflation rate edged up to 211 percent by the end of 1983.

During the 1984 electoral campaign, Brazil was most preoccupied with the political ramifications of the long-awaited transition from military rule to civilian government, and no attempt was made to bring inflation under control. During these national campaigns, however, a broad agreement emerged about the need for implementing a social pact among various groups of society that would reduce inflation without increasing unemployment and undermining the wage claims of the working people. While such a social pact never materialized, it became clear that controlling inflation was a national priority.

The Cruzado Plan

In 1985, Tancredo Neves, a mild-mannered, highly respected, and popular seventy-four-year-old man, was to become the first civilian president of Brazil after almost a quarter century of military dictatorship. For the Brazilian people, Tancredo embodied hope for a better future free of repression; for the military he represented a link to conservatism. Tancredo was a man trusted both by the left and the right, respected by liberals and conservatives alike, and as such he was a rare actor on the political stage of Brazil. As Brazilians were preparing for March 15, 1985, the date of Tancredo's inauguration, fate had other plans. The night before the scheduled inauguration, Tancredo was rushed to the hospital. He died a month later. Brazil, a nation in grief, watched as José Sarney, the vice president–elect, was sworn in as the Brazilian president, as dictated by the constitution. The task before Sarney was daunting, as he himself summarized the challenge that faced him:

> When I assumed the presidency, my inheritance included the deepest recession in Brazil's history, the highest rate of unemployment, an unprecedented climate of violence, potential political disintegration, and the highest rate of inflation ever recorded in our country's history—250 percent a year, with the prospect of reaching 1,000 percent.[27]

By the time the new democratic government took office in March 1985, stabilization policies based on demand management had proven ineffective and had caused an economic slowdown. In April 1985, Sarney's New Republic government implemented a combination of fiscal and monetary policies together with a limited price-control plan to control inflation.[28] A severe drought in August caused a 20 percent rise in food prices that undermined the partial price freeze program.[29]

In the first few months of Sarney's administration, a rift between those who wanted a speedy adjustment through more orthodox means and those who claimed growth and adjustment could be accomplished simultaneously surfaced in the form of an open conflict between Finance Minister Francisco Dornelles and Planning Secretary João Sayad. This conflict resembled the 1979 Delfim–Simonsen clash. Similar to Delfim Neto in 1979, João Sayad painted a rosy picture of Brazilian economic conditions, and with the popular support for his PMDB (the Brazilian Democratic Movement Party), he won out. As in the Delfim–Simonsen case, the proponent of orthodoxy, Finance Minister Dornelles was forced out of the cabinet and replaced by Dilson Funaro, a supporter of Sayad. Soon Sayad and Funaro, together with other PMDB economists including Francisco Lopes, Edmar Bacha, Persio Arida, and André Lara Resende sketched a plan for fighting inflation without sacrificing output and employment.[30]

On February 28, 1986, as the annual inflation rate exceeded 265 percent, the government of José Sarney introduced its first comprehensive heterodox anti-inflation plan: the Cruzado Plan. For the first time in Brazil, economists who had argued that the neostructuralist framework best explained the nature of Brazilian inflation were given an opportunity to test the effectiveness of their prescriptions. As discussed in chapter 1, the neostructuralists' heterodox approach was based on the view that Brazilian inflation was fundamentally different from inflation in advanced industrialized countries. Brazilian inflation, it was argued, was caused by structural idiosyncrasies such as wage indexation, distributive conflicts, and fights for shares of national income. The Cruzado Plan economists concluded that since inertia was the central characteristic of Brazilian inflation, demand management policies alone could not quell it. The remedy to this type of persistent, self-propelling inflation was to be found in heterodox anti-inflationary shocks that eliminated the "inflationary memory" of economic agents.[31]

The architects of the Cruzado Plan therefore prescribed a policy package similar to the recent Argentine Austral Plan[32] (see chapter 5), which included temporary price and exchange rate freezes, the elimination of most indexing mechanisms, and the introduction of a new monetary unit (the cruzado), which replaced the old currency (the cruzeiro) at the rate of 1:1,000.[33] The plan effectively froze wages for one year by reintroducing annual wage indexation.[34] Prior to the freeze, wages were increased based on real average wages of the previous six months plus a bonus of 15 percent for the minimum wage and 8 percent for all other indexed wages.[35]

The architects of the plan argued that this particular wage scheme was needed because staggered contracts had resulted in unsynchronized adjustment of wages for inflation. In other words, since some workers did not have their wages corrected for inflation prior to the wage freeze, wage bonuses were given to all workers. While the unsynchronized nature of wage contracts may explain why the planners decided to grant across-the-board wage increases, the *size* of wage bonuses was chosen in an *ad hoc* way. As Eduardo Modiano (1988a, 225), one of the architects of the plan, described it, "there was no economic rationale for the magnitude of the wage bonus. This resulted from a political decision to promote a redistribution of income toward wage earners, favoring still further the lower classes." While Planning Minister João Sayad later recounted that from a distributive perspective the plan was designed to be essentially neutral,[36] the government seemed to have had in mind a redistribution of income in favor of lower classes.

While wages were boosted, prices were frozen at their level of February 27 for an indefinite period of time. For about five hundred consumer products, the government published a list of maximum prices that could be charged and relied on official inspectors and a vigilant public to monitor prices.[37]

As the price freeze continued, inflationary pressure was exerted on two fronts. First, the wage increases that immediately preceded the freeze led to a substantial rise in demand for goods, which, in an environment of fixed prices, led to shortages, hoarding, and an increase in the activity of the underground economy. Compared to the first half of 1985, in the first six months of 1986 retail sales increased by 24 percent. Despite a capacity utilization of close to 100 percent in some industries and an average utilization of 82 percent for the entire industrial sector, shortages spread.[38] In this environment, consumers were often forced to pay *ágios*, premiums above the official price, to get scarce items at inflated prices.

On the second front, the government placed itself in a tenuous financial position by attempting to maintain a price freeze at any cost. The wage–price squeeze worsened the government's budgetary problems by increasing the production cost of state enterprises while forbidding compensatory increases in their prices. The financial pressure was even more pronounced for firms that had not adjusted their prices prior to the freeze. Moreover, to maintain the price freeze, the government gave certain producers costly financial incentives. Of these the most expensive was a 30 percent subsidy given to the producers of dairy products that cost the government 1.5 billion cruzados between June and December 1986.[39] As a result of these financial pressures, the budget deficit rose by 70.5 percent from September 1986 until the end of the year while the inflation rate averaged only 3.1 percent.[40]

In July the government introduced the Cruzadinho—"the little cruzado"—Plan with the intention of cooling down demand and promoting investment through forced saving. This plan imposed a tax of 28 to 30 percent on gasoline and new car purchases in the form of "compulsory loans." These were considered "loans" because the payees of the tax were to be given equity shares in the National Development Fund.[41] The government, therefore, justified not including the resulting price increases in calculating the inflation rate.[42]

The Cruzado Plan resulted in significant balance-of-payments difficulties. As can be seen from Figure 2.2, the trade balance turned from a strong surplus position to a deficit. The plan caused this deterioration in two ways.

Figure 2.2 **Trade Balance and Balance of Payments, 1986:1–1987:4**

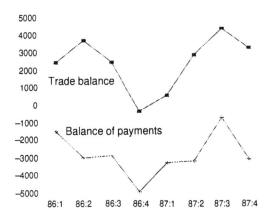

First, the exchange rate was fixed for seven months and was subsequently devalued at rates lower than the inflation rate. Second, to alleviate shortages, the government increased imports. The overvalued cruzado and increased imports reversed the country's strong trade balance position. For the first time since the first quarter of 1981, Brazil faced a trade deficit, which, combined with difficulties in the capital account, exerted enormous pressures on the balance of payments.

Because of the popularity of the Cruzado Plan, the government was unwilling to unfreeze prices before the elections. A few days after the November elections, the government introduced the Cruzado II Plan. The plan was designed to correct imbalances and to reduce the government deficit. The Cruzado II program increased prices of public utility services, gasoline, automobiles, and products with highly inelastic demand such as cigarettes and dairy products. But these price increases set in motion an automatic wage adjustment mechanism built into the Cruzado Plan that would increase wages in response to an annual inflation rate of 20 percent.[43] The reincarnation of the wage–price spiral undermined the Cruzado Plan as the inflation rate reached 16.8 percent in January and thereafter continued to increase steadily until June, when the Bresser Plan was introduced.

The first comprehensive heterodox plan for combating Brazilian inflation failed quickly.[44] By August 1986, the black market premium on the U.S. dollar approached 90 percent, prompting Finance Minister Funaro to attempt to abolish parallel foreign-exchange markets. As shortages spread and long lines formed, the use of *ágios* became common practice. The Cruzado Plan failed for a number of important reasons. First, it never suc-

Figure 2.3 **Monthly Budget Deficit (Nominal Government Revenues—
Nominal Government Expenditures): 1986:3–1986:12** (in millions cruzeriros)

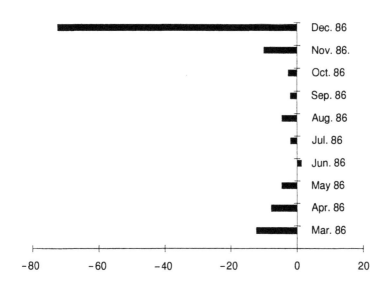

Source: Banco Central do Brasil.

ceeded in controlling the government deficit (see Figure 2.3). In a way, the Cruzado Plan sowed the seeds of its own destruction by creating a budgetary crisis for important state enterprises that had not adjusted their prices prior to the freeze. High and persistent public sector deficits, together with the government's objective of keeping interest rates low, led to substantial increases in the money supply, which fueled inflation. The policy of simultaneous wage increases and price freezes was another costly mistake that contributed to the failure of the plan by creating widespread imbalances.

Supporters of the inertialist approach to the inflation problem often blame political factors for the failure of the Cruzado Plan. Both Werner Baer (1989) and Luiz Bresser Pereira (1990) suggest that the plan may have succeeded had President Sarney accepted the recommendation of the architects of the plan to unfreeze prices in a timely fashion. Obviously, it is important to establish what the planners meant by a short-term price freeze. Baer observes that "while the Cruzado Plan economists agreed that the price freeze would be temporary, they had reached no consensus about how long it should last, since they did not know how long it would take to reverse inflationary expectations."[45]

Since in the framework adopted by the designers of the Cruzado Plan expectations did not play an important role, it was difficult to establish how long the price freeze was to last. The available evidence, however, suggests that the architects of the Cruzado Plan simply assumed that economic agents were backward-looking in forming their expectations. A closer look at how the designers of the plan decided to deal with the problem of conversion of financial liabilities with preset monetary indexing into cruzados sheds light on this issue. It was determined that the liabilities preset indexing clauses that were contracted before February 28, 1986, were to be settled on the day of maturity with 0.45 percent per day discount. This discount rate was figured based on the assumption that inflationary expectations built into contracts were formed from the average of the previous three months' inflation rates.

Since the architects of the plan assumed that the public formed its inflationary expectations by taking into consideration only the average of recent inflation rates, they reasoned that maintaining low inflation rates for a number of months would eliminate the inertial component of inflation and stop the inflationary fight for shares among different classes and sectors. The significance of drastically and quickly reducing the government fiscal deficit was downplayed, at least in practice, even though originally the plan was supposed to create an opportunity for the government to attack the underlying causes of inflation by bringing its budget deficit under control. But the initial success of the plan made the government unenthusiastic about applying the bitter medicine of fiscal restraint. The official inflation rates were low only because of the government's intervention in the marketplace, and with the fundamental causes of inflation still intact, high inflation rates were expected to return as soon as price controls were lifted. Not having addressed the underlying causes of inflation, the relief provided by the Cruzado Plan was only temporary.

The failure of the Cruzado Plan proved costly as it resulted in a deep economic crisis. Between May and October 1987, investment levels fell to their lowest since 1964, real wages declined by 65 percent, the balance of payments deteriorated rapidly and, in São Paulo alone, more than 2,500 businesses filed for bankruptcy. Those who had often criticized the orthodox approach because of its recessionary impact had themselves implemented a plan that brought about severe economic hardship.

The Bresser Plan and the Summer Plan

On June 12, 1987, Luiz Bresser Pereira, the newly appointed finance minister, introduced a second heterodox plan that came to be known as the

Bresser Plan. Unlike the Cruzado Plan, the main objective of the Bresser Plan was not to eliminate inflation, but to bring it down to manageable levels. Moreover, the Bresser Plan aimed at restoring the economic health of the country, as Bresser Pereira was warned by President Sarney in their first meeting that the government foreign reserves were expected to be entirely depleted by September.[46]

The Bresser Plan and the Cruzado Plan had three important characteristics in common. First, both plans adopted a heterodox approach to solving the inflation problem. In the same spirit as the Cruzado Plan, the Bresser Plan also contained price and wage freeze components, but it set in advance the time horizon of the freeze at three months.

Second, both plans implemented policies that were incompatible with price control programs. The Cruzado Plan, as explained above, created inadvertent inflationary pressures by increasing wages prior to the freeze. The Bresser Plan, reacting to balance-of-payments problems caused by the Cruzado Plan, devalued the cruzado on the day of the freeze and proceeded with a policy of continuous mini-devaluations. Between May and December 1987, the cruzado was devalued by more than 65 percent without a corresponding adjustment in domestic prices.[47]

Third, both the Cruzado Plan and the Bresser Plan proved ineffective in less than a year. If monthly double-digit inflation rates show the failure of anti-inflationary measures, the Cruzado and Bresser plans floundered in ten and three months, respectively (see Table 2.4). In September 1987 the Bresser Plan's price-wage control mechanism broke down when government employees were given substantial wage increases. By October it was clear that like the Cruzado Plan, the Bresser Plan had failed to bring the public sector deficit under control and to stabilize prices.

In the first two weeks of January 1989, prices increased by 28 percent. On January 15, the Sarney government introduced its third heterodox stabilization plan. The so-called Summer Plan (also called the New Cruzado Plan) gave the inertialists yet another opportunity to control inflation.

Like the two previous plans, the Summer Plan imposed a price and wage freeze that was designed to last four to eight weeks. To avoid comparisons with the price controls of the two previous plans, the government called the freeze "prefixing of inflation at the zero level." The Summer Plan eliminated monthly correction of wages for inflation and introduced yet another currency (the cruzado novo) that replaced the three-year-old cruzado at the rate 1:1,000. The government ambition was to reduce its deficit by selling or closing forty state enterprises and thirty government agencies and foun-

Table 2.4

Monthly Inflation Rate, Exchange Rate, and Trade Balance: 1986–87

Period	Inflation rate (percent)	Exchange rate (cruzado/U.S.$)	Trade balance
1986			
January	17.8	12.15	698
February	22.4	13.84	627
March	−1.0	13.84	—
April	−0.6	13.84	1,291
May	0.3	13.84	1,383
June	0.5	13.84	1,071
July	0.6	13.84	1,005
August	1.3	13.84	945
September	1.1	14.09	534
October	1.4	14.09	−83
November	2.5	14.20	−38
December	7.6	14.94	−218
1987			
January	12.0	16.54	−36
February	14.1	19.80	320
March	15.0	22.14	302
April	20.1	25.43	502
May	27.7	34.00	960
June	25.9	43.38	1,430
July	9.3	46.02	1,457
August	4.5	48.36	1,429
September	8.0	51.28	1,497
October	11.2	55.90	1,193
November	14.5	63.07	1,001
December	15.9	71.71	1,117

Sources: Exchange rate from Fundaço Getulio Vargas; trade balance from Banco Central do Brasil, *Boletim Mensal* (April 1990).

dations, abolishing five ministries, and laying off ninety thousand government employees. But political factors in the form of strong resistance from the national congress and protests by public sector employees forced the government to modify the plan. By January 1990 the monthly inflation rate had reached 72 percent. But as Brazil awaited the inauguration of its new president, no forceful government anti-inflation measures were adopted. During the presidential campaign, president-elect Fernando Collor had repeatedly promised to kill the inflation beast with one magic bullet. The Brazilians later found out that what President Collor had in mind was not a bullet but a bomb that would badly damage the economy but leave the inflation beast untouched.

Table 2.5

Key Domestic Variables and the Collor Plan, 1990:1–1991:4

Period	Industrial production (1981 = 100)	Inflation rate (monthly)	% change in monetary base	% change in money (M₁)	Real wages (% change, annual)
1990					
January	111.7	71.9	19.1	13.4	7.3
February	106.0	71.7	74.3	91.8	16.1
March	108.5	81.3	144.3	194.1	6.0
April	80.5	11.3	70.2	35.6	−21.1
May	109.3	9.1	58.4	36.0	−26.7
June	111.9	9.0	−9.2	−0.5	−16.3
July	125.3	13.0	−9.0	0.0	−13.4
August	132.9	12.9	2.6	9.3	−11.1
September	125.1	11.7	17.8	14.7	−12.1
October	128.8	14.2	−0.1	0.2	−22.8
November	116.1	17.4	11.5	19.2	−22.9
December	92.3	16.5	58.0	38.6	−32.1
1991					
January	94.3	19.9	−19.3	−14.8	−33.8
February	85.7	21.1	38.4	54.5	−34.2
March	95.0	7.2	11.7	4.6	−34.1
April	106.9	8.7	0.2	1.8	−4.7

Source: Conjuntura Econômica (November 1991).

The Collor Plan

In March 1990, when Fernando Collor was sworn in as the first democratically elected president of Brazil in thirty years, the signs of hyperinflation were conspicuously present.[48] In the first three months of the year the monthly inflation rate averaged 75 percent (see Table 2.5), and triple-digit monthly rates of money expansion and inflation seemed imminent. As the economy moved along a course destined to lead to the breakdown of the monetary system, confidence in the domestic currency declined significantly, as evidenced by a 150 percent increase in the black market premium on the U.S. dollar. The hyperinflationary environment, with inflation rates of 72 and 81 percent in February and March, respectively, offered the Collor government a golden opportunity to bring the inflation problem under control at a low output cost (see chapter 1). However, this opportunity was lost as the Collor economic team adopted counterproductive policies.

On March 16, 1990, as the annual inflation rate reached 37,000 percent, President Fernando Collor introduced overnight the most audacious stabilization plan ever implemented in Latin America. Following the heterodox strategy, the Collor Plan's income policy temporarily stopped the inflationary spiral by imposing wage and price freezes. All prices were frozen at the level of March 12 and could be adjusted at a later date according to the *expected* rate of inflation as determined by the government. After a correction of 72.8 percent for the February inflation, wages were also frozen. As it was the case with prices, wages were to be adjusted according to the expected rate of inflation. If the actual rate of inflation differed from the expected rate of inflation, workers and employers were to negotiate wage adjustments accordingly.

The Collor Plan's monetary reform had three major components: (1) a substantial reduction in the stock of money; (2) a moderation in the rate of money growth; and (3) the introduction of a new monetary unit.

The centerpiece of the Collor Plan was Provisional Decree 168, which immediately reduced the money stock (M_4) by about 80 percent by imposing stringent restrictions on financial markets and by freezing all private and business bank accounts for a period of eighteen months. The maximum amount that could be withdrawn from checking and saving accounts was 50,000 cruzeiros (less than $1,000). Only 25,000 cruzeiros, or 25 percent of the balance, whichever was greater, could be withdrawn from overnight accounts. These restrictions resulted in an unprecedented liquidity squeeze.

The architects of the plan claimed that this squeeze was designed to bring down the liquidity level from about 26 percent of gross domestic product ($120 billion) to less than 9 percent ($40 billion). The planners found the 9 percent level attractive because it resembled the liquidity/GDP ratio in countries with stable, low inflation rates. In the Brazilian case, however, the reduction in liquidity as a means of fighting inflation is of dubious value. Table 2.6 clearly shows the lack of a historical correlation between the liquidity/GDP ratio and the rate of inflation in Brazil.

While the government used the liquidity reduction argument to justify the restrictions it imposed on bank accounts, a more vital reason motivated such restrictions. The Brazilian government had succeeded in paying a negative effective average rate of interest on its domestic debt in the twelve months preceding the introduction of the Collor Plan.[49] This, however, could not continue if inflation was to be controlled and inflation taxation was to end. In the short run, the Collor Plan's provisions enabled the government to finance its deficit in a noninflationary way. By freezing all bank accounts, the government brought about the largest temporary transfer of private wealth into the public sector in history. From the very beginning, it was clear that the government's objective was not zero inflation. The stated goal of the plan was to bring down the monthly inflation rate to 10 percent within one hundred days. By paying a "monetary correction" factor on bank

Table 2.6

The Rate of Inflation and Liquidity, 1970–89 (as a percentage of GDP)

Year	Inflation rate	(percentage of GDP)			
		M_1	M_2	M_3	M_4
1970	19.30	15.71	20.08	20.77	22.50
1971	19.50	15.31	19.87	21.02	23.55
1972	15.70	14.97	20.35	22.02	25.83
1973	15.50	14.93	20.88	23.00	27.39
1974	34.50	14.19	19.46	22.22	26.15
1975	29.40	13.52	19.74	23.81	28.01
1976	46.30	12.41	19.56	24.59	28.56
1977	38.80	11.31	18.39	24.31	28.41
1978	40.80	10.99	18.35	24.66	29.55
1979	77.20	10.24	16.65	23.39	28.42
1980	11.20	8.75	12.96	19.30	23.25
1981	95.20	7.30	12.74	19.77	23.49
1982	99.70	6.50	13.26	21.33	25.86
1983	211.00	5.15	11.20	20.35	25.33
1984	223.80	3.79	10.35	19.79	25.49
1985	224.40	3.73	14.12	23.32	29.49
1986	62.40	8.20	17.53	25.63	31.68
1987	365.51	4.62	14.71	24.41	29.27
1988	933.62	2.71	14.79	25.43	29.49
1989	1,764.87	2.05	16.06	24.21	26.98

Source: Yoshino, and Lopes (1990, 9).

accounts that lagged behind the rate of inflation, the government effectively taxed all bank deposits and thus enhanced its revenues.

Despite a substantial reduction in the stock of money, the money supply continued to increase. After a shock such as the one administered by the Collor Plan, it is essential to reliquify the economy to avoid excessively high real interest rates.[50] The German stabilization program of 1923 and the Hungarian experience with hyperinflation in 1947 provide two important historical case studies that show that substantial increases in the monetary base in the aftermath of a shock is prudent monetary policy.[51] The difficulty lies in finding the appropriate monetary targets for the post-shock period. To see the necessity of increasing real balances in the aftermath of a shock, consider the money market equilibrium condition:[52]

$$\frac{M_0}{P_0} = L(i_0, P^e, \dots)$$

where M and i show the nominal money stock and the interest rate, respectively; P and P^e are the actual and the expected price variables. From this equation the equilibrium interest rate can be obtained:

$$i_0 = f(\frac{M_0}{P_0}, P^e, \dots)$$

For a fixed money stock, policies such as the heterodox plans adopted by Brazil, which freeze prices and, in the short run, reduce inflationary expectations, result in an upward shift in the L function. Frozen prices and unchanged money stock then imply higher interest rates: i_1 ($i_1 > i_0$). To stabilize the interest rate at its pre-shock level, the government needs to increase the money stock. In the aftermath of the Collor Plan, the Brazilian monetary authorities increased the money supply at the substantial rate of 29 percent per month.[53]

Finally, the third component of the Collor Plan's monetary policy was the introduction of a new currency, the cruzeiro, which replaced the cruzado novo at the rate of 1:1. As in previous plans, the introduction of a new monetary unit was meant to increase confidence in the domestic economy and to help erase inflationary expectations associated with the weak currency. But more importantly, a new currency was needed to make it possible for banks to separate the frozen accounts (all in cruzado novo) from active accounts (all in cruzeiro).

The central fiscal goal of the Collor Plan was to move from a deficit of 8 percent of GDP to a surplus of 1 to 2 percent by the end of the year. In addition to decreasing the cost of financing its deficit through freezing bank accounts, the government employed seven other instruments for attaining this goal: (1) a tax known as IOF (Imposto sobre Operações Financeiras) was levied on financial transactions; (2) a nationwide three-day bank holiday, which saved the government the equivalent of $6 billion, was observed; (3) the government raised prices of state-produced products such as fuel (57 percent), electricity (32 percent), telephone (32 percent), and postal services (72 percent); (4) new income taxes were imposed on the agricultural sector; (5) the majority of government subsidies to private enterprises were cut or reduced; (6) the government announced administrative reforms, which included the goal of laying off 360,000 state employees by the end of June; and (7) a privatization program aimed at reducing the deficit by 2.5 percent of GDP was launched.

The goal of dismissing federal employees proved unrealistic both because the Brazilian constitution gave most of these employees "tenured" positions and because of objections raised by the Congress. While the government claimed that it had dismissed 160,000 federal employees, most estimates put the actual number at 50,000. The privatization program also

Figure 2.4 **Monthly Government Revenues, Expenditures, and Surplus (Deficit), 1989:1–1990:12**

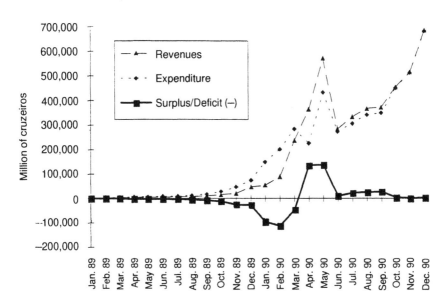

progressed more slowly than anticipated as it faced formidable challenges from the unions and the Congress. Despite these setbacks, the government succeeded in achieving a fourfold increase in its nominal revenues (see Table 2.7) partly through the privatization program and partly through rules it put in place when it sequestered citizens' and businesses' bank accounts. In particular, while individuals and businesses had their bank accounts frozen for an eighteen-month period, they could use their frozen funds to prepay taxes and fulfill their financial obligations to the government. The government boasted that in its two months in office it had turned a deficit of 113 billion cruzeiros (February 1990) into a surplus of 136 billion cruzeiros (April 1990) (see Figure 2.4 and Table 2.7).

Such seemingly impressive improvements on the deficit front, however, should be regarded cautiously for three reasons. First, as mentioned before, a large part of the increase in government's revenues was a one-time increase due to the prepayment of taxes in the frozen currency, the cruzado novo. Second, the government used a highly innovative accounting method for calculating its deficit. In particular, the government was discounting its expenses by the current month's inflation rate while it was paying a monetary correction on its entitlement payments based on the previous month's inflation rate. As a result, in an environment of increasing inflation, the

Table 2.7

Revenues, Expenditure, and Surplus/Deficit, 1986:1–1991:12 (in millions of cruzeiros)

Date	Revenues	Expenditure	Surplus/deficit	Date	Revenues	Expenditure	Surplus/deficit
Jan. 86	31.052	26.649	4.403	Jan. 89	2,177	2,250	−73
Feb. 86	31.73	25.888	5.842	Feb. 89	2,084	2,076	8
Mar. 86	25.99	38.283	−12.293	Mar. 89	3,357	3,912	−555
Apr. 86	25.447	33.131	−7.684	Apr. 89	3,219	5,817	−2,598
May 86	27.461	32.012	−4.551	May 89	4,678	6,605	−1,927
Jun. 86	30.57	29.208	1.362	Jun. 89	4,696	7,509	−2,813
Jul. 86	31.174	33.081	−1.907	Jul. 89	6,338	9,696	−3,358
Aug. 86	27.692	32.112	−4.42	Aug. 89	7,795	12,401	−4,606
Sep. 86	33.026	34.984	−1.958	Sep. 89	10,422	18,152	−7,730
Oct. 86	43.592	46.17	−2.578	Oct. 89	15,544	27,327	−11,783
Nov. 86	38.666	48.599	−9.933	Nov. 89	20,508	46,033	−25,525
Dec. 86	47.636	120.061	−72.425	Dec. 89	48,439	75,745	−27,306
Jan. 87	36.392	35.653	0.739	Jan. 90	54,757	150,013	−95,256
Feb. 87	38.693	37.594	1.099	Feb. 90	88,655	201,335	−112,680
Mar. 87	41.031	28.007	13.024	Mar. 90	236,317	284,229	−47,912
Apr. 87	80.03	79.299	0.731	Apr. 90	363,607	227,351	136,256
May 87	71.479	77.439	−5.96	May 90	571,297	432,584	138,713
Jun. 87	97.94	121.977	−24.037	Jun. 90	285,147	274,343	108,04
Jul. 87	92.737	113.768	−21.031	Jul. 90	334,061	307,824	23,560

Aug. 87	104.904	95.716	9.188	Aug. 90	368,677	343,827	25,334
Sep. 87	107.961	133.366	−25.405	Sep. 90	374,280	349,827	27,851
Oct. 87	129.497	156.216	−26.719	Oct. 90	456,104	452,549	4,249
Nov. 87	132.445	178.06	−45.615	Nov. 90	516,223	514,605	1,618
Dec. 87	269.278	335.038	−65.76	Dec. 90	687,505	683,913	3,592
Jan. 88	197	276	−79	Jan. 91	624,199	621,446	2,753
Feb. 88	219	294	−75	Feb. 91	701,035	699,431	1,604
Mar. 88	273	477	−204	Mar. 91	852,276	846,802	5,474
Apr. 88	336	493	−157	Apr. 91	962,241	958,009	4,232
May 88	450	628	−178	May 91	1,314,233	1,303,260	10,973
Jun. 88	580	894	−314	Jun. 91	1,320,216	1,312,629	7,587
Jul. 88	586	571	15	Jul. 91	1,554,004	1,544,211	9,793
Aug. 88	876	1,364	−488	Aug. 91	1,444,295	1,327,893	116,402
Sep. 88	1,125	1,371	−246	Sep. 91	1,642,016	1,539,355	102,661
Oct. 88	1,160	1,566	−406	Oct. 91	2,055,661	1,926,027	129,634
Nov. 88	2,045	2,389	−344	Nov. 91	2,202,520	2,066,547	135,973
Dec. 88	11,672	5,188	6,484	Dec. 91	3,410,709	3,255,049	155,660

Sources: Banco Central do Brasil and Serfina/Apef data bank.

government ended up with a brighter budgetary picture. In the first six months of 1990, the inflation rate and the monetary correction factors used for calculating the government deficit (surplus) were 632 and 301 percent, respectively.[54] Third, the government unilaterally limited its foreign debt service payments. These payments were reduced from $10.7 billion paid out in January and February to $0.5 billion in April.

The Collor Plan also initiated a pronounced reversal in Brazilian trade policies. The government announced its commitment to removing the majority of import restrictions and reducing tariffs. In one year, the average tariff rate was reduced from 40 to 20 percent, and further reductions were planned for July 1993.[55] Furthermore, the government brought the official exchange rate more in line with the black market rate. In the few months following the inception of the plan, the black market premium on the U.S. dollar decreased significantly, signaling the government's decision not to rely on export taxation. The architects of the plan hoped that a more open economy would reduce price pressures.

The drastic measures introduced by the Collor Plan did not result in deflation. Normally, an unanticipated reduction in the money stock causes a one-time decrease in the price level and/or the output level. In Brazil, however, the institutional setting of widespread indexation made prices and wages highly rigid downward. According to calculations of the Institute for Economic Research (FIPE) at the University of São Paulo (USP), despite the liquidity squeeze and a general price and wage freeze, prices rose by 3 percent between March 15 and May 15. While wages and prices resisted the downward pressure caused by the liquidity squeeze, the dramatic reduction in the money stock significantly constricted the output level.

The recessionary impact of the plan was sharp, immediate, and widespread. The National Confederation of Industries (CNI) estimated that in the two weeks following implementation of the plan, the level of economic activity declined by 24 percent. The industrial work force was reduced by half a million in four weeks. In only one month the production level in the capital goods sector fell by 36 percent.[56] A lackluster demand for consumer products reduced production of clothing, shoes, and textiles significantly. Of the nineteen major industries surveyed by the Instituto Brasileiro de Geografia e Estatística (IBGE), all except the tobacco industry showed dramatic contractions. The capacity utilization rate in the consumer goods sector declined from 81 percent in January to 53 percent in April.[57] The capital utilization rate in the transportation and capital goods sectors declined by 46 and 26 percent, respectively. Table 2.8 shows the average rate of capacity utilization for these nineteen industries for the period April 1988 through April 1990.

Table 2.8

Average Capacity Utilization for Various Industries, 1988–90

Industry	April 1988	April 1989	April 1990
Consumer goods	77	76	53
Capital goods	75	74	48
Construction material	77	71	52
Mineral products (nonmetallic)	78	74	55
Transportation	78	73	27
Metallurgy	85	86	63
Plastic products	70	74	53
Chemical	86	84	74
Pharmaceutical	81	78	66
Textile	85	88	73
Food products	71	70	66
Beverages	85	85	66
Tobacco	95	76	85
Wood products	77	88	69
Rubber products	86	82	67
Machinery	75	73	56
Electrical equipment	74	74	58
Leather products	76	77	67
Printing and publishing	77	84	68

Source: *Conjuntura Econômica* (August 1991).

As economic conditions worsened, the government reformed its monetary policy to help various sectors of the economy. In April, a $500 million line of credit was given to the construction sector. A few weeks later, the heavy machinery and agricultural sectors were given access to $1.8 billion and $1.1 billion, respectively. These steps, however, were too little and too late; the recession showed no signs of receding.

Then, in July 1990, the government lifted price controls. As repressed prices adjusted upwards toward equilibrium, inflation reappeared. The government required that all businesses open their books for inspection so that it could be determined if their pricing practices were "fair." Despite the government's attempts to end wage indexation through "social pacts" and presidential vetoes, informal indexation of wages continued in the private sector as the official Fator de Recomposição Salarial (FRS), which was used to adjust wages for inflation, fell behind the inflation rate. In the face of declining real wages, labor militancy and strikes increased. In July and August more than three million workers from industries as diverse as the automotive, transportation, textiles, and plastics initiated widespread strikes. In the face of continued pressure from labor, most wages were adjusted for inflation and the wage–price spiral reemerged. In the last quarter of 1990, as the inflation rate mounted, firms increased their prices further in response to wage increases and as a hedge against another heterodox shock.

On January 31, 1991, in the face of a monthly inflation rate of 20 percent, the widely anticipated Collor Plan II was ushered in.[58] The heart of the plan was another price freeze and the requirement that wages had to be adjusted in February for the inflation of the preceding twelve months. Thereafter, wages were to be adjusted through biannual negotiations between employers and employees. In order to change the indexation mechanism used in the financial markets, in April the government announced the replacement of the National Treasury Bond Rates (BTN) with the Referential Rate of Interest (Taxa Referencial, TR). TR was to be a forward-looking rate based on the expected rate of inflation as determined by the government. In the inflationary environment of Brazil, the widely used *overnight* bank accounts, which paid interest on deposits left in the banks overnight, became the most popular financial instrument for "parking" cash. As speculations in the financial markets approached dangerous levels, the government reduced returns to short term investments, especially the overnight, and forced all short-term investments into Fundos de Aplicações Financeiros (FAF) in private banks.[59] Banks were then required to use a part of deposited funds to purchase government bonds. The government also enhanced its revenue by increasing prices of fuel (47 percent), utility (60 percent), and postal services (71 percent), and promised rigorous fiscal discipline. This heterodox shock also proved costly: in the first quarter of 1991 the level of industrial production dropped by 8 percent.

May 1991 marked the end of Brazil's experimentation with heterodox stabilization plans. President Collor replaced Finance Minister Zélia Cardoso do Mello with Marcilio Marques Moreira, who promised to put an end to futile heterodox shocks and return to more orthodox prescriptions for fighting inflation.

The Real Plan

After the impeachment of Fernando Collor in 1992, his vice president, Itamar Franco, became the thirty-seventh president of Brazil. In his first eight months in office, Franco named four different finance ministers (*ministros da fazenda*). The fourth was none other than Fernando Henrique Cardoso, who introduced the successful Real Plan (also referred to as the *Plano Fernando Henrique Cardoso*) for controlling Brazilian inflation. The success of the plan in bringing down inflation paved the way for the election of Cardoso as the president of Brazil in October 1994.

The Real Plan, as envisioned by Cardoso, Edmar Bacha, and André Lara Resende (two architects of the Cruzado Plan), with frequent input from Mário Henrique Simonsen, was a three-phase attack on inflation.

The plan, introduced in December 1993, identified the fiscal crises as the main source of inflationary pressure in Brazil (see Cardoso 1994). Yet it also recognized the need for fighting the inertial component of inflation and establishing a stable currency. The plan thus anticipated the creation of the Real Unit of Value (URV, Unidade Real de Valor) as a stable currency that could be used as a measure of real value (the index currency).

The goal of the first phase of the plan was to bring about fiscal equilibrium by introducing fiscal and administrative reforms. In particular, it proposed a reduction of U.S. $44.2 billion in public expenditures and an across-the-board 5 percent increase in federal taxes. The plan also created the Social Emergency Fund for financing social (especially health and education) programs in a noninflationary way by allocating 15 percent of federal tax and contribution receipts to the fund.[60] Given the transitory nature of the Franco government and the pending inauguration of Cardoso, the Congress postponed acting on the fiscal reform package until 1995.

The second phase of the plan was designed to introduce a strong currency that was immune to inflation. It was initiated on February 27, 1994, when the government introduced Provisional Measure number 434 and the Real Unit of Value (URV). The URV was set at 647.50 cruzeiros reáis and entered the Brazilian monetary system as a complement to the cruzeiro real. The Central Bank was given the task of adjusting the value of the URV in terms of the cruzeiro real such that the purchasing power of the URV remained constant. In other words, as an alternative to the "dollarization" of the economy, the URV played the role of a strong currency whose purchasing power did not deteriorate with inflation. Beginning with March 1, 1994, wages and public sector prices were all quoted in terms of URV. The URV thus became the index according to which most nominal variables such as rents, wages, and prices were measured.

The third and final phase of the plan was the creation of the real, which replaced the cruzeiro real as the new currency of the country. The real was set at one-to-one parity with the URV and de facto became the strong currency. The real was allowed to fluctuate freely under the R$1 per U.S. $1 exchange rate. The government thus imposed a floor on the dollar value of the real, but allowed the real to fluctuate above this floor. This gave the Central Bank a certain degree of flexibility in managing the money supply.[61] It is important to remember that unlike the Cavallo Plan in Argentina (see chapter 5), the Real Plan did not guarantee the convertibility of the

Table 2.9

Capital Inflow, 1992–94

	1992	1993 Quarters				1994 Quarters	
		I	II	III	IV	I	II
Total	17,791	4,958	6,627	8,544	12,538	10,450	10,857
Investments	5,188	1,562	2,667	4,585	7,114	6,841	6,473
Portfolios	3,863	1,394	2,535	4,399	6,646	5,916	4,530
Direct	3,863	1,394	2,532	4,399	6,646	5,916	4,530
Fixed income	—	—	—	—	80	266	638
Currency loans	7,979	1,625	2,762	2,978	3,666	2,230	1,520
Financing	2,332	1,321	877	203	881	745	1,697
Leasing & rent	1,173	276	106	98	525	72	248
Prepaid exports	1,119	174	215	680	352	562	919

Source: Banco Central do Brasil, *Boletim Mensal,* September 1994, pp. 148–49.

domestic currency to the dollar at par; nor did it impose any legal restrictions regarding the management of the exchange rate and the money supply. It relied on the exchange rate as the nominal anchor for stabilizing prices, however.

During the period 1992–94, Brazil experienced a substantial inflow of foreign capital. Foreign capital was attracted to Brazil because of Brazil's fast-growing economy, its promising future and sizzling equity markets, and high interest rates. In the first half of 1994, foreign capital inflow surpassed U.S. $21 billion, of which more than U.S. $13 billion was in the form of foreign investment (see Table 2.9). The substantial inflow of foreign capital helped the Central Bank to accumulate international reserves totaling U.S. $40.13 billion by June 1994.[62] (see Figure 2.5). The capital inflow, the strong foreign reserves position of the country, and the confidence in the plan's ability to tame inflation pushed the real value above the 1:1 parity as soon as the new currency was introduced. The real stabilized at around 0.85 per U.S. dollar in the second half of 1994.

Inflation dropped significantly after the introduction of the Real Plan from about 50 percent in June 1994 to 7.7 percent and 1.8 percent in July and August, respectively. For the remainder of 1994, inflation stayed under control as the monthly rates oscillated between 1.4 to 2.9 percent (see Figure 2.6).

The initial success of the Real Plan in controlling inflation translated into a consumption boom typical of exchange rate–based stabilization plans.

Figure 2.5 **Brazilian International Reserves, 1987–94** (in millions of U.S.$)

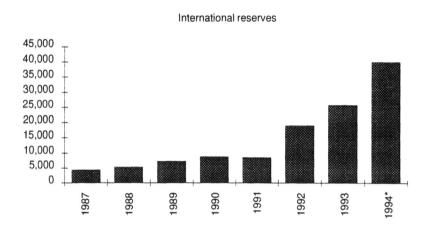

International reserves

Source: Banco Central do Brasil.
*Only for the first half of the year.

Figure 2.6 **Monthly Rates of Inflation, 1992:6–1994:12**

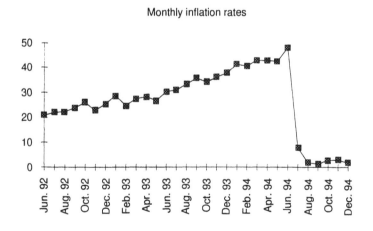

Monthly inflation rates

*Source:*INPC-IBGE.

Between July and August, the production of capital, intermediate, and durable goods jumped by about 16, 8, and 20 percent, respectively, while industrial production rose by 11 percent.[63] Calvo (1986) and others have
identified a lack of credibility as the source of the economic boom associ-

ated with exchange rate–based stabilization (see chapter 3). In the case of the Real Plan, however, the initial boom in output and consumption could not be attributed to a lack of credibility because of the behavior of the exchange rate. The public did not regard the policymakers' success against inflation as only temporary as it did not substitute dollars for *reals*. Bruno's (1993) and Gregorio et al.'s (1993) explanations of such booms based on a wealth effect may come closer to the Brazilian reality. (See chapter 3 for further explanation.)

The Real Plan thus used the introduction of a strong currency, a temporary control of the budget deficit, and the exchange rate anchor to bring the monthly inflation rate from 50 percent to about 2 to 3 percent. This impressive initial success, however, can lead to an eventual victory over inflation only if the government eliminates the public deficit.

Conclusion

In summary, the roots of the Brazilian inflation are to be traced to a number of factors including terms-of-trade shocks, balance-of-payments shocks, and fiscal imbalances that were accommodated by monetary authorities. During the 1970s and 1980s, these three important destabilizing forces undermined the internal and external balance of the Brazilian economy and combined to bring about a sustained inflationary environment. First, a significant terms-of-trade shock that resulted from the oil price jumps of the 1970s was not neutralized through domestic adjustment. Brazilian policymakers responded aggressively to the oil shocks by relying on foreign capital to avoid recession and unemployment at the cost of higher prices. Second, the capital outflow of the 1980s associated with the outbreak of the debt crises resulted in balance-of-payments shocks and significant external account disequilibrium. These two external shocks together with the third factor of persistent budget deficits exerted mounting inflationary pressure on the economy.

In addition to the failure of monetary and fiscal authorities to neutralize the inflationary impact of various shocks of the 1973–86 period, the institutional settings of Brazil that included widespread indexation of nominal contracts helped propagate the inflationary impact of each of these shocks well into the future, thus making fighting inflation solely through orthodox measures problematic.

The only successful orthodox anti-inflation program implemented in Brazil in the last thirty years was a gradualist prescription adopted in the 1960s under the military dictatorship. But since the success of this program coincided with and benefited from widespread repression, the policy lessons that can be drawn from this experiment are of limited value for newly democratized societies. The more recent success of the Real Plan and the overall Brazilian experience with fighting inflation over the last decade offers a number of valuable lessons for designing stabilization programs in newly industrialized countries.

First, the Brazilian experience demonstrates that it is hard, if not entirely impossible, to eradicate the roots of inflation using one-bladed scissors. Policies that focus solely on demand management and disregard the inertia nature of inflation are likely to fail. And policies that focus solely on the inflation inertia and overlook the necessity of fiscal and monetary discipline are certain to fail. The Brazilian experience shows that the heterodox approach, devoid of monetary and fiscal discipline, is ineffective and costly.[64] The dismal economic performance of the country in the aftermath of various heterodox shocks shows that the pledge of fighting inflation with no tears is a quixotic promise. In the absence of credible monetary and fiscal policies, heterodox policies designed to remove the inertial component of inflation cannot succeed.

In the case of developing countries such as Brazil, where readily available financial instruments for financing government deficits do not exist and independent monetary authorities are absent, public deficits make it difficult to pursue effective anti-inflationary policies. Several studies, including Alesina (1988, 1989), Grilli, Masciandaro, and Tabellini (1991) and Alesina and Summers (1993), have established a positive link between the degree of central bank independence and lower inflation. Monetary policy needs to be insulated from the political process. The two important and interrelated aspects of the Brazilian economy—namely, large, sustained public deficit and a central bank dependent on the political process—have made fighting inflation from either a heterodox or an orthodox front highly problematic. There is a growing consensus among economists that the key to prudent monetary policy and low inflation rates lies in either an independent central bank or in the "dollarization" of the economy à la Menem's plan in Argentina (see chapter 5).[65]

Second, the Brazilian experience shows that political factors that emerge in the aftermath of a return to democracy complicate the implementation of economic stabilization programs. The transition from a dictatorial rule that silences legitimate claims of different social groups to a democratic system is often characterized by the lack of political stability as the recent experiences of the former Soviet Union, Argentina, Bolivia, and Brazil show.[66] In such transitional and uncertain environments, the success of economic stabilization plans is less likely. The redemocratization process that created tenuous political conditions during the 1970s and 1980s made it difficult for Brazilian administrations to respond to major shocks forcefully. Instead, various Brazilian governments followed accommodating policies and avoided stabilization measures that could result in significant output and employment costs. In retrospect, overly optimistic and perhaps politically driven evaluations of growth prospects and unrealistic outlook of the designers of various stabilization plans were detrimental to effective stabilization.

3

Chile: Economic Reform, Transformation, and Progress

Introduction

Chile began its abrupt and decisive break with macroeconomic populism, import substitution industrialization, and Keynesian economics in 1973, long before neoconservatism swept Latin America as the dominant economic doctrine in the 1980s and 1990s. The military dictatorship that routinely violated the civil liberties of Chileans introduced unprecedented economic liberalization and reforms.

The profound pro-market structural changes of the last two decades have turned Chile into a vibrant, fast growing, and stable economy often vaunted as a model for developing nations. While the Chilean experience is considered successful by almost every yardstick, it also demonstrates that the transformation from a highly regulated and protected economy to a relatively unregulated and open economy is difficult and slow and may require huge sacrifices.

In this chapter, we analyze the Chilean success story and the difficulties Chile faced along the transformation road. We look for broad lessons regarding stabilization policy and the timing and sequencing of trade and capital market liberalization. We also consider the costs and benefits of market reforms such as privatization and deregulation.

The organization of this chapter is as follows. In the next section we analyze economic policies of the immediate postcoup period of 1973–78. "The Exchange Rate Stabilization Anchor and the Mini-Miracle" examines the 1978–81 stabilization plan that relied on the exchange rate as the nominal anchor for controlling inflation. The next section analyzes the causes of the economic crisis of the early 1980s and the final section examines the economic turnaround and the export-led growth of the last decade. These sections are followed by a conclusion.

Damage Control and Economic Stabilization: 1973–78

In September 1973, the Popular Unity government of President Salvador Allende, the first democratically elected socialist president in the Western hemisphere, was ousted by a *coup d'état* led by General Augusto Pinochet. The new military rulers inherited an economy plagued with runaway inflation, budget shortfalls, and balance-of-payments difficulties.[1] As in the cases of Brazil (1964) and Argentina (1976)—which are discussed in chapters 2 and 5, respectively—the Chilean generals sought to restore price stability without incurring substantial output and employment costs.

The military regime's initial economic goals were modest. As in Brazil in the aftermath of the 1964 coup, the Chilean government adopted a gradual approach to stabilization. In order to reestablish macroeconomic balance and control the economic damage of the 1972–73 period, the government sought to (1) cut the public sector deficit, which had reached one-quarter of GDP; (2) (re)privatize state-owned enterprises, particularly those nationalized by the Popular Unity government; (3) restore external (current account) balance; (4) remove price controls and interest rate regulations imposed by the previous administration; and, above all, (5) reduce the inflation rate.

The annual inflation rate had reached an unprecedented 600 percent in October 1973. High inflation was partially caused by the decision to remove price controls imposed by the Allende government. As previously distorted prices adjusted upward to their equilibrium levels, inflation surged. While accepting this short-term "corrective inflation," Pinochet's government set out to eradicate the roots of inflation in the long run through bold policy initiatives. The most important of these initiatives aimed at making a noninflationary monetary policy possible by eliminating the public deficit quickly and significantly.

The government succeeded in increasing its revenues substantially by implementing a tax reform that reassessed real estate taxes, increased income and sales tax rates, and introduced stiffer penalties for tax evasion. As a result of these actions, public revenues nearly doubled from 9.9 million pesos in 1973 to 19.3 million pesos in 1974. Public expenditures, on the other hand, increased by about 15 percent between 1973 and 1974 as the government reduced its current expenditure only marginally and raised its capital spending considerably.

While the government focused its attention on restoring fiscal balance, it adopted a relatively loose monetary policy and avoided shock therapy in its fight against inflation. The accommodative monetary policy, coupled with a money overhang that had been accumulating since 1971,[2] revived price

Table 3.1

Major Macroeconomic Variables for Chile, 1970–94

	GDP growth	Public sector deficit (% GDP)	Copper prices	Inflation	Unemploy- ment rate
1970	2.1	2.7	64.2	36.1	5.7
1971	9.0	10.7	49.3	28.2	3.9
1972	-1.2	13.0	48.6	255.4	3.3
1973	-5.6	24.7	80.8	608.7	5.0
1974	1.0	3.5	93.3	369.2	9.5
1975	-12.9	0.9	55.9	343.3	14.8
1976	3.5	-0.6	63.6	198.0	12.7
1977	9.9	-0.1	59.3	84.2	11.8
1978	8.2	-1.5	61.9	37.2	14.2
1979	8.3	-3.3	89.8	38.9	13.6
1980	7.8	-4.5	99.2	31.2	10.4
1981	5.5	-0.8	78.9	9.5	11.3
1982	-14.1	3.5	67.1	20.7	19.6
1983	-0.7	3.2	72.2	23.1	14.6
1984	6.3	4.3	62.4	23.0	13.9
1985	2.4	2.5	64.3	26.4	12.0
1986	5.7	2.1	62.3	17.4	8.8
1987	5.7	0.2	81.1	21.5	7.9
1988	7.4	-0.1	117.9	12.7	6.3
1989	10.0	-1.2	129.1	21.4	5.3
1990	3.3	0.7	120.9	27.3	6.0
1991	7.3	-1.0	106.1	18.7	6.5
1992	11.0	-0.5	103.6	12.7	4.9
1993	6.3	2.0	86.86	12.2	4.6
1994	4.3	2.0	NA	8.9	6.0

Sources: Banco Central de Chile, *Indicadores Económicos y Sociales,* and Universidad Católica de Chile.

pressures and resulted in inflation rates in excess of 340 percent for both 1974 and 1975.

In response to unabating inflation, on April 24, 1975, Finance Minister (*Ministro de Hacienda*) Jorge Cauas introduced the Program for Economic Recuperation (PRE). The PRE was essentially a full-fledged orthodox attack on the inflation problem. The government also forged full speed ahead with reforming foreign trade, deregulating domestic capital markets, and privatizing state enterprises.

On the fiscal side, by increasing tax revenues and implementing new austerity measures that curtailed expenditures, the government registered budget surpluses for the entire 1975–78 period (see Table 3.1). Public revenues were increased through a new tax code that fully indexed taxes to inflation, imposed a 20 percent value-added tax, eliminated many tax exemptions, and unified personal and corporate tax structures.[3] On the expenditures side, the government reduced its real total expenditures by 27 percent and cut public investment by about 50 percent.[4]

Chile's public sector streamlining included an ambitious privatization program aimed at reducing the burden of state-owned enterprises on public finances. The program centered around facilitating the privatization drive by encouraging privileged economic groups to engage in the privatization process. This was accomplished by offering attractive ownership options, which included generous financing incentives (see below). The number of state-owned enterprises, which stood at 529 (including 19 banks and 259 seized firms[5]), was quickly reduced. The government returned all 259 seized firms to their original owners and initiated a comprehensive privatization program. CORFO (Corporación de Fomento de la Producción) which was established in 1939 to facilitate the government's role in the industrialization drive, was given the task of divesting state-owned enterprises. For those enterprises that remained in the public sector, the government eliminated subsidies and adopted the profit-maximizing principle of the private sector.[6]

The goal of speedy privatization led the government to offer investors easy long-term loans that used the assets of the privatized companies as collateral. This resulted in dangerously high ownership concentration among private parties, many of whom did not have financial resources needed for operating these firms. According to CORFO statistics, forty Chileans bought 22 percent of all privatized enterprises while almost half were taken over by other Chilean firms.[7] Thus, a handful of *grupos* (conglomerates) emerged that controlled most Chilean corporations and banks.

In addition to fiscal restraint, monetary contraction was used to help fight the inflation problem. While Harberger (1982) and others doubt that the 1975 expansion of 313 percent in the monetary base and 245 percent in M_1 could be classified as overly restrictive, the rate of monetary expansion did fall well below the rate of inflation. In particular, as more recent evidence makes clear, in 1975 there was considerable positive excess demand for money and the monetary policy remained restrictive.[8]

Contractionary fiscal and monetary measures, together with adverse external factors, ushered in an expectedly deep recession. The oil price revolution of the 1973–75 period, a global recession that severely limited Chile's export revenues, and a sharp fall in the price of copper (see Table 3.1) jeopardized Chile's external balance. In 1975, Chile's trade and current-account deficits reached, respectively, 2 and 5 percent of GDP; output tumbled by close to 13 percent; and the unemployment rate bordered on 15 percent.

The economy showed signs of recuperation in 1976, but despite fiscal equilibrium and monetary restraint, the bold anti-inflation measures of 1975 proved only modestly successful. The inflation rate declined from the 300-plus range of the 1974–75 period to 198 percent in 1976.

Two factors help explain the persistence of inflation in the face of a strong contraction in aggregate demand. First, beginning with October 1974, Chile instituted full indexation of salaries and wages to inflation carried out quarterly. Second, the exchange rate was also indexed to the inflation rate as the government periodically and gradually devalued the peso based on the rate of price increases. The indexing of wages and the exchange rate to inflation gave inflation an inertial characteristic that could not be controlled by relying on traditional demand management measures (see chapter 1).[9]

The Exchange Rate Stabilization Anchor and the Mini-Miracle: 1978–81

Still unsatisfied with its progress in defeating inflation, in 1978 Chile chose the exchange rate instead of the supply of money as the nominal anchor for stabilization. Chilean policymakers saw in Chile a small and increasingly open economy that almost perfectly matched textbook examples they had studied in American universities. For such an economy, the exchange rate offered an effective way for bringing the domestic inflation rate in line with international inflation rates. In particular, it was expected, based on purchasing power parity, that the Chilean inflation rate would soon equal the world inflation rate plus the rate of peso devaluation.[10]

Chile thus introduced a *Tablita* plan which offered a schedule for peso devaluations. The *Tablita* was essentially an active crawling peg exchange rate system that set the devaluation rate at 21.8 percent and mapped into the future a gradual reduction in the rate of devaluation. In accordance with exchange rate devaluations, tariff rates were reduced gradually.

The inflation rate did not converge quickly to the international rates, but it declined from 198 percent in 1976 to 84 percent in 1977 and 37 percent in 1978 (see Table 3.1). The persistence of inflation was caused by a fundamental policy inconsistency: while the exchange rate was indexed forward to the expected inflation rate, wages were indexed backward to past inflation. Despite the slow decline in the inflation rate, policymakers decided to continue using the exchange rate as the nominal anchor. Thus, in 1979, Chile abandoned the *Tablita* and fixed the exchange rate at 39 pesos per U.S. dollar. The inflation rate remained in the 31–39 percent range until 1981, when it dropped to 9.5 percent.

During the 1977–80 period Chile went through a so-called economic miracle phase and registered average annual GDP growth rates of more than

Figure 3.1 **High-Powered Money, 1977:1–1982:4** (1978: 1 = 100)

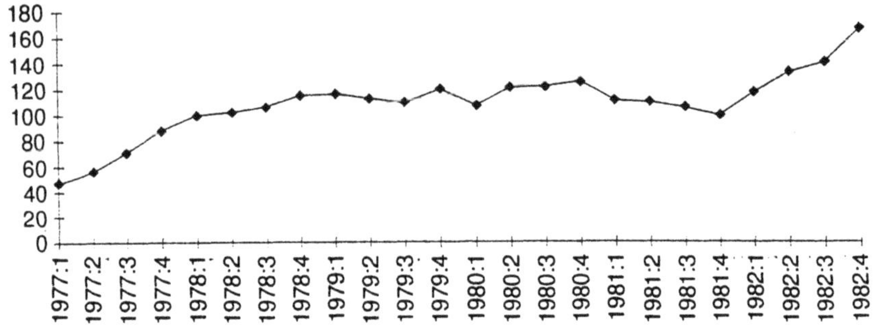

Source: Edwards (1985, Table 7).

8.5 percent. The economic boom of this period was caused by two principle factors. First, the decline in the rate of inflation resulted in higher real wages and brought about a 26 percent increase in real consumption.[11] The Chilean consumption expansion is typical of countries that achieve price stability by using the exchange rate as the nominal anchor. Three possible explanations have been offered in the literature for exchange rate–based stabilization booms. Calvo (1986) and others have suggested that the initial boom in consumption may be due to the lack of credibility. The public perception regarding the temporary nature of policymakers' success against inflation motivates the public to trade off future consumption for current consumption. Bruno (1993), among others,[12] doubts the credibility hypothesis and offers an alternative based on a wealth effect caused by the success of the program. Gregorio et al. (1993) also offer a model based on a wealth effect associated with the initial fall of inflation which results in increased consumption of durable goods and a general consumption boom. Helpman and Razin (1987) construct a model in which an intertemporal spending substitution occurs because the present value of future tax liabilities is smaller than the capital gain from an exchange rate freeze.

Second, a substantial growth in capital inflow contributed to the boom. During the 1978–80 period, about half of the surplus from the capital account was used to cover the current account deficit, and the rest accumulated as foreign reserves.[13] With the hesitation of monetary authorities to sterilize the increased reserves, and with the fixed exchange rate acting as a ceiling on tradable prices, increased capital inflow resulted in increases in price and output of nontradables (especially in the construction industry) and higher wages. As can be seen in Figure 3.1, during the 1977–82 period

Table 3.2

Total External Debt, 1970–87 (in millions of 1987 U.S.$)

Year	U.S.$ millions	Year	U.S.$ millions	Year	U.S.$ millions
1970	8,703	1976	8,794	1982	17,631
1971	8,619	1977	8,888	1983	18,303
1972	9,303	1978	10,301	1984	19,486
1973	9,241	1979	11,310	1985	20,313
1974	9,172	1980	12,820	1986	21,266
1975	9,301	1981	16.343	1987	20,551

Source: Corporación de Investigaciones Económicas para América Latina (CIPLAN).

Chile experienced a sizable increase in high-power money, which, in turn, undermined the fight against inflation.

The considerable rise in capital inflow was caused mainly by the deregulation of the capital account and by very high domestic interest rates. The deregulation of the capital account of the balance of payments began in mid-1979 when the government eliminated restrictions on nonspeculative (medium and long-run) capital movements. By 1980, the capital account was pretty much unregulated as limits on monthly capital inflows were lifted.

At a time when the cost of domestic borrowing was unusually high, the fixed exchange rate resulted in negative real interest rates on foreign loans.[14] As a result, many Chilean companies borrowed heavily abroad, significantly increasing Chile's external debt. (See Table 3.2.) In 1980 and 1981, capital inflows jumped to U.S. $2.5 billion and U.S. $4.5 billion, respectively, from the 1979 level of only U.S. $1.2 billion.[15]

The impressive output expansion of the 1977–80 period occurred despite unusually high unemployment rates (see Table 3.1) and a widening current account deficit. The inflation differential (relative to the United States) together with the fixed exchange rate, the opening of the capital account, and the massive inflow of foreign capital resulted in a seriously overvalued currency. The overvalued peso, in turn, put the balance of payments in extreme jeopardy.

Economic Crises: 1981–84

In the fourth quarter of 1981, a combination of internal and external factors jolted the Chilean economy into a severe and prolonged crisis. On the external side, three major events combined to play the role of the proverbial straw that broke the back of the Chilean economy. First, the U.S. Federal

Reserve Bank's resolve to fight American inflation through a highly restrictive monetary policy resulted in a considerable increase in world interest rates. For Chile, which had contracted a substantial amount of foreign debt and had fast become one of the most indebted countries in the region, higher international interest rates translated into a heavier debt-service burden and created significant difficulties in the capital account of the balance of payments.

Second, as the U.S. dollar began a prolonged period of appreciation relative to other major currencies, the peso, which was fixed vis-à-vis the dollar, became grossly overvalued relative to other major currencies. This overvaluation, in turn, encouraged increased imports and reduced exports by undermining the competitiveness of the export sector abroad. Third, the price of copper (the single most important source of foreign exchange for Chile) began a six-year slide in 1981. Between 1980 and 1981, copper prices fell by more than 32 percent, while trade and current account deficits more than doubled.

Policy mistakes of the early 1980s added to external account problems to result in an unprecedented economic crisis. Policymakers adopted a laissez-faire approach to economics. They waited for the "automatic adjustment" mechanism of the free market to work its magic and refrained from responding to economic problems that were fast assuming crisis magnitude. The government's hands-off policy extended to the financial sector where, compared to advanced industrialized countries, institutions faced less monitoring and fewer regulations.

The dangers inherent in allowing the banking system to operate without close supervision became apparent during the 1981–82 meltdown. Chilean companies and conglomerates that had borrowed heavily abroad found themselves in financial dire straits and unable to pay back their loans. With danger signs conspicuously present, the government attempted to rescue the financial system. But it was too late, and scores of financial institutions went bankrupt. The difficulties with the haphazard privatization program of the 1970s (see "Damage Control and Economic Stabilization: 1973–78, above) became clear as 70 percent of privatized banks and enterprises went into bankruptcy.[16] The collapse of the financial system and widespread bankruptcies forced the government to take over many banks and enterprises that had been privatized a few years earlier.

In retrospect, the quick opening of the capital account may have been partially responsible for the economic problems of the 1981–83 period. The sequencing and timing of the opening of external accounts are important factors in determining the success of stabilization policies. The sequencing of the opening of external accounts (capital account deregulations following trade liberalization) is often needed for two reasons. First, goods markets adjust more slowly to deregulation than capital markets; second, goods market distortions may result in an inefficient allocation of capital.[17] In addition to sequencing, sufficient time must elapse after deregulating the current account before the capital account is opened. The very success of the exchange rate in stabilizing the economy can lead to increased capital inflow, which, in turn, undermines the external sector (current account) by causing overvaluation.[18]

In retrospect, the timing of the opening of the capital account relative to the opening of the current account may have compounded Chilean difficulties.[19] While Chile initially reduced tariffs and kept the capital account closed, the time that elapsed between the opening of the two accounts may not have been long enough.[20] As explained before, the continuous use of the exchange rate as the stabilizing anchor, and the substantial capital inflow made possible by capital account deregulations resulted in a highly overvalued peso and subsequent balance-of-payments difficulties.

The Chilean experience shows that even if current and capital account liberalizations are sequenced properly (i.e., the current account is opened before a complete opening of the capital account), special attention should be given to the timing of the capital account opening.

By the end of 1981, the Chilean economy was in great difficulty despite an apparent victory over inflation. The inflation rate finally stood in the single-digit range, but output plummeted, unemployment rate soared, and bankruptcies became prevalent.

The situation deteriorated in 1982 as the GDP fell by more than 14 percent, the official unemployment rate neared 20 percent, and inflation reached 20.7 percent. Output continued to decline in 1983, inflation inched up to 23 percent, and, excluding government-sponsored employment in PEM[21] and POJH[22] programs, the unemployment rate reached 30 percent.[23] Finally, in 1984, the economy began to grow again but the inflation and unemployment rates remained high (see Table 3.1). Continued macroeconomic instability and anemic growth in 1985 encouraged policymakers to rethink economic policy in search of a fresh approach to economic growth and stability.

A Decade of Reform and Growth: 1985–94

In 1985, the new finance minister, Hernán Büchi, negotiated a structural adjustment program with the World Bank. The government streamlined its expenditures and introduced a privatization program dubbed as "popular capitalism" with the intent of returning to the private sector many companies it had taken over during the crisis year. This time around, the privatiza-

Table 3.3

The Performance of the Chilean Export Sector: 1986 and 1991
(FOB, millions of U.S.$)

Sector	1986	1991	Percentage change
Unprocessed natural resources	2,168.2	4,341.2	14.9
Processed natural resources	993.7	2,390.5	19.2
Industrial products	145.2	720.4	37.8
Total	3,307.1	7,452.2	17.6

Source: Banco Central de Chile.

tion program operated under a much more stringent set of criteria for determining the ownership of state-owned enterprises.

One important priority of the adjustment program was restoring order to the balance of payments by focusing on the export sector as the engine of economic growth. The export promotion program was designed to take advantage of Chile's comparative advantage to expand traditional as well as nontraditional exports.

Chile thus chose a growth strategy based on the production and export of new farming, forestry, fishing, mining, and cellulose products. In an attempt to support export-led economic growth, the government devalued the peso substantially and introduced the "crawling band" nominal exchange rate system, which resulted in a 40 percent peso devaluation between 1984 and 1990.[24]

Between 1986 and 1991 Chilean exports increased by more than 17.5 percent, with exports of processed natural resources growing by 14.9 percent, and exports of unprocessed natural resources rising by 19.2 percent. While natural resources remained the most important Chilean exports by accounting for approximately 90 percent of all exports in 1991, their relative significance diminished from 1986, when they accounted for 96 percent of all exports (see Table 3.3).

The mining sector continued play an important role in the Chilean economy in general and the export sector in particular. For the period 1980–90, mining production grew at the average annual rate of close to 36 percent and was responsible for 8 percent of the Chilean GDP.[25] Copper remains the heart of the Chilean export sector, representing about 82 percent of total mining exports, followed by gold, which accounts for approximately 6 percent of mining exports (see Table 3.4).

The mining sector has also been successful in attracting direct foreign

Table 3.4

Exports of Mining Products, 1988–94 (thousands metric tons)

Product	1988	1989	1990	1991	1992	1993	1994 (January– March)
Metallic copper	3,357	4,058	3,907	3,586	3,902	3,336	756
Metallic gold	110	101	104	110	95	39	11
Metallic silver	83	90	90	59	92	81	23
Other	571	636	669	658	689	631	181
Total	4,121	4,885	4,770	4,413	4,778	4,087	971
% of all exports	58.5	59.6	55.6	48.8	47.2	43.4	38.7

Source: Banco Central de Chile, *Foreign Trade Indicators*, March 1994.

investment. The 1982 Mining Law and the 1983 Mining Code defined a legal framework that gave the Chilean state the ownership of all mineral resources, but granted the concession holders full ownership and concessionary rights for the period under concession. The concession itself requires the payment of annual licensing fees in return for exclusive exploration and exploitation rights. As a result of better defined property rights and protection for foreign investors, a dramatic surge in direct investment in the mining sector occurred. Between 1987 and 1994, Chile attracted U.S. $4.8 billion in direct foreign investment in mining with U.S. $432 million in debt-equity swaps.[26] It is expected that during the 1994–97 period new mining ventures by American, Japanese, Australian, British, Canadian firms and CODELCO (Corporación Nacional del Cobre de Chile) will bring in U.S. $6 billion in direct foreign investment.

As can be seen from Table 3.4, in 1990, Chile's export of mineral products stood at U.S. $4.1 billion, accounting for 43.4 percent of total exports. In 1988, the same dollar amount of mining exports (U.S. $4.1 billion) accounted for 58.5 percent of all Chilean exports, showing an increasingly important role played by nontraditional exports.

Between 1984 and 1993, forestry products exports increased by about 215 percent (see Table 3.5), and in one decade (1983–93) fruit and vegetable exports rose by more than 1,000 percent while exports of wine products grew by more than 1,200 percent (see Table 3.6). For the same decade, the exports of livestock and agricultural products showed an eightfold jump.

In addition to impressive gains in the export of agricultural goods and

Table 3.5

Chilean Forestry Production and Exports, 1980–93 (in millions of U.S.$)

Year	Forestry production	Exports	Exports/production (%)
1980	774.3	468.1	60.4
1982	514.1	332.1	64.6
1984	575.0	382.7	66.5
1986	574.5	403.1	70.1
1988	976.9	730.1	74.7
1990	1,165.3	855.3	73.4
1991	1,275.7	913.1	71.6
1992	1,632.1	1,125.8	69.0
1993	1,658.0	1,207.1	72.8

Source: CONAF-INFOR, 1994.

Table 3.6

Chile's Exports of Livestock and Agricultural Products, 1983–94
(in millions of U.S.$)

Product/year	1983	1985	1987	1989	1991	1993	1994 (January–March)
Livestock & related	6.3	5.2	3.6	7.4	7.4	6.4	2.1
Fruits & vegetables	20.2	29.7	73.1	125.8	191.1	231.9	56.4
Wheat	4.6	2.0	0.3	0.1	0.0	0.0	0.0
Wine	9.3	11.0	17.5	35.4	84.2	128.5	27.6
Total	40.4	47.9	94.5	168.7	282.7	366.8	86.1

Source: Banco Central de Chile.

livestock, and forestry products, Chile became the sixth-largest fishing nation in the world. Between 1981 and 1991 fish production increased by more than 76 percent, and in three years (1989 to 1992) fishing exports jumped by 54.8 percent. Today, the fishing sector's share of total exports is 10 percent and the fishing industry accounts for 1 percent of GDP and 4.8 percent of the total workforce.

Two factors played an important role in helping Chile achieve its impressive export growth of the past decade. First, the Chilean government redirected its investment dollars into projects with spillover effects that helped the private sector. For example, the Ministry of Public Works (MOP) spent nearly U.S. $1.1 billion on the infrastructure investment (see

Figure 3.2 **Public Investment in Infrastructure, 1987–90** (in millions of U.S.$)

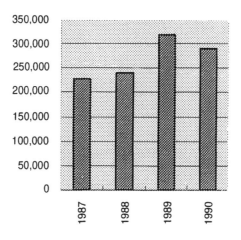

Source: Ministry of Public Works, *Public Works Annual Report*, 1990.

Figure 3.3 **Real Urban Minimum Wage: Annual Index** (1980=100)

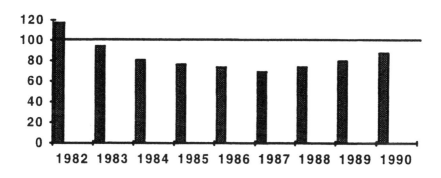

Source: United Nations, *Economic Survey of Latin America and the Caribbean*, 1990.

Figure 3.2.) and, for the period 1991–94, the Chilean government devised a development plan that allocated U.S. $2.32 billion to infrastructure investment.

Second, the Chilean economy in general and its export sector in particular benefited from low and declining labor costs. Figure 3.3 shows that in the aftermath of the 1982 economic crisis the Chilean real minimum wage

Table 3.7

Chile's Imports Breakdown, 1988–94

	1988	1989	1990	1991	1992	1993	1994 (January–March)
Consumer goods	563	894	826	1,136	1,691	1,905	439
Capital goods	1,317	1,917	2,130	1,840	2,571	3,040	772
Intermediate goods	2,822	3,666	4,046	4,449	5,176	5,591	1,275
Others	29	19	23	28	18	8	2
Duty-free zones	193	238	249	233	214	228	45
Total	4,924	6,734	7,272	7,686	9,670	10,771	2,533

Source: Banco Central de Chile.

declined significantly. Even by 1990, the minimum wage had not yet returned to its 1980 levels. Furthermore, Chile's nonwage labor costs significantly declined both in absolute terms and relative to other Latin American countries, making the Chilean labor force one of the least expensive in the region.[27]

Despite the strong performance of nontraditional exports, Chile remains heavily dependent on imported capital and intermediate products. As can be seen from Table 3.7, in 1993 more than 80 percent of the Chilean imports were capital goods and intermediate goods imports. Moreover, the capital goods imports jumped by more than 130 percent between 1988 and 1993, while for the same period the intermediate products imports nearly doubled. While capital goods production increased by 6.8 percent for the period 1986–90, it still accounts for less than 5 percent of total manufacturing.[28]

Relative price stability has characterized the Chilean economy since the mid-1980s. For the period 1986–94, the Chilean inflation rate averaged 6.2 percent per annum. In addition to noninflationary fiscal policy, two other initiatives introduced in 1989 helped control inflation.

First, Chile became the first Latin American country with a truly independent central bank. Because economic stabilization and the success of economic policy depend on the credibility of the government and its policies,[29] the Central Bank's independence helped establish credibility by protecting monetary policy from fiscal mismanagement.

Second, Chile adopted a diagonal band for the exchange rate. The exchange rate band thus gave the Central Bank some flexibility in conducting monetary policy and made a gradual reduction in inflation possible without compromising the strong position of the export sector.[30]

Inflation has been kept in check despite a substantial increase in foreign capital inflow. With the return of democracy and an affirmation by President Aylwin that the civilian government was going to continue with market-oriented economic policies, and increased confidence in the economy, Chile again experienced a substantial inflow of foreign capital. Decree Law 600 helped attract more foreign investments by allowing for the unconditional remittance of foreign capital one year after the date of entry and by removing all restrictions on the remittance of profits.[31] Real interest rates, which were much higher than international interest rates, also helped attract foreign capital. Much of this new wave of capital inflow seems to have been targeted for directed foreign investment. For example, in 1989 alone, direct foreign investment reached 6 percent of GDP[32] and for the period 1990–92 direct foreign investment exceeded U.S. $1.5 billion.[33] The high share of capital inflow from direct foreign investment meant that no serious sterilization was needed because direct investment is not usually mediated through the domestic banking system and hence does not cause credit expansion.[34]

In 1990, the large influx of foreign capital pushed the exchange rate to the lower bound of the plus-or-minus 5 percent band established in 1989 and increased the country's foreign reserves substantially. In January 1992, the government widened the band to plus-or-minus 10 percent, yet the exchange rate immediately resettled at the lower bound.[35]

Conclusion

The Chilean experience shows that the success and failure of exchange rate–based stabilization programs depends on the performance of the external sector and the current account position of the country. The external position of the country can be improved by policies that seek and support areas of production and export in which a dynamic comparative advantage exists. Chile has successfully explored its comparative advantage in cheap labor and natural resources to expand exports of traditional and nontraditional products.

Despite the Persian Gulf War and the subsequent increase in the price of oil, the resilience of the export-dependent Chilean economy to external shocks has not been tested yet. Nevertheless, the commitment Chile has made to maintaining fiscal balance, to encouraging nonspeculative foreign investment, to freeing monetary policy from politics and fiscal policy, to keeping the export sector competitive, and to reducing the burden of foreign debt has left the country better prepared than other Latin American countries to withstand external shocks such as a severe global recession or a significant drop in the price of copper.

The Chilean privatization experience was largely successful in bringing order to public finances. The other leg of market reforms—that is, deregulation—was sometimes implemented with too much haste and unrealistic convictions in laissez-faire. In particular, as discussed above, the 1981–82 crisis was needlessly worsened by the collapse of a financial system that had been poorly managed and monitored. While much of Chile's economic difficulties during the last two decades were triggered by external factors, like the experience of other Latin American countries policy, mistakes compounded the negative effect of external shocks and propagated their impact into the future.

4

Mexico: Reform and Stability

Introduction

In this chapter we examine the Mexican experience with economic policymaking as it relates to the questions of inflation, stabilization, and economic growth. In less than three decades Mexico underwent a profound transformation that turned a predominantly agricultural society into a newly industrialized country. Not surprisingly, this metamorphosis brought a great many changes in the social fabric and the economic structure of Mexico.

Since the 1950s, the Mexican government has alternated between active and reactive economic policies.[1] To understand Mexico's broad policy shifts, it is helpful to consider three distinct time periods: (1) the period of the "Mexican miracle" of 1955–72, characterized by economic stability and rapid growth; (2) the external shocks decade of 1972–82, marked by economic expansion based on macroeconomic populism;[2] (3) the crash and reform period of 1982–93.

The plan of this chapter is as follows. In the first section, economic policies of the 1950s and the 1960s that led to the "miracle years" are considered prior to an analysis of inflationary fiscal and balance-of-payments disequilibriums of the 1970–82 period. In the following section, we analyze the origins of the 1976 and 1982 crises and evaluate policy responses. We shall see that the structural factors responsible for the outbreak of the 1982 crises were in existence during the 1975–76 crises. We shall also see that sustained price stability in the 1980s was achieved with the help of nominal anchors and through structural reforms that included sound public finance. In the final section, we focus on the social costs of stabilization and ask what stabilization without growth has meant for the Mexican people. The chapter ends with our conclusions.

From Stabilizing Development to Economic Instability

For close to two decades (1954–72), Mexico's reliance on a program of so-called "stabilizing development" (*desarrollo estabilizador*, hereafter, SD) resulted in respectable rates of economic growth, low inflation, exchange rate stability, and a low and manageable external debt–GDP ratio.[3]

The prime goal of SD was to foster sustained growth with low inflation by cultivating a stable economic environment. For price stability, the government avoided large budget deficits through tight expenditure controls. Mexico financed its inconsequential budget shortfalls primarily through external borrowing.[4] To pave the way for economic growth, Mexican policymakers protected domestic industries from foreign competition, pampering the manufacturing sector at the expense of the export and agricultural sectors. Beginning in the 1950s, Mexico pursued import substitution industrialization by imposing quantitative restrictions on imports and increasing nominal tariffs.

Mexico's plan was to encourage domestic production of consumer goods. Once a consumer goods industry was developed, an intermediate goods industry was supposed to appear in order to supply inputs for the consumer goods industry. Pursuant to these ends, Mexico employed import license requirements to discourage the importation of most consumer goods. To nurture domestic production of intermediate products, Mexico then imposed domestic-content rules for inputs in the consumer goods industry.[5]

Economic growth was thus fueled by inward-looking industrialization policies that attempted to establish backward linkages in the economy. In this process, a major role was given to the private sector as the engine of development. The government actively encouraged private sector investment through tax policy and generous subsidies and through public investments in complementary infrastructure projects and invested heavily in public projects that complemented private investment.[6] As a result, during the SD period private sector investment in the economy rose from about 8 percent to 20 percent of GDP.[7]

The response of the Mexican economy to the import substitution strategy and the government's active yet fiscally responsible policies was impressively positive. During the 1954–70 period, Mexico grew at an average annual rate of 6.8 percent while the annual inflation rate was only about 3.5 percent. But the artificiality of import substitution together with the policy biases against the agricultural and export sectors created long-term structural problems. First, the protective trade policy of SD created industries that could not compete in the international arena. Thus Mexico became vulnerable to external shocks, as it could not generate the current account surpluses it would need to support its increasingly precarious balance-of-payments position. Second, SD introduced a pronounced bias against exporters and the agricultural sector. By overvaluing the exchange rate, Mexico hurt all exporters (including the agricultural sector) and benefited importers. Moreover, by imposing price controls on some agricultural products and by turning the industrial-agricultural terms of trade decidedly against the agricultural sector, the SD strategy proved detrimental to Mexican agriculture.[8] Third, the overvalued exchange rate together with high tariff barriers resulted in cheap input-imports and expensive consumer goods imports. As a result, capital goods imports were subsidized at the same time that consumer goods imports were penalized. Thus the government helped the industrialists at the expense of consumers. Fourth, to control inflation, the government introduced price controls on a variety of key products ranging from foodstuffs to utility and transportation, thereby causing distortions that had to be corrected in the future.[9] Fifth, the prosperity brought about by SD did not benefit all Mexicans equally and accentuated the already perverse distribution of income. Despite these problems, sound public finance in an economy that did not suffer from adverse external shocks, together with the benefits of the "easy" phase of import substitution, resulted in a remarkable period of economic growth and stability.

Import substitution industrialization had started to become an impediment to growth instead of a motivation for it. Difficulty in building a political consensus had arisen in part because of what these policies had engendered.

Mexico's focus on building a manufacturing sector through trade protectionism and exchange rate manipulation had not simply created industry, but inefficient industry. Productivity was low and finished products were costly. Moreover, while the government had devoted much energy to fostering manufacturing activity, more basic efforts at the creation of human capital had received less attention. The government had foregone necessary investments in health, education, and human services.[10]

Growth in manufacturing through protectionism, together with inattention to the public creation of human capital, aggravated the nation's uneven income distribution and imposed new strains on the consensus that the nation's ruling political party had traditionally worked to create. The distortions imposed not only by protectionism and exchange rate overvaluations, but by a government-organized collective farm system that discouraged agricultural investment, resulted in the migration of armies of poor to the large cities. Squatter communities of the underemployed coalesced in Mexico's principal urban areas.

The social strains imposed by increasing distortions in income distribution, together with the government's inattention to human capital development, resulted—among other things—in a coalition between students and the poor, and the ensuing, tragic conflicts between these groups and the government. This social unrest climaxed in 1968, when the army massacred students in the plaza at Tlatelolco, further undermining the government's legitimacy.

It was in the midst of this turmoil that in 1970, for the first time in more than four and one-half decades, the political elite failed to choose a consensus presidential candidate. Luis Echeverría Álvarez, who, as minister of the interior, was accused of responsibility for the Tlatelolco massacre, was unenthusiastically elected as the new president of a country about to experience profound political and economic changes.

Faced with mounting public pressure to open up the political system, Echeverría reweighted the government economic objectives away from industrial growth and toward development blended with what was perceived as social justice. In an attempt to strengthen his political base among various socioeconomic groups, Echeverría opened the national coffers to embark on an economic program of "shared development." The program called for income redistribution and increased help for the neglected agricultural sector. It also spelled increased public expenditures on infrastructure, the welfare system, education, and health services.

Government expenditures rose from 22 percent of GDP in 1970 to 32 percent in 1976. The public sector's share of total investment increased to 46 percent in 1975 from 35 percent in 1970. Government expenditure in the agricultural sector doubled in less than five years.[11] Mexico expanded coverage by its social security system, and increased its expenditures on such basic yardsticks of social development as health, education, and housing. During Echeverría's administration, education's share of public spending increased from 13.2 percent to 19.4 percent while health services' share increased from 3.1 percent to 4.5 percent.[12] Echeverría also granted considerable public sector wage hikes and created new public sector employment opportunities to enhance the economic conditions of the middle and working classes. The increased public expenditure coincided with the government's political inability to enhance its revenues as the administration's initial attempts to introduce a meaningful tax reform were met with derailing opposition from the private sector.[13]

While these economic efforts at political consolidation were pursued by means of deficit spending, the implications of the inflation they might stimulate were given scant attention.[14] In the midst of these inflationary, spend-now-pay-later policies and the ensuing fiscal imbalance, the oil shock of

1973 compounded Mexican economic difficulties. For Mexico, then an importer of oil, the oil price jump translated into considerable pressure on the current account of the balance of payments.

Like Brazil and other developing countries adversely affected by the 1973 oil shock, Mexico decided to fight the recessionary impact of the oil price increase by adopting pro-growth policies that were financed by foreign resources.[15] Foreign banks, eager to recycle petrodollars, were offering creditworthy developing countries loans with highly attractive terms, including very low real interest rates (see chapter 2).

Mexican policymakers believed that by financing development projects through present borrowing it was possible to engineer economic growth rapid enough to ensure repayment. Total foreign debt increased from about $9 billion in 1971 to close to $17 billion in 1974, thereafter increasing steadily at an annual average rate of 24.5 percent until 1982.

The 1970–76 economic populist policies brought about average real GDP growth of more than 6.2 percent per year, but by the end of Echeverría's presidential term, signs of widespread imbalances in the economy were conspicuously present. The government turned out to have engineered current economic expansion at the expense of future contractions and at the cost of significant deficits in the country's internal and external accounts. In 1976, the ratio of fiscal deficit to GDP reached 9.9 percent and the balance of payments registered unprecedented deficits.

Nevertheless, the most visible symptom of troubled policies was an inflation rate that reached 16 percent in 1976 and rose to 29 percent in 1977. Mounting pressures in the current account and balance of payments coupled with high inflation forced Mexico to abandon the fixed exchange rate regime it had maintained since 1954. In dire need of external resources, the Mexican government signed an extended fund facility agreement with the IMF. This 1976–77 stabilization program sought to bring about adjustment not only through devaluation but through large government expenditure cuts. In line with the usual IMF-sponsored programs, the peso was devalued by 64.8 percent in August 1976.

In another typical reaction to, and ultimately against, IMF policies, Mexico reduced its fiscal deficit—for a while. The public sector's primary deficit[16] declined from 6.5 percent of GDP in 1975 to 2.3 percent in 1977; thereafter, it consistently increased, exceeding 8 percent by 1981. This return to expansionary fiscal policy was motivated by the oil bonanza of 1976, and the anticipation of more to come. The unexpected discovery of abundant oil reserves in Chiapas, Tabasco, and Campeche clearly meant that macroeconomic austerity was no longer needed. In oil-rich Mexico, the new role of policymakers was perceived as "administering the abundance."[17] This optimism about economic prospects discounted the fact Mexico was showing the symptoms of a classic case of "Dutch disease," (see below) with its well-known side effects of economic instability, current account difficulties, and inflation. (See "The 1982–87 Economic Crises," below.)

Mexico targeted ambitious growth rates under the assumption that at a minimum its petroleum exports would be 1.5 million barrels a day and that the international price of oil would increase by 5 to 7 percent annually.[18] Mexican policymakers anticipated a current account surplus of 3.4 billion dollars by the end of the *sexenio* and real GDP growth of 7 to 10 percent between 1979 and 1982.[19] In the short term, these forecasts seemed accurate. Between 1975 and 1978 Mexican petroleum production increased by more than 71 percent to 1.2 million barrels a day, and by 1980 petroleum production approached 2 million barrels a day while the price of oil reached $31. Real GDP grew at better than expected rates of 9.1 and 13.3 percent in 1979 and 1980, respectively; in 1981, the economy grew at the respectable rate of 7.7 percent (see Table 4.1). But Mexico's was not the only supply response to higher prices. Rising world production and lagged demand reactions to past price increases caught Mexican policymakers by surprise and shattered the illusion of oil-financed fast growth.

The 1982–87 Economic Crises

As the price of oil increased substantially in late 1970s, so did Mexico's dependence on oil revenues. By the end of 1980, the price of Mexican oil exceeded $31 per barrel, and petroleum revenues accounted for 45 percent of Mexico's merchandise exports and 30 percent of the government's revenues.[20] The oil windfall also made Mexico a more creditworthy country in the eyes of foreign bankers and resulted in a sizable inflow of external resources in the form of new lending.

The Mexican central bank failed to sterilize the increased reserves. Increased credit and the associated rise in demand had their usual inflationary effect. More would come. In 1981, the government's revenues increased by under 7 percent, while public sector expenditure rose by close to 25 percent. Public sector borrowing requirements doubled to more than 14 percent of the GDP. Meanwhile, despite an annual inflation rate of 28 percent in 1981, President López Portillo declared he would defend the peso "like a dog." The increasingly overvalued exchange rate played the typical role in expanding demand for imports. In a process made famous in the Netherlands ("Dutch disease"), the tension between a pegged exchange rate and accelerating inflation made Mexican nonoil exports lose their competitiveness altogether. The current account of the balance of pay-

Table 4.1

Nominal GDP, Real GDP, GDP Growth Rates, and Inflation Rate, 1970–93

Year	Nominal GDP (millions of pesos)	GDP in 1970 prices (millions of pesos)	GDP in 1980 prices (millions of pesos)	GDP growth rate (1970 prices)	GDP growth rate (1980 prices)	Inflation[a] annual average (%)	Inflation[a] December–December (%)
1970	444	444	—	—	—	5.2	4.8
1971	490	463	—	4.28	—	5.3	5.2
1972	565	502	—	8.42	—	5.0	5.5
1973	691	544	—	8.37	—	12.0	21.3
1974	890	578	—	6.25	—	23.8	20.7
1975	1,100	610	—	5.54	—	15.2	11.2
1976	1,371	636	—	4.26	—	15.8	27.2
1977	1,850	658	—	3.46	—	28.9	20.7
1978	2,338	712	—	8.21	—	17.5	16.2
1979	3,068	777	—	9.13	—	18.2	20.0
1980	4,470	880	4,470	13.26	—	26.3	29.8
1981	6,128	948	4,862	7.73	8.77	28.0	28.7
1982	9,798	941	4,832	−0.74	−0.62	58.9	98.9
1983	17,879	893	4,629	−5.10	−4.20	101.9	80.8
1984	29,472	910	4,796	1.90	3.61	65.4	59.2
1985	47,392	948	4,920	4.18	2.59	57.7	63.7
1986	79,191	893	4,736	−5.80	−3.74	86.2	105.7
1987	193,312	909	4,824	1.79	1.86	131.8	159.2
1988	390,451	—	4,884	—	1.24	114.2	51.7
1989	507,618	—	5,047	—	3.34	20.0	19.7
1990	686,406	—	5,272	—	4.46	26.7	29.9
1991	865,166	—	5,463	—	3.62	22.7	18.8
1992	1,019,156	—	5,616	—	2.80	15.5	11.9
1993	1,122,928	—	5,641	—	0.45	9.8	8.0

Sources: Banco de México, *Informe Annual,* 1989 and 1993. (In 1987, stopped reporting the GDP in 1970 prices.) Banco de México, *Indicadores Económicos*, 1989 and 1994.

[a] Based on consumer price index.

ments came under considerable pressure, registering an unsurpassed deficit of $16.1 billion, or about 6 percent of GDP in 1981 (see Table 4.2).

The Mexican government turned to foreign banks for new loans with short maturities and variable interest rates.[21] International bankers, eager to recycle petrodollars, and just as certain about the direction of oil prices as the Mexicans were, opened their coffers. By 1982, 75 percent of Mexico's external debt was owed by the public sector and the Mexican debt burden exceeded $92 billion, compared to only $30 billion in 1978.

Although Mexican borrowing and spending represented a bet on higher

Table 4.2

External Sector Performance: Current Account, Merchandise Exports and Imports, Trade Balance, and Balance of Payments, 1960–90 (in millions of U.S.$)

	Current account	Merchandise exports	Merchandise imports	Trade balance	Balance of payments
1960	−324	778	−1,132	−354	—
1961	−241	826	−1,086	−260	−30
1962	−182	930	−1,097	−167	14
1963	−218	985	−1,186	−201	116
1964	−423	1,054	−1,424	−370	46
1965	−392	1,146	−1,498	−352	−67
1966	−343	1,244	−1,581	−337	25
1967	−685	1,152	−1,760	−608	15
1968	−743	1,258	−1,892	−634	72
1969	−592	1,454	−1,983	−529	1
1970	−1,068	1,348	−2,236	−888	29
1971	−835	1,409	−2,158	−749	130
1972	−916	1,717	−2,610	−894	178
1973	−1,415	2,141	−3,656	−1,515	157
1974	−2,876	2,999	−5,791	−2,791	74
1975	−4,042	3,007	−6,278	−3,272	204
1976	−3,409	3,475	−5,771	−2,295	−860
1977	−1,854	4,604	−5,625	−1,021	622
1978	−3,171	6,246	−7,992	−1,745	386
1979	−5,459	9,301	−12,131	−2,830	315
1980	−10,750	15,511	−18,896	−3,385	818
1981	−16,061	20,102	−23,948	−3,846	1,275
1982	−6,307	21,230	−14,435	6,795	−11,635
1983	5,403	22,312	−8,550	13,762	−4,308
1984	4,194	24,196	−11,255	12,941	−677
1985	1,130	21,663	−13,212	8,451	−3,706
1986	−1,673	16,031	−11,432	4,599	−451
1987	3,968	20,655	−12,222	8,433	4,120
1988	−2,443	20,566	−18,898	1,668	−11,153
1989	−3,958	22,765	−23,410	−645	−210
1990	−5,255	26,773	−29,799	−3,026	2,219

Source: International Monetary Fund, *International Financial Statistics,* CD–ROM Version, 12/91, Washington, D.C.: IMF.

oil prices, oil prices actually declined sharply, from about $33 a barrel in 1981 to $28 in 1982 and $25 in 1983 (see Table 4.3). Another factor contributing to the decline in Mexico's oil revenues was the pricing strategy of the government-owned oil company (PEMEX), which resulted in a market-share loss. As OPEC members failed to reach a production agreement in May 1981, it became clear that the oil glut in the international markets was

Table 4.3

Mexican Oil Price, Export Volume, and Revenues, 1980–89

	1980	1981	1982	1983	1984
Price per barrel (dollars)	31.06	33.01	28.08	25.2	26.39
Export volume (billions of dollars)	10.41	14.57	16.59	16.17	16.47
Export volume (millions of barrels)	335.16	441.38	590.81	641.67	624.10

	1985	1986	1987	1988	1989
Price per barrel (dollars)	25.33	11.84	16.36	12.18	15.96
Export volume (billions of dollars)	14.61	6.14	8.47	6.51	7.84
Export volume (millions of barrels)	576.79	518.58	517.73	534.48	491.23

Sources: Price per barrel from *Energy Information Administration/Monthly Energy Review,* February 1994; export volume from *PEMEX: Memoria de Labores,* 1980–89.

not going to end soon. Immediately after OPEC's failure to cut production, PEMEX announced that these developments would not have an impact on the calculus of Mexican oil production and prices. Less than a week later, Mexico cut its oil prices by more than 10 percent. In yet another pricing policy flip-flop,[22] PEMEX increased the price of Mexican oil by about 6 percent, somehow believing that Mexican oil was immune to the dictates of market forces. The uncompetitive pricing of Mexican oil quickly translated into a smaller market share.[23]

To add to Mexico's balance-of-payments woes, international interest rates rose substantially when the U.S. Federal Reserve Bank resolved to bring U.S. inflation under control. The prime rate charged by U.S. banks, which stood at 6.8 percent in the 1976–77 period, rose to 15.3 percent in 1981 and to 18.9 percent in 1982.[24] Because of the hefty size of Mexican short-term debt (which had to be rolled over) and variable interest rate obligations, the interest rate hike meant an immediate increase in resource transfer abroad and capital account difficulties. Still believing that adverse external conditions were temporary, the Mexican government continued its spending spree, and resisted the needed currency devaluation and structural adjustments.

As the inflation rate outpaced both the nominal interest rate and the controlled slide of the peso, a significant devaluation began to seem imminent. In response to increased probability of a devaluation, investors shifted out of the peso. As a result, during the 1981–82 period, Mexico experienced a capital outflow of close to $12 billion,[25] exceeding 15 percent of the country's export revenues for the period. In 1982, the anticipated devaluation became a self-fulfilling prophecy: as Mexicans restructured their port-

96

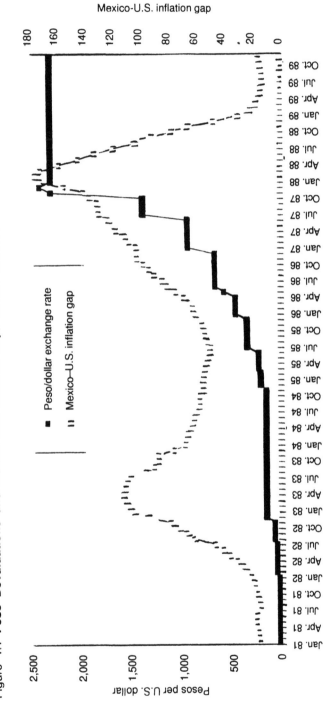

Figure 4.1 Peso Devaluations and Mexico–U.S. Inflation Gap, 1981:1–1989:12

folios by moving out of the peso, a substantial capital flight depleted the central bank's foreign reserves and caused a major devaluation.

On February 17, 1982, the peso lost more than 40 percent of its value (see Figure 4.1). Two days later, a stabilization plan that promised monetary and fiscal corrections was announced, followed by a cut in the price of Mexican oil. The oil price cut resulted in an anticipated reduction in government revenues and increased the public sector deficit. The budgetary picture deteriorated as public sector borrowing requirements reached 16.9 percent of GDP. These changes seem to have affected inflationary expectations; the peso suffered another massive devaluation of close to 20 percent.

As the Mexican financial situation deteriorated to the point of collapse, the United States and its European allies came to the rescue. The U.S. government, the World Bank, and the Paris Club committed more than $4.5 billion in emergency aid to Mexico. Despite this, in August 1982, Mexico was forced to impose a moratorium on the payment of its foreign debt. Meanwhile, in retaliation for capital flight that his own policies had inspired, López Portillo surprised the financial community by nationalizing all banks.[26] By the end of 1982, the Mexican annual inflation rate had more than tripled, approaching the unprecedented triple-digit range.

In December 1982, soon after Miguel de la Madrid Hurtado took over as president, the Program of Immediate Economic Reorganization (*Programa Inmediato de Reordenación Económica*—PIRE) was introduced to restore economic order. PIRE was essentially an orthodox plan and as such it benefited from the IMF's blessing, which translated into an extended fund facility and nearly U.S. $4 billion. PIRE was a limited reform program designed to generate trade surpluses needed for servicing the country's huge foreign debt. It did not include significant trade reforms and privatization programs.

The program consisted of provisions that were designed to attack the inflation problem immediately through shock therapy measures. It also included features that were to be implemented in the 1984–85 period with the intention of gradually bringing about prolonged economic recovery and sustained stability. The shock therapy had a number of components that were implemented simultaneously. First, in an attempt to control the inertial component of inflation (see chapter 1), the government abandoned the practice of indexing wages to past inflation in favor of wage indexation based on expected inflation. Second, on December 20, 1982, the government devalued the peso by 114 percent. Third, the government also acted to reduce the public deficit immediately and substantially. In one year, the government achieved its goal of halving the public sector borrowing requirement from 16.9 percent of GDP to about 8.5 percent of GDP. In cutting its expenditure, the government substantially reduced its investment in infrastructure and human and social development projects that had traditionally complemented private sector investment. Recent evidence suggests that these cutbacks in public investment adversely affected private investment and undermined economic growth.[27]

In the early 1980s, the concepts of inertial inflation and credibility were not well appreciated. The administration and the IMF economists believed that by quickly and significantly reducing the deficit, they could reduce the inflation rate abruptly and substantially. The inflation rate dropped modestly from about 99 percent in 1982 to 81 percent in 1983 (see Table 4.1). IMF economists had projected an inflation rate of 55 percent for that year. The persistence of inflation and the resistance of the IMF and Mexican policymakers to changing nominal targets translated into a more drastic fiscal cutback than was originally planned. The resulting significant fiscal contraction pushed the economy hard down the recessionary path. Despite this overshooting, the IMF experts predicted flat output growth for 1983. Output fell by 4.2 percent (see Table 4.1).

In the second half of 1983, Mexico and its foreign creditors finally reached a debt restructuring agreement involving new loans with more attractive terms. The time structure of loans was set at eight years with 1.875 percent over the London Inter-Bank Offer Rate (LIBOR). A year later, Mexico reached another favorable agreement with its major creditors for restructuring another $48 billion.

As signs of economic life remained weak in 1984, the government attempted to reignite the economy with tax credits for purchases of equipment and machinery. The resulting increased domestic expenditure was especially beneficial to the important automotive sector.[28] Yet the overall economy remained sluggish—after a decline of 6.3 percent in 1983, the real GDP per capita grew by only 1.4 percent in 1984.[29]

A spread between U.S. and Mexican inflation rates (see Figure 4.1) that was uncompensated by exchange rate fluctuations in an era of dirty float, together with deteriorating economic conditions, led to exodus of capital. To stop the capital flight and to improve the country's external accounts, on July 11, 1985, the government brought the peso more in line with purchasing power parity levels by devaluing it by 53 percent (see Figure 4.1).

The economy remained listless as the important gubernatorial and local elections of July were approaching, causing concern for the ruling Institutional Revolutionary Party (PRI). In anticipation of the upcoming elections, the government increased public expenditure significantly. In response to Mexico's failure to comply with IMF targets, the IMF suspended the inflow of new money to Mexico. On the very same day that the IMF announced it was suspending the last 25 percent of its $3.6 billion loan to Mexico, a disastrous earthquake ravaged Mexico City.[30] In response to the devastation caused by the earthquake, the government increased its spending considerably, expanding the deficit.

The combination of oil price declines, the IMF's vote of no confidence, and the growing budget deficit resulted in a run on the peso and a quick deterioration of the capital account.[31] The lingering peso overvaluation placed the export sector under considerable pressure in two ways. First, the overvalued currency made Mexican exports more expensive on the world market and undermined the competitiveness of Mexican exports. Second, it squeezed exporters' profit margins by making the imported products needed in the production process more expensive. The current account surplus fell from $4.2 billion in 1984 to $714 million in 1985 while the capital account surplus of $39 million in 1984 sank into a deficit of $1.8 billion in 1985, resulting in a decline of 172 percent in Mexico's reserves.[32]

In July 1985, as the limitations of import substitution industrialization and the dangers inherent in overreliance on oil exports had become clear, Mexico introduced a major trade reform. The reform included tariff reductions, phasing out of imports license requirements, and gradual elimination of quantitative restrictions on imports and import price controls.[33] In a drastic turnaround, Mexico made more than 64 percent of all imports exempt from the imports license requirements. In accordance with General Agreement on Trade and Tariffs (GATT) mandates, by the end of 1987 Mexico moved toward a trade system relatively free from import-licensing provisions and extended import license requirement exemptions to more than 78 percent of all imports. Moreover, Mexico gradually reduced import tariffs from an average of 27 percent in 1982 to 10.4 percent by 1988.[34]

Despite their long-run implications, the short-run impact of these reforms on the economy was negligible. While nonpetroleum exports grew smartly by about 12 percent in the 1985–88 period, it must be remembered that in the year before the reforms took effect, these exports had registered an impressive increase of 28 percent.[35] Moreover, for the same period, the manufacturing sector experienced zero growth.

Meanwhile, energy-sector conflicts far beyond the control of Mexico offered new pressures to develop nonoil exports. The price of oil fell from more than $25 a barrel in 1985 to $12 a barrel in 1986 (see Table 4.3, page 95), and Mexican terms of trade dropped by more than 26 percent. Government revenues from oil exports fell from 10.8 percent of the GDP in 1983 to 4.9 percent in 1986[36] and the current account turned from a surplus of $1.1 billion to a deficit of $1.7 billion (see Table 4.2, page 94).

As the price of oil plunged, so did government finances. In 1986, the public sector borrowing requirements reached 16 percent of the GDP and the annual inflation rate (December over December) surged to 106 percent. It was in the midst of these distressing developments that the international financial community began cooperating with Mexico again. In July 1986, the IMF, under pressure from the Reagan administration, agreed to use an operational definition of budget deficit as requested by Mexico and pegged lending levels to changes in oil prices. A few months later, Mexico signed a loan rescheduling agreement with its foreign creditors.[37]

In December 1986, the Mexican government tried to impose its own austerity program aimed at fighting inflation through demand containment, adopting a highly restrictive credit policy that practically stopped new loans to the private sector by requiring reserves of close to 100 percent. The authorities also devalued the peso by 41 percent. On the fiscal side, the government reduced its discretionary expenditures from 22 percent of GDP in 1986 to 20 percent in 1987 (see Table 4.4). But high domestic interest rates resulted in a considerable jump in public sector interest expenses. Government expenditures devoted to paying off the interest on public domestic debt increased from 12 percent of GDP in 1986 to 15.3 percent in 1987. Moreover, the persistence of recession translated into essentially flat revenues for the government. As a result of these adverse conditions, public sector borrowing requirements swelled to about 16 percent of GDP in 1987. In the meanwhile, inflation rose steadily from 59 percent in 1984 to 159 percent in 1987.

The Mexican government enjoyed the good fortune of a temporary increase in oil prices in 1987. After a decline of 3.7 percent in 1986, real GDP grew modestly by 1.5 percent in 1987. Despite surpluses in both primary and operational fiscal balance in 1987 and very high nominal interest rates, inflation did not retreat. The stock market plunge of October 1987, an inflation that remained stubbornly high, and the overvaluation of the peso resulted in widespread dollarization in anticipation of a pending devaluation. Finally, in November 1987, the value of the peso in terms of U.S. dollar fell by more than 67 percent.

The Long Road to Stabilization

In response to all these threatening economic developments, in December 1987 President de la Madrid introduced the Economic Solidarity Pact (*Pacto de Solidaridad Económico*, hereafter referred to as the Pact). To restore order to economic conditions that were fast deteriorating, the Pact brought government, labor, and business representatives together to agree on a platform for cutting the monthly inflation rate down to 2 percent in one

Table 4.4

Public Sector Indicators As a Percentage of GDP, 1983–92

	1984	1985	1986	1987	1988	1989	1990	1991	1992
Total expenditure	37.6	37.2	42.1	43.2	38.7	33.2	29.5	25.6	24.2
Discretionary expenditure	20.8	21.5	22.0	20.4	18.2	16.8	16.4	16.6	16.7
Salaries & wages	6.2	6.2	6.1	6.0	5.4	5.4	5.1	5.5	5.9
Capital	4.2	3.8	3.8	3.7	3.1	2.8	3.0	3.2	2.9
Nondiscretionary expenditure									
Net transfer	2.9	3.1	3.6	3.3	2.6	2.3	2.3	2.6	2.8
Interest payments	11.7	11.3	16.3	19.6	16.7	12.8	9.4	5.5	3.9
Domestic	7.8	7.7	12.0	15.3	13.2	9.5	7.2	3.4	—
External	3.9	3.6	4.3	4.3	3.6	3.2	2.2	2.0	—
Others	6.1	5.4	4.8	4.2	3.8	4.6	3.7	3.5	3.6
Total revenues	31.3	30.4	29.2	29.5	29.1	27.7	27.5	29.4	28.8
Deficit (+) or surplus (−)	6.3	6.9	12.8	13.7	9.7	5.5	2.0	−3.8	−4.6
PSBR	8.5	9.6	15.9	16.0	12.5	5.6	3.9	−2.0	−3.4

Source: Banco de México, *Indicadores Económicos* (February 1994): e and f.

year. To achieve this goal, the Pact combined heterodox elements of price controls and wage freezes with orthodox tools of currency devaluation and public deficit reduction. While relying on the IMF's support through a standby agreement, the Mexican government restructured its foreign debt, streamlined its expenditures, and forged ahead with trade liberalization and public sector privatization programs.

The Pact was designed to offer both long-run and short-run solutions to the inflation problem. To bring inflation under control quickly, the government relied on multiple nominal anchors. It committed itself to a fixed exchange rate of one peso per 0.04 U.S. dollar, and, for the first time in Mexico, introduced an incomes policy in the form of wage and price freezes. The prime objective of the incomes policy was to eradicate inertial inflation. From the 1985–87 stabilization failures in Brazil and Argentina (see chapters 2 and 5), Mexican policymakers concluded that in the absence of meaningful fiscal and structural reforms heterodox policies were ineffective.

To bring about effective, long-run stabilization, the Pact initiated structural reforms in two fronts. First, it targeted the fiscal deficit. Given the substantial debt-service obligations, the plan aimed at reaching a primary public sector surplus of 6 to 7 percent of GDP so that it could service its debt without running any operational deficit. To reach this goal, the government implemented a fiscal austerity program that (1) eliminated many non-agricultural subsidies, (2) dismissed 13,000 executives who worked for the government and reduced the size of the public sector workforce by 50,000 through voluntary retirements, and (3) cut its discretionary expenditures substantially from 20.4 percent of GDP in 1987 to 16.7 percent in 1989. Impressively, for the 1987–89 period the total government expenditure was reduced from 43.2 percent of GDP to 32.2 percent (see Table 4.4). As a result of these measures, the public sector borrowing requirements that stood at 16 percent of GDP in 1987 were slashed to 5.6 percent in 1989.

Second, the government liberalized foreign trade to an extent that would have been unimaginable a short decade before. In 1986, Mexico had finally signed the General Agreement on Trade and Tariffs (GATT), and in 1987 it had entered into bilateral agreements with the United States that strengthened the trade relations between the two countries and set the groundwork for the North American Free Trade Agreement. The Pact further moved Mexico down the free trade path by cutting the maximum import tariffs in half from 40 percent to 20 percent and by abolishing import license requirements.

As a means of fighting inflation, the Mexican government imposed restraints on exchange rate devaluation and allowed the real exchange rate to remain overvalued (see Figure 4.1, page 96). This, together with trade liberalization program started in 1985, helped to hold the line on prices by making cheaper imports available to both consumers and producers. Despite overvalued exchange rates, exports expanded impressively in the 1988–90 period (see Table 4.2, page 94) for three reasons. First, Mexico's competitiveness in international markets improved as a result of a decline in real wages and cheaper imported inputs. Second, there was a growing sentiment among producers that the Mexican government was not going to revert to a trade policy that was detrimental to the export sector.[38] Finally, the strength of the U.S. economy, Mexico's largest export market, translated into a 13 percent increase in demand for imports in the United States, which benefited Mexico directly.[39]

The implementation of far-reaching trade liberalization initiatives was perceived as untimely by some analysts who feared that it could jeopardize the use of a fixed exchange rate as the nominal anchor for stabilization. If the country's current account and balance of payments were to suffer because of trade reforms, the prospects of a devaluation and the associated exodus from the domestic currency could have undermined the peso and the Pact. To safeguard against such a scenario and to prevent capital flight, the government set the domestic interest rate very high, thus hindering economic growth.

In the immediate aftermath of the plan, the demand for durable goods and high ticket items increased, as the long-run success of the stability plan was still in question.[40] But as the demand for durable goods cooled down, so did the rest of the economy. The economy remained anemic: in 1987 the real GDP grew by only 1.9 percent. While the annual inflation rate dropped from about 159 percent in December 1987 to 52 percent in December 1988, in the aftermath of the Pact the inflation rate continued to outpace the rise in nominal wages (see Figure 4.2). This contributed to pronounced declines in real wages (see Figure 4.3 and "Economic Stability for Whom?" below).

In summary, the six years of the Miguel de la Madrid (1982–88) administration were years of extreme sacrifice in terms of output and employment. The sacrifice was deemed necessary for restoring balance in the budget and current account and for achieving effective stabilization. Some of the need for a pronounced adjustment was created by external factors. First, the virtual halt of foreign capital inflow, especially in 1985–86, put enormous pressure on Mexico's capital account. Second, the drastic reduction in world oil prices proved disastrous for Mexico's terms of trade, export revenues, and trade balance. But in the end, it was the reckless economic policymaking of the 1970s and early 1980s caused by internal political constraints that created fiscal imbalances and made Mexico vulnerable to external shocks. On the one hand, the lower and middle classes

Figure 4.2 **Inflation and Percentage Change in Nominal Minimum Salary** (annual averages)

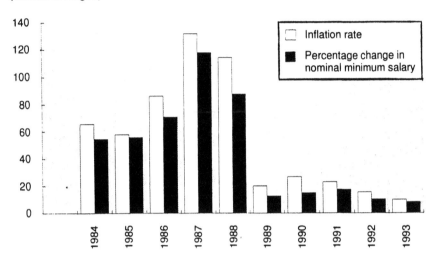

Figure 4.3 **Real Wages (Annual Average and December–December), 1983–93**

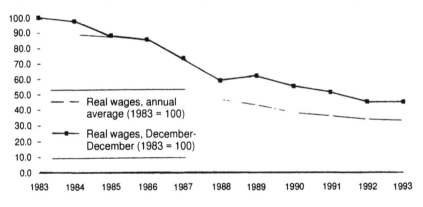

demanded and, through popular pressure, won increased government investment and expenditure on social programs; on the other hand, political and economic elites effectively opposed increased taxation needed for financing public programs. As a result, the government resorted to deficit spending financed by external borrowing to increase its expenditure without enhancing its revenues.

The de la Madrid administration resorted to the strong medicine of cutting expenditures to bring order to the fiscal and balance-of-payments conditions. It succeeded in turning a primary deficit of 7.3 percent of GDP in 1982 into a surplus of 7.5 percent of GDP by 1988, an improvement of close to 14.8 percent of GDP.[41] By 1988, Mexico had its fiscal deficit and inflation under control.

The eventual success of the Pact can be attributed to a number of factors. First, the government managed its fiscal house responsibly and pursued a decidedly noninflationary monetary policy. Second, use of the fixed exchange rate as the nominal anchor worked effectively because the country's abundant foreign reserves made the policy credible. Third, the overvaluation brought about by the Solidarity Pact slowed down the rate of decline of real wages and generated political support for the Pact with labor.[42]

In December 1988, Carlos Salinas de Gortari took office as the new president of Mexico with the intention of adding growth to stability. The Salinas administration continued to employ a consensus-based pact for maintaining price stability and introducing the growth element. The Pact for Stability and Economic Growth (hereafter PSG) was an agreement among government, labor, and business representatives to continue with reforms, keep inflation under control, and map a growth strategy.

Under the auspices of a debt reduction and restructuring plan put forth by the United States (the Brady Plan), in July 1989, Mexico signed an important debt reduction package that resulted in the much-needed annual debt relief of about $3 billion. Between 1980 and 1988 the Mexican total external debt had almost doubled. In 1988, Mexico's foreign debt exceeded 60 percent of its GNP and claimed more than 300 percent of the country's total export revenues (see Table 4.5). To help Mexico better cope with these financial burdens, the Brady Plan brought about a 35 percent reduction of Mexico's foreign debt. Mexico's foreign creditors, totaling five hundred banks, were given two options. Under one option, the face value of the loan was to remain unchanged while the interest rate was reduced to a fixed 6.2 percent. Under the other option, the face value of the loan was set at the London Inter-Bank Offer Rate (LIBOR) plus thirteen-sixteenths of 1 percent. The banks could also choose to participate in the Mexican government's privatization program through debt-for-equity swaps.[43] Indeed, between 1986 and 1990, Mexico benefited from a capital inflow of $4.24 billion through debt-for-equity swaps and another $2.6 billion from bonds-equity swaps.[44]

Between 1989 and 1993, the Salinas administration continued far-reaching reforms in three major areas. First, it accelerated the privatization program, including the reprivatization of the banks. Second, it initiated the constitutional provisions that made the privatization of the *ejido* land tenure

Table 4.5

Foreign Debt Indicators, 1970–89

	1970	1975	1980	1981	1982	1983	1984	1985	1986	1987	1988	1989
Total External Debt (EDT)	—	—	57,378	78,270	86,019	92,964	94,822	96,865	100,872	109,447	100,752	95,541
Long-term debt	5,966	15,609	41,215	53,287	59,651	81,565	86,022	88,446	90,912	98,484	86,492	80,256
Public	3,196	11,414	33,915	43,087	51,551	66,765	69,726	72,701	75,809	84,336	80,561	76,257
Private	2,770	4,195	7300	10,200	8,100	14,800	16,296	15,745	15,103	14,148	5,931	3,999
Short-term debt	—	—	16,163	24,983	26,147	10,139	6,440	5,450	5,900	5,800	9,456	10,295
Interest payment (INT)	—	829.2	3,890	4,833	11,153	9,994	11,302	10,220	8,375	8,325	8,710	9,292
Total debt service (TDS)	—	1,584	7,901	8,551	15,684	14,822	16,958	15,293	12,945	12,085	15,469	14,352
International reserves (RES)	756	1,897	4,175	4,972	1,778	4,794	8,019	5,679	6,674	13,692	6,327	6,740
EDT/Exports of goods & services (XGS) (%)	—	—	259	257	312	324	291	326	423	364	312	263
EDT/GNP(%)	—	—	30.3	31.9	52.5	66.4	57.1	55.2	82.6	82.3	60.9	51.2
TDS/XGS(%)	—	24.9	32.1	28.1	56.8	51.7	52.1	51.5	54.2	40.1	47.9	39.5

Source: World Bank, *World Bank Tables*, 1987–88 and 1990–91.

Figure 4.4 **Monetary Aggregates and Inflation, 1984–93**

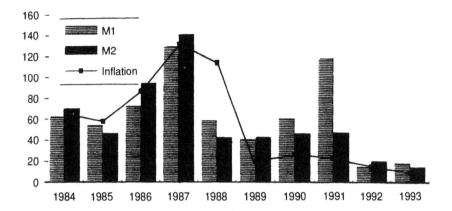

system possible. Third, it put into effect the North American Free Trade Agreement (NAFTA).

In the 1992–93 period, Mexico continued highly restrictive monetary policy to assure low inflation. Figure 4.4 shows the evolution of monetary aggregates M_1 and M_2 and the inflation rate for the period 1984–93. The drastic monetary contraction of the 1992–93 period, which coincided with negative real per capita output growth and single-digit inflation for the first time in two decades is especially noteworthy. In addition to using the monetary anchor, the strong position in the country's external balance helped the government use the exchange rate as an additional anchor for price stability. The balance-of-payments surplus of $1.2 billion in 1992 was increased to a surplus of $6.1 billion in 1993. This improvement was mostly due to a substantial increase in foreign investment from $22.4 billion in 1992 to $33.3 billion in 1993. As a result, the capital account position of the country improved from a surplus of $26.5 billion in 1992 to a surplus of $30.9 billion in 1993. Most of this impressive improvement in the capital account, however, was due to a substantial increase in foreign speculative investment in the Mexican stock market due to optimism stemming from NAFTA. In particular, foreign investment in the Mexican stock market rose from $4.8 billion in 1992 to $10.8 billion in 1993, while direct foreign investment rose only modestly from $4.4 billion to $4.9 billion. In the absence of credible restraints on capital flows, foreign capital can speed in and out of the country with potentially sobering consequences for the country's balance-of-payments position.

As economic growth remained elusive in 1993 and 1994, signs of underlying social discontent emerged across the nation. Rebels in the state of Chiapas challenged the central government and the PRI's first presidential candidate was assassinated in Baja California. In response to popular demands, as the important August presidential elections were approaching, PRI presidential candidate Ernesto Zedillo outlined a ten-point economic program in June 1994 designed to restore economic growth and bring about income redistribution. In August, Zedillo was elected as the new Mexican president with a mandate to bring about "economic growth with income redistribution," recalling Echeverría's objective of "shared development."

Economic Stability for Whom?

Mexico has thus achieved what very few observers thought possible a decade ago. In about ten years, it has restored order to its balance of payments, put the debt crisis behind it, brought its public finance and inflation under control, and adopted free trade. In other words, Mexico has revamped its economic system. But what has this metamorphosis meant for the Mexican people? What have been the social costs and benefits of stabilization and modernization?

The majority of Mexican people are worse off today than they were ten years ago. This deterioration of living standards has occurred in both relative and absolute terms. In relative terms, income distribution has become more skewed: the most privileged portion of the population has increased its share of national income at the expense of other Mexicans. As can be seen in Table 4.6, while the top decile of the population claimed close to 33 percent of national income in 1984, its share increased to over 38 percent by 1992. Thus in nine years, the top 10 percent of the population enhanced its share of national income by 5.3 percent in relative terms and 16.4 percent in absolute terms. The other 90 percent of the population, however, fought a loosing battle and saw their living standard decline relative to both their own past living standard and the living standard of the most privileged 10 percent of the population (see Table 4.6).

For the majority of Mexican people, the decline in their relative income share came at a time when real income was contracting significantly. Thus, both the size of the national pie and the share given to 90 percent of Mexicans were shrinking. As can be seen from Table 4.1 (page 93), in the decade of 1983–93, the Mexican real GDP fell by an annual average rate of 1.8 percent. The decline in per capita income was even more pronounced because the population continued to grow by between 2 and 3 percent per year. During the same period real minimum wages, earned by two out of every three Mexican workers,[45] dropped significantly. Figure 4.2 (page

Table 4.6

Income Distribution in Mexico, 1984–92 (percentages)

Decile	1984	1989	1992	Relative difference, 1984-92	Absolute difference, 1984-91
		Percentages			
I	1.72	1.58	1.55	−0.17	−9.9
II	3.11	2.81	2.73	−0.38	−12.1
III	4.21	3.74	3.70	−0.51	−12.0
IV	5.32	4.73	4.70	−0.62	−11.6
V	6.40	5.90	5.74	−0.66	−10.3
VI	7.86	7.29	7.11	−0.75	−9.6
VII	9.72	8.98	8.92	−0.80	−8.2
VIII	12.17	11.42	11.37	−0.80	−6.5
IX	16.73	15.62	16.02	−0.71	−4.3
X	32.77	37.93	38.16	5.39	16.4
Gini coefficient	0.429	0.469	0.475	0.046	10.6
Decile X/ decile I	19.1	24.0	24.6	1.046	29.1

Sources: Departmento de Estudios Económicos de BANAMEX, Instituto Nacional de Estatísticas, Geografía e Informática, *Encuesta nacional ingreso-gasto de los hogares,* 1984, 1989, and 1992; Grupo Financiero BANAMEX–ACCIVAL: *Exémen de la Situación Económica de México,* 20, no. 821 (1994).

104) shows the inflation rate and percentage increases in nominal wages for the period 1984–93. It can be seen that in each year inflation outpaced nominal wages, thus squeezing real wages. Figure 4.3 (page 104) shows the decline in real wages—measured as an annual average and end-of-year change—for the period 1983–93. During this period, average annual real wages declined by a whopping 67 percent while the December-to-December measure of real wages shows a decline of 55 percent.

To confront this drastic reduction in income per capita and living standards, the Mexican government allocated a larger percentage of its discretionary expenditures to social programs. Table 4.7 shows that the public sector expenditure on social programs rose from about 31 percent in 1980 to over 53 percent of all the government's budgeted expenditures in 1993. Similarly, Table 4.7 shows that expenditures on education and health were increased as a percentage of total government budgeted expenditures. But it must be remembered that while the government was allocating a larger percentage of its discretionary expenditures to social programs, it was

Table 4.7

Public Sector Expenditure on Social Programs As a Percentage of Total Budgeted Expenditure

	1980	1982	1985	1990	1991	1992	1993
Social programs	31.1	33.9	31.2	38.1	44.4	49.1	53.6
Education	12.1	14.0	12.9	15.8	18.4	20.2	22.4
Health	13.6	13.6	12.6	18.6	21.3	22.1	24.0
Regional programs	2.3	3.9	2.2	2.4	3.0	3.9	3.9
Urban programs	3.1	2.4	3.5	1.3	1.6	1.4	1.8

Source: El Nacional, *Reporte económico* (July 7, 1993).

Table 4.8

Government Expenditure in 1980 Pesos by Category, 1983–90

Year	Total		Education		Medical services		Public administration & defense	
	Millions 1980 pesos	% change	Millions 1980 pesos	% change	Millions 1980 pesos	% change	Millions 1980 pesos	% change
1983	518.6	—	201.3	—	111.3	—	206.0	—
1984	552.8	6.6	214.9	6.8	114.1	2.5	223.8	8.6
1985	557.8	0.9	217.2	1.0	116.8	2.4	223.8	0.0
1986	569.6	2.1	226.9	4.5	120.9	3.6	221.8	−0.9
1987	559.2	−1.8	223.1	−1.6	122.4	1.2	213.7	−3.6
1988	556.4	−0.5	222.9	0.1	127.3	4.0	206.2	−3.5
1989	552.6	−0.7	225.1	1.0	133.2	4.6	194.3	−5.8
1990	562.1	1.7	228.6	1.6	137.0	2.8	196.6	1.2

Source: Macro Asesoría Económica, S.C., *Realidad Económica de México, 1992*: 279.

cutting back on its total expenditures. As can be seen from Table 4.8, in inflation-adjusted terms, government expenditures on education were virtually unchanged for the post-stabilization period of 1987–90. For the same period, expenditures on medical services show an average annual increase of 3 percent, roughly in line with population growth.

Table 4.4 (page 101) shows that during the adjustment period, government expenditures on salaries and wages and capital expenditure were reduced. This implies that employment offered by the public sector directly and indirectly (through future growth) was reduced as a result of austerity. But while the government cut its expenditures in these areas, it had to continue paying considerable sums in interest payments on its domestic debt. Thus, by its very structure, the government quest for reaching balance in its fiscal accounts brought about a redistribution of income and rent away from the lower classes to the owners of capital.

Conclusion

In this chapter we have traced the origins of the economic crises that engulfed Mexico in the 1980s to external shocks, most of which were due to significant swings in oil prices and policies that unrealistically discounted growth constraints faced by the economy. We also identified fiscal and balance-of-payments imbalances as the source of price instability and examined failed stabilization attempts of the 1970s and 1980s.

Stabilization was finally achieved in the post-1987 period via a program that brought public finances under control and used multiple nominal anchors, including price and wage freezes, managed exchange rate, and restrictive monetary policy. The exchange variable played an important role in shaping the economic destiny of Mexico. On the one hand, overvalued exchange rates were used to control inflation and to stop wage erosions; on the other hand, undervalued exchange rates were employed as a means of encouraging exports. This conflict in policy objectives led to wide swings in the real exchange rate such that exchange rate overvaluation was employed during periods of stabilization followed by periods of exchange rate devaluations aimed at helping exporters.[46]

The relentless fight of the Mexican government against inflation has brought annual inflation down to the 6 to 8 percent range. As impressive as the triumph over inflation may be, one cannot help but think of overkill, as this taming of inflation has been achieved at significant output and income costs. It is also important to evaluate the success of the Mexican stabilization in the context of a political environment that is not democratic.[47] The social problems of highly skewed income distribution, poverty, and malnutrition are distressingly conspicuous in Mexico. The profound and bold reforms introduced during the last decade may have paved the way for long-term economic growth and justice, but meanwhile Mexico suffers from slow growth and a formidable array of social problems that detract from the lives of ordinary Mexicans.

5

Argentina and Bolivia: The Road from Inflation to Stabilization

Introduction

Despite the vast differences that exist between the economies of Argentina and Bolivia (see introduction), by 1985 both countries had identified runaway inflation as their prime economic foe. In both countries economic instability was triggered by external shocks, and the fundamental driving force behind price increases was public sector disequilibrium. In 1985, disenchanted by orthodox stabilization policies favored by the International Monetary Fund (IMF), Argentina introduced the first comprehensive heterodox anti-inflation plan in Latin America. In the same year, Bolivia chose to bring order to its economy through an orthodox shock. While various Argentine stabilization attempts failed in the 1986–90 period, Bolivia restored price stability quickly. In the post-1990 period, Argentina returned to the orthodox blueprint of economic management and restored stability. In the end, Argentina and Bolivia brought their inflation under control by using tactics that were essentially identical. Both countries streamlined their public finances, introduced market oriented structural reforms, and adopted a fixed exchange rate that functioned as the nominal anchor for stabilization.

In this chapter we examine the inflation problem that plagued both Argentina and Bolivia in the 1980s and the nature of various stabilization plans that were introduced in hopes of ending runaway inflation. In the first section, "Modern Stabilization Policies in Argentina," we analyze the Argentine experience with inflation and macroeconomic (in)stability for the period 1976–93. The second section, "The Bolivian Experience: From Hy-

perinflation to Stabilization," is devoted to a brief study of Bolivian hyperinflation. This is followed by the conclusion.

Modern Stabilization Policies in Argentina

Inflation and Stabilization: 1976–1985

One of the most important goals of the military government that ousted the
1973–76 Perónist administration was controlling inflation. During the administration of Isabel Perón (1974–76), economic mismanagement had resulted in severe macroeconomic disequilibria. In 1975, the gross domestic
product (GDP) declined by about 0.6 percent, the fiscal deficit stood at
about 15 percent of GDP, the current account deficit approached the unprecedented level of $1.3 billion, and inflation had jumped from 24 percent
in the previous year to 183 percent.

The military regime sought to engineer long-term economic growth by
implementing significant reforms that included reducing the role of the state
in the economy, liberalizing foreign trade, and implementing structural
changes.[1] As in the aftermath of the 1964 coup in Brazil, the Argentine
generals hoped to achieve these goals gradually, avoiding a drastic reduction in output and employment.

To achieve short-term stabilization, the authorities following an orthodox
blueprint, adopted a restrictive monetary policy, and freed prices of all goods
(except for medicine). The government also overhauled the financial sector by
freeing regulated interest rates, which had remained negative in real terms for
six consecutive years,[2] and by cutting the reserve requirement for banks from
100 percent to 10 percent.[3] In an attempt to gradually liberalize foreign trade,
tariffs were reduced from an average of 55 percent to 41 percent,[4] and export
taxes on corn and meat were eliminated. The black market premium on the
dollar vanished as the government allowed unrestricted foreign exchange transactions on capital account, adopted a unified exchange rate, and opted for a
"dirty float" regime that amounted to daily devaluations of the peso.

In spite of these far reaching reforms, macroeconomic stability proved
elusive. The military dictatorship that had taken over political power in the
name of restoring economic order could not, after two years in office, claim
a victory over the inflation foe. Inflation had declined significantly, but it
still persisted at around 170 percent per year (see Table 5.1). As a "final
solution" to the inflation problem, in December 1978 Economic Minister
Martínez de Hoz introduced the *Tablita* plan.

The overriding purpose of the *Tablita* plan was to reduce inflation
expectations by linking a managed and reduced currency depreciation rate
to a managed and reduced rate of inflation. In essence, the plan attempted to

Table 5.1

**Argentina: GDP Per Capita Annual Growth Rates
and Annual Inflation Rates, 1976–85**

Year	% change in per capita GDP	Annual inflation rate
1976	-2.0	347.5
1977	4.6	150.4
1978	-4.9	169.8
1979	4.9	139.7
1980	-0.5	87.6
1981	-8.2	131.2
1982	-6.8	208.7
1983	0.7	433.7
1984	0.7	688.0
1985	-0.1	385.4

map the evolution of the inflation rate by managing expectations through pre-announcing the exchange rate.[5] The exchange rate was to depreciate by 5.4 percent in January 1979, 5.2 percent in February, 5.0 percent in March, and so on, until August, when the exchange rate was to depreciate by 3.8 percent. Wages and prices in the public sector were to grow by about 4 percent a month. As required by the plan's reliance on the law of one price, Argentina introduced radical reforms in the financial markets by removing restrictions on foreign capital and promoting the integration of the domestic and international capital markets.

The plan was successful at first as reduced inflationary expectations led to a decline in demand for real cash balances and inflation declined in line with the purchasing power parity levels. But as the inflation rate continued to exceed the scheduled rate of depreciation, real appreciation and a pronounced decline in the tradables–nontradables price ratio resulted.[6] The overvaluation of the peso undermined Argentina's external competitiveness considerably as the gap between the domestic and the international inflation rate widened further without a corresponding adjustment in the exchange rate. The *Tablita* plan's designers had singled out the export sector as the stabilization anchor. Martínez de Hoz summarized his economic team's decision by stating,

> We preferred to take the exporting sector, rather than the whole economy, as a variable for adjustment. The former was enjoying surpluses in its trade balance while the latter would have to undergo a strong monetary adjustment with dubious results, as the examples of stagflation have shown.[7]

Thus, overvaluation together with lower tariff rates for consumer products damaged the country's current account significantly. The strong trade surplus of $2.6 billion in 1978 turned into a deficit of $2.5 billion by 1980. As the import–export ratio increased from 25 percent in 1978 to 140 percent in 1980 and 1981,[8] the current account came under considerable pressure. The noninterest current account turned from a surplus of $2.2 billion in 1978 to a deficit of $3.8 billion in 1980. A surplus of $1.8 billion in the current account in 1978 turned into deficits of $536 million and $4.8 billion in 1979 and 1980, respectively.

Difficulties in the capital account further undermined Argentina's balance of payments. Initially, the government's removal of restrictions on foreign capital mobility resulted in a substantial capital inflow as high interest rates in Argentina enticed foreign capital. In the meantime, the Argentine private sector sought to reduce its capital cost by borrowing abroad, contributing to a dramatic increase in Argentina's foreign debt. As a result, in the 1978–79 period, the Central Bank's foreign reserves almost doubled, with a corresponding increase in private sector foreign debt.[9] In 1979 alone, private foreign debt increased by about 100 percent, and in two years (from 1979 to 1981) the total external debt tripled.[10] As the real appreciation of the peso persisted, the probability of a large devaluation increased considerably. This, in turn, resulted in massive capital flight and further undermined the country's capital account position.

To make matters worse, a prolonged financial crisis began in the second quarter of 1980. In March 1980, Argentina's largest private bank, Banco de Intercambio Regional (BIR), faced a solvency problem. Following a neoliberal perspective, the government decided not to bail out the BIR and other cash-strapped banks. As these banks failed, the Central Bank printed more money to pay off the depositors of federally insured bank accounts. As a result, in April alone, the monetary base increased by 27 percent.[11]

In addition to the financial crises that enveloped the economy, a fiscal disequilibrium that resulted in a lack of consistency between deficit and the *Tablita* emerged.[12] In 1980 the deficit–GDP ratio increased to 11.3 percent from 9 percent in the preceding year. To combat the outflow of capital, the Argentine government resorted to a policy of tight credit and high interest rates at the cost of declining output.[13] The eroding public confidence in the economy and the continued overvaluation of the peso brought about increased capital flight and put considerable pressure on the country's balance of payments. In response to fast deteriorating economic conditions, in February 1981, Martínez de Hoz devalued the peso by 10 percent, which was too little, too late. By the first quarter of 1981, it was evident that the *Tablita* plan could not stem the inflationary tide.

While the factors discussed above contributed to the failure of the

Tablita plan, persistent fiscal disequilibrium was the detrimental force that undermined the plan from the very beginning. The government's inability to establish fiscal discipline meant the plan was not credible. As a result, the public's deep-rooted skepticism about the government's ability to tame the inflation beast brought about persistent inflation through the expectation mechanism (see chapter 1), which outpaced the scheduled devaluation rates. During the first four quarters of the plan the peso was devalued by about 68 percent while the inflation rate surpassed 167 percent, and during the last quarter of the plan the inflation rate was about 89 percent while the devaluation rate was only 23 percent. During the life of the plan the peso appreciated by about 47 percent in real terms. This real appreciation resulted in turn in significant balance-of-payments problems and the eventual undoing of the plan. In summary, the fatal flaw of the plan was its resolve to use the exchange rate as a nominal anchor in the presence of pronounced internal disequilibrium. This led to disequilibrium in the external accounts which destroyed the nominal anchor for stabilization.

The four economic ministers that followed Martínez de Hoz stayed in office an average of eight months. In April 1981, a month after he replaced Martínez de Hoz, Lorenzo Sigaut announced a 30 percent devaluation, which was later followed by another massive devaluation of 20 percent. In December 1981, Sigaut was replaced by Roberto Alémann, who was replaced seven months later by José Pastore. In July 1982, José Pastore and Domingo Cavallo introduced the so-called Pastore-Cavallo Plan[14] with the main objective of lessening the heavy burden of private and public debts, and the intention of reviving the stagnating economy and controlling inflation.

To alleviate the serious debt crises faced by the private sector, the government set the nominal interest rate below the rate of inflation, thus again creating a negative real rate of interest. The government also repurchased the entire internal public debt and external private debt. Because money creation was used to finance debt purchases, a substantial increase in demand for black market dollars resulted, as evidenced by a one-day rise of 100 percent in the black market dollar premium.[15] The government created three different exchange rates: commercial, official, and financial. The commercial rate was then devalued 27.3 percent to encourage exports since a strong trade balance was needed to help alleviate the capital account disequilibrium caused by foreign debt. In addition to feeding inflation by its monetary policy, the government followed an inflationary fiscal policy. The fiscal deficit exceeded 17 percent of the gross domestic product (GDP) in 1982. The uncertainty associated with the elections that marked the transition from military rule to democracy exerted additional pressure on prices.[16] Thus, after six years of economic mismanagement, the generals gave back to the civilians an economy that was suffering from a great many problems, including high foreign debt, inflation, and instability.

Post-Redemocratization Stabilization Plans

When the Alfonsín administration took office in December 1983, it identified the taming of an inflation that exceeded 400 percent a year as its highest economic priority. The Argentine government turned to the IMF for stabilization assistance. The IMF adjustment program included the usual demand management measures aimed at reducing public expenditures, controlling wages, and devaluing the domestic currency. The program resulted in the expected short-term output decline and compressed real wages significantly. But inflation did not show signs of abating, forcing the government to grant considerable wage increases to compensate wage earners for lost purchasing power. These wage hikes restrained the budget and undermined external competitiveness, thereby causing substantial devaluations.[17] As the IMF-type approach failed, policymakers were reminded that various orthodox plans adopted between 1976 and 1985 had resulted in an average annual inflation rate of 245 percent and a decline in real per capita income of 1.7 percent. Meanwhile, di Tella (1979), Canitrot (1981), and Frenkel (1984), among others, concluded that the Argentine inflation was essentially different from inflation in industrialized countries because it was shaped by inertia and wage indexation (see chapter 1). It was therefore imperative that a new set of policies that differed from orthodox prescriptions and addressed the underlying characteristics of the Argentine inflation be employed.

On June 14, 1985, as important November elections were approaching and the annual inflation rate was surpassing 1,100 percent, the Alfonsín government introduced the first comprehensive heterodox stabilization plan in Latin America: the Austral Plan.[18] The two primary goals of the plan were to control inflation and to restore fiscal balance. Achieving the second goal was not deemed as a necessary condition for reaching the first because authorities believed fiscal imbalances were a consequence of inflation and not a cause of it.

The centerpiece of the Austral Plan was a wage, price, and exchange rate freeze program coupled with fiscal and monetary reforms.[19] The plan froze prices (except for products of a seasonal nature), wages, and the exchange rate for an unspecified period. In an attempt to minimize imbalances, prior to the freeze the government adjusted public sector prices, wages, and the exchange rate.[20] Beginning in May 1985, the government had introduced a number of important measures aimed at preparing the public sector for the plan. First, it reduced the time horizon for the payment of value-added taxes (VAT) from an average of fifty-five to forty days. As a result, the government succeeded in increasing VAT receipts by about 160 percent in the first month of the plan.[21] Second, the prices of products produced by state enterprises were readjusted for inflation. From May 1 until June 12, public sector prices increased by 108 percent, and in June alone the price of gasoline products rose by between 43 and 56 percent.[22]

In an attempt to maintain the approximate average real purchasing power of wage earners, wages were increased by 22.6 percent before the freeze took effect. Unlike the Brazilian pre-shock wage bonuses (see chapter 2), which resulted in a 1.2 percent increase in the real purchasing power of economic agents, the Austral wage-adjustment scheme brought about a reduction of 1 percent in the average real wage bill.[23]

In an attempt to give credibility to the domestic currency, the plan replaced the inflation-ridden peso with a new currency (the austral) at the rate of 1,000:1. Initially, the austral was valued at 874 pesos, but the peso was to be devalued against the austral at the daily rate of 0.85 percent which resulted in a 1,000:1 peso/austral exchange rate by July first.

On the fiscal side, the government pledged to reduce the deficit–GDP ratio by 6.7 percent and to stop printing new money as a means of financing its deficit. Initially, the government succeeded in restoring fiscal balance by turning a deficit of 56 billion australs into a surplus of 17 billion australs by November 1985 (see Table 5.2). The government achieved this turnaround by reducing its expenditure–GDP ratio by 5.1 percent and by augmenting its revenues–GDP ratio by 2.6 percent through new fees and tariffs in addition to higher taxes.[24] The drastic reduction in the inflation rate brought about by the Austral Plan also helped the budget by maintaining the real value of tax receipts in accordance with the Olivera-Tanzi effect. Moreover, thanks to lower interest rates, the government benefited from a significant reduction in the domestic cost of servicing its debt.[25] A month after the introduction of the plan, the Argentine government received a confidence-building signal from abroad as the IMF and the United States agreed to provide Argentina with $4.7 and $0.5 billion, respectively, in financial support.[26]

The immediate success of the Austral Plan was spectacular (see Figure 5.1). The inflation rate (in terms of consumer prices) declined from 30 percent in June to 7 percent in July and 2 percent in August (see Table 5.2). Despite the price freeze program, from January to April 1986 consumer and wholesale prices increased by 12 and 5 percent, respectively. Because of the uneven effectiveness of price controls and the ever-widening gap between the frozen prices and the market equilibrium prices, in April the government

Figure 5.1 **Argentine Inflation Rate, 1978:1–1985–12** (annual)

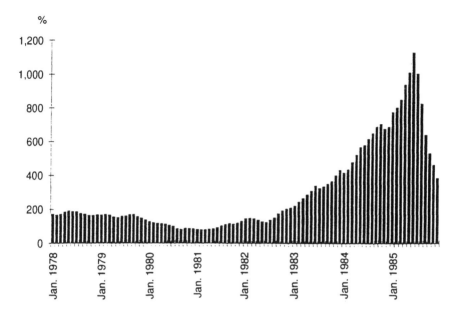

replaced the rigid price controls with a system of "administered" prices. Moreover, the government granted an 8.5 percent wage increase and put aside the fixed exchange rate in favor of a return to the crawling peg system.

As with the introduction of the Cruzadinho (the little cruzado) Plan in Brazil (see chapter 2), the Alfonsín administration introduced the Australito (the little austral) Plan when in January 1987 the annual inflation rate reached 90 percent. The Australito Plan imposed another price and wage freeze program that was to last six months. Despite this, by March 1987 the annual inflation rate once again reached the three-digit range, signaling the failure of the Austral Plan.

The failure of the Austral Plan can be attributed to three factors. First, despite early success, the government failed to maintain fiscal balance and to refrain from excessive money creation.[27] Second, cost-push factors, especially increases in nominal wages, exerted continuous pressure on prices.[28] Third, the imbalances introduced by the Austral Plan had to be resolved through realignment of prices and the removal of the freeze.[29] The end of the freeze then revived inflation as relative prices moved to restore market equilibrium.[30]

In August 1988, as the monthly and annual inflation rates reached 38

Table 5.2

Prices, Inflation, and Government Deficit in Argentina, 1985:1–1990:12

	Wholesale prices index (1985 = base)	Annual changes in consumer prices (percent)	Consumer prices index (1985 = base)	Deficit (–) or surplus (millions of *austrais*)
1985				
January	35	776	36	–4,766
February	41	804	44	–8,099
March	52	851	55	–3,020
April	69	939	71	–24,843
May	90	1,010	89	–19,118
June	129	1,129	116	–56,139
July	127	1,003	124	–7,580
August	129	826	127	540
September	130	640	130	1,480
October	131	532	132	4,720
November	132	463	136	17,800
December	133	385	140	–184,720
1986				
January	133	300	144	–5,570
February	134	237	147	–15,650
March	136	179	153	–29,020
April	140	125	161	–7,010
May	144	87	167	7,510
June	151	50	175	–37,430
July	158	51	186	–7,200
August	173	59	203	6,640
September	185	67	218	–32,630
October	195	74	231	–9,670
November	204	79	243	–39,270
December	211	82	254	–70,060
1987				
January	222	90	274	–16,690
February	237	99	291	–36,530
March	256	106	315	–23,220
April	261	103	326	–52,330
May	273	103	340	–18,650
June	292	110	367	–68,660
July	319	117	404	–26,080
August	366	126	459	–40,890
September	427	136	513	–57,170
October	556	166	613	–52,160
November	580	178	676	–101,940
December	593	175	699	–133,930
1988				
January	665	179	763	–120,370
February	755	189	842	–89,420
March	877	206	966	–99,780
April	1,025	248	1,133	–67,340

(continued)

Table 5.2 *(continued)*

	Wholesale prices index (1985 = base)	Annual changes in consumer prices (percent)	Consumer prices index (1985 = base)	Deficit (−) or surplus (millions of *austrais*)
1988 *(continued)*				
May	1,263	286	1,310	−54,890
June	1,567	322	1,547	−89,500
July	1,958	381	1,944	−151,380
August	2,584	440	2,479	−93,950
September	2,750	440	2,769	−178,230
October	2,876	392	3,019	−176,880
November	2,986	372	3,192	−104,580
December	3,156	388	3,410	−260,750
1989				
January	3,376	387	3,714	148,100
February	3,659	383	4,070	921,280
March	4,351	393	4,761	609,370
April	6,874	460	6,352	867,440
May	14,054	765	11,335	3,561,110
June	32,813	1,471	24,311	−3,440
July	101,425	3,610	72,112	5,733,350
August	110,017	3,910	99,415	590,450
September	112,770	3,826	108,716	5,523,760
October	114,492	3,703	114,799	89,160
November	116,543	3,731	122,284	620,060
December	173,153	4,923	171,287	4,600,730

Source: International Monetary Fund (IMF), *International Financial Statistics* (various issues.

and 440 percent, respectively, the government introduced another heterodox stabilization plan known as the Spring Plan (*Plan Primavera*). To bring the economy back from the brink of hyperinflation, the plan froze prices, devalued the austral by 11 percent, and set a 4 percent monthly devaluation schedule. The government also introduced a multiple exchange rate system to bring about increased revenues for the Central Bank. This scheme forced exporters to exchange their foreign currency for austrais at the official rate and importers to purchase foreign currency from the Central Bank at the parallel rate. Despite windfall profits generated by this scheme, the fiscal deficit persisted.[31] To maintain the disequilibrium exchange rate, interest rates had to remain artificially high. High interest rates, in turn, undermined the government's efforts to bring about fiscal discipline.[32] High interest rates adversely affected the budget in two ways. First, they reduced government revenues by depressing economic activity; second, they increased government expenditure by increasing public debt service.

As it became clear that public finance was deteriorating and high inflation was reemerging, and in response to uncertainty on the political horizon
caused by the presidential elections, the public shifted its assets from the
austral to the U.S. dollar. Despite the government's attempts to stop the
flight to foreign capital by adopting a tighter monetary policy, the trend
of substituting dollars for austrais continued; in the first week of February alone, the Central Bank's reserves declined by $0.5 billion.[33] Two
statistics from the first half of 1989 show that the public had no confidence in the government's ability to fight inflation and defend the austral: the average monthly inflation rate during this period bordered on 44
percent, while the U.S. dollar's value in austrais increased at an average
monthly rate of 87 percent. Sensing the ensuing financial crisis, the
Argentines soon withdrew approximately $1 billion from the local
banks, thus exerting enormous pressure on the Central Bank's foreign reserves.[34] In July 1989, five months before the scheduled transition of power
to a new president, as the annual inflation rate exceeded 3,600 percent and
the recession deepened, Alfonsín stepped down in favor of the newly
elected president Carlos Menem.

The Perónist Menem put aside the economic populist ethos of his
presidential campaign and recruited the top officials of Bunge y Born
(BB), a major grain-trading multinational corporation, to mastermind his
economic policies. The principal goal of the BB plan was to stabilize
domestic prices immediately by (1) introducing extensive economic reforms, and (2) utilizing the exchange rate as the stabilizing anchor. BB's
reform package included provisions for economic deregulation and public sector deficit reductions. The government brought the budget deficit
down to about 4 percent of the GDP and requested that wage increases
be held to under 15 percent until March 1990. The BB team devalued
the austral by about 16 percent to eliminate the black market premium
on the U.S. dollar and planned to keep the exchange rate fixed at 650
austrais per U.S. dollar until March 1990.[35] The IMF supported the plan
with a new standby loan of U.S. $220 million.

These measures proved successful in the short run as the inflation rate
dropped from about 200 percent in July to an average of about 6 percent in
October and November of 1989. In December, the relative price tranquil-
lity came to an abrupt end. Government finances caved in under the enormous pressure of very expensive short-term debt, and labor unions
demanded, and through strikes won, wage increases that ranged between 70
and 80 percent. As the exchange rate remained fixed and inflation continued, alas at lower rates, the austral became overvalued again. The
government's use of the fixed exchange rate as a nominal anchor in the

presence of persistent inflation had resulted in a highly overvalued currency and had fueled speculation regarding currency devaluation. To hedge against high inflation rates and the pending devaluation, the Argentines restructured their portfolios by shifting away from the austral in favor of dollar-denominated assets. By the end of 1989, the BB plan had failed to achieve its stabilization objectives and a run on the Central Bank ensued in December, despite 20 percent monthly interest rates and a 35 percent devaluation. The BB economic team resigned in December and Erman Gonzáles was appointed economic minister.

In an attempt to stop the run on the banking system and inflation, on December 28 the government rescheduled the public debt by mandating a conversion of interest-bearing deposits into ten-year dollar-denominated bonds (BONEX). This enabled it to convert all short-term public debt with seven day maturities into long-term obligations and reduce the inflationary pressure caused by public debt financing through monetary expansion.

The drastic reduction in the cost of financing the public debt and the associated improvements in the fiscal accounts, together with the introduction of the Economic Emergency Law in March, helped bring inflation down from hyperinflation levels in the first quarter of 1990 to the low double-digit range in the second and third quarters, and to the single-digit range by the last quarter. The Economic Emergency Law separated the Central Bank from the Treasury Department and introduced structural reforms aimed at streamlining public finances and opening up the economy. Despite these measures, public finances deteriorated when the government was forced to increase its expenditures on pension funds by about 1 percent of GDP to cover a deficit in the social security system. Despite a Central Bank intervention, the austral plummeted and inflation reached 27 percent in February (see Table 5.3).

On March 20, 1991, newly appointed Economic Minister Domingo Cavallo introduced the Convertibility Plan, also known as the Cavallo Plan. This plan committed the Argentine government to maintaining the full convertibility of the austral into the U.S. dollar at the rate of 10,000:1. As announced, four zeros were later removed from the exchange rate as a new currency (the peso) replaced the austral at the rate of 1:10,000.

Unlike other stabilization plans implemented in Argentina that used the exchange rate variable as the nominal anchor, Cavallo's Convertibility Plan succeeded in quelling inflation. The key to the success of Cavallo's plan was the "Law of Convertibility," which made it illegal for the government to increase the money supply without sufficient gold or dollar reserves. By using the legal apparatus, the government in effect created an independent monetary authority, eliminated wage indexation, and froze public sector

Table 5.3

Monthly Inflation Rate in Argentina, 1990:1-1991:12

Date	Inflation rate
1990	
January	79.2
February	61.6
March	95.5
April	11.4
May	13.6
June	13.9
July	10.8
August	15.3
September	15.7
October	7.7
November	6.2
December	4.7
1991	
January	7.7
February	27.0
March	11.0
April	5.5
May	2.8
June	1.3
July	1.8
August	1.4
September	1.7
October	1.3
November	.3
December	.7

Source: Boletín Económico (various issues).

workers' wages and public utility prices. The success of the Cavallo Plan in fighting inflation is apparent from results summarized in Table 5.3. The monthly inflation rate dropped from 27 percent in February 1991 to 5.5 percent in April, and 1.3 percent in July.

The success of stabilization plans that use the nominal exchange rate as the stabilization factor is contingent upon the fulfillment of two requirements: the budget deficit has to be under control and the government should be able to defend the domestic currency. In Argentina, both of these conditions were in place.

On the fiscal front, the Cavallo team showed that the government was serious about running a tight ship. First, to reduce the size of the federal government, the Cavallo Plan transferred a significant part of economic decision making from the federal level to the state and municipal levels.

The federal government provided the state and municipal governments with 56 percent of all tax revenues. In return, local authorities were given the responsibility to finance various services such as education, law enforcement, the judicial system, and so forth, without contracting new debt. Second, privatization played a significant role in improving the government's financial position. After initial resistance from public sector employees, the privatization process got under way successfully. By March 1992, one year after the inception of the plan, privatization brought in more than $6.5 billion. These funds were used strictly for cutting foreign debt, thus reducing government's debt-service expenses. Third, the government increased its revenues by enhancing tax receipts through improved collection as more tax auditors were hired to discourage tax evasion. Fourth, the government decreased its expenditures by reducing the size of state enterprises. In 1991 alone, the public sector workforce was cut by 8 percent (60,000 people).[36]

The strong foreign reserves position of Argentina made adhering to a fixed exchange rate policy and defending the austral possible. Beginning in 1990, the external sector's conditions began to improve substantially as the current account surplus increased by 59 percent because of a 27 percent decline in imports and an export expansion of more than 11 percent. As a result, Argentina's foreign reserves reached $2 billion in 1990, a tenfold increase over 1989.[37]

In April 1992, one year after the introduction of the Cavallo Plan, Argentina and its foreign creditors reached an important agreement for rescheduling $31 billion of Argentina's $61 billion foreign debt. This agreement (which was signed in December 1992) cut Argentina's medium- and long-term obligations by $10 billion and restructured Argentina's foreign debt along the lines outlined by the Brady Plan and applied in 1989 to the Mexican case (see chapter 4). In particular, the majority of the seven hundred banks that had extended credit to Argentina exchanged between 30 and 40 percent of their loans for guaranteed U.S. Treasury bills at a discount or at par. The former took the form of a 35 percent reduction in the face value of the original obligation in exchange for new debt guaranteed by the U.S. Treasury, which pays an interest rate 0.8125 points above the London Inter-Bank Offering Rate (LIBOR). The latter constituted a restructuring of the interest rate paid on the debt in exchange for new obligations guaranteed by the U.S. government. In this case, no reduction in the principal of the debt obligation occurs; instead, Argentina will pay reduced but accelerating interest on its obligations. Specifically, in the first year of the plan, Argentina will pay an interest rate of 4 percent. The rate of interest will increase by 0.25 percent every year until the seventh year. Thereafter, the rate of interest will remain fixed at 7 percent.

The Bolivian Experience: From Hyperinflation to Stabilization

Despite brief flirtations with high inflation during the 1950s and early 1970s, runaway inflation was an anomaly in Bolivia until the high inflation and hyperinflation episodes of the 1982–85 period. Interestingly, unlike the experiences of Argentina and Brazil, these episodes developed in the absence of indexation of wages, prices and other nominal variables. Thus, while the formal propagation mechanism of inflation was not present and inertia was not an embedded feature of the Bolivian economy, inflation gathered frightening momentum.[38]

As in the cases of Argentina, Brazil, and Mexico considered above, the combination of a significant external shock and the government's reaction in the form of expansionary policies set in motion an inflationary process that was soon out of control. In the case of Bolivia, the external shock began in 1978 when the demand for and the price of Bolivia's main exports, mineral and hydrocarbon products, started to decline. As a result of a significant deterioration in terms of trade, current account difficulties emerged, which, combined with Bolivia's large foreign debt,[39] brought about a dangerous balance-of-payments disequilibrium. Political factors complicated the calculus of sound economic policy as the 1980s began with the dictatorship of General Luis García Meza (1980–81), who resorted to deficit spending as a way of legitimizing his repressive regime. As a percentage of GDP, the public deficit reached about 5.7 percent in 1981 and jumped to 22.3 percent in 1982.[40]

To finance its continued high deficit, the García Meza administration employed inflationary tactics as it relied on seigniorage to transfer resources from the private sector to the public sector. The seigniorage, measured in constant pesos, increased from 232 million in 1980–81 period to 981 million in the following twenty-one months.[41] An especially drastic increase in seigniorage occurred in 1981; thereafter it stabilized, but the inflation rate continued its steep upward trend.[42]

When on October 10, 1982, the newly chosen president Hernán Siles Zuazo began governing the country with the help of the predominantly Marxist United Democratic and Popular Front (UDP)[43], the annual inflation rate was about 210 percent and the black market premium on the U.S. dollar had reached 50 percent.[44] The balance-of-payments position of the country deteriorated significantly as multilateral agencies—which were Bolivia's main source of foreign capital—practically stopped granting it new loans, in part because of the nature of the Bolivian government and in part because of the Mexican moratorium on debt payments (see chapter 4). The Bolivian government, which had relied on foreign resources for financing about 13 percent of its deficit (relative to GDP) was forced either to decrease its expenditures and reduce its deficit drastically or to continue with its established spending patterns at the cost of higher inflation. Given the populist nature of the government in office, it comes as no surprise that the latter option was chosen.

To fight the inflation problem, between 1982 and 1985, President Siles Zuazo introduced five "economic pacts" in November 1982, March 1983, November 1983, April 1984, November 1984, and February 1985. Most of these stabilization plans amounted to haphazard measures that corrected nominal prices, wages, and exchange rates for inflation,45 but did not address the underlying financial disequilibrium in the public sector. For example, the November 1982 plan devalued the exchange rate and increased prices of basic foodstuffs and petroleum while giving compensatory wage hikes to offset the impact of price increases. The plan was thus entirely ineffectual in terms of demand management and fighting inflation. The most promising of these plans was introduced in March 1983. This plan had a decidedly orthodox overtone but also relied on some heterodox tools.

Following the usual orthodox recipe, the Bolivian government devalued the peso by 78 percent, and attempted to reduce its deficit by increasing the prices of state-produced products. It also implemented heterodox measures of price and exchange rate controls[46] and introduced wage indexation with the intention of reducing the disastrous impact of inflation on real wages. According to this indexation scheme, minimum wages were to be increased by 100 percent in response to an increase of 40 percent in prices.[47] This triggering mechanism was repeatedly activated as prices rose relentlessly, causing drastic increases in government expenditures and public deficit. The ratio of the deficit of the nonfinancial public sector to the gross domestic product approached 30 percent by 1984.[48] As the deficit surged, so did the inflation rate; in the last quarter of 1984 alone prices rose by 234 percent.

The high inflation rate undermined public finance in two ways. First, through the well-known Olivera-Tanzi effect, real taxes declined. Second, by bringing about a highly overvalued official exchange rate—as evidenced by a more than 400 percent black market premium on the U.S. dollar—high inflation undermined the export sector. Because the export sector benefited the government directly (through exports by state enterprises) and indirectly (through export taxation), government revenues suffered significantly.[49] As public finance came under enormous pressure, the inflation rate continued to increase, reaching hyperinflationary proportions by April 1984.[50] In April, the government changed the indexation mechanism to a once-every-

Table 5.4

Money, Exchange Rate, Prices, and Industrial Production for Bolivia, 1974:1–1990:4

Year/quarter	M₁	Exchange rate (U.S. dollar)	Price index	Industrial production
1974:1	33.41	49,975.01	69.40	240.50
1974:2	44.29	49,975.01	76.23	233.80
1974:3	47.41	49,975.01	66.67	242.80
1974:4	44.58	49,975.01	43.52	198.80
1975:1	37.79	49,975.01	11.32	168.80
1975:2	26.79	49,975.01	4.68	215.00
1975:3	17.73	49,975.01	7.98	217.10
1975:4	12.76	49,975.01	8.17	209.60
1976:1	10.88	49,975.01	6.35	202.70
1976:2	9.54	49,975.01	5.08	205.50
1976:3	19.19	49,975.01	2.70	209.50
1976:4	34.97	49,975.01	3.93	202.00
1977:1	39.24	49,975.01	6.15	176.70
1977:2	40.73	49,975.01	6.67	177.50
1977:3	29.65	49,975.01	8.93	173.80
1977:4	21.63	49,975.01	10.58	171.60
1978:1	19.07	49,975.01	7.75	156.50
1978:2	12.59	49,975.01	8.26	169.30
1978:3	12.35	49,975.01	11.24	168.80
1978:4	10.83	49,975.01	13.89	159.10
1979:1	12.56	49,975.01	16.22	147.30
1979:2	10.91	49,975.01	17.80	145.00
1979:3	13.79	49,975.01	17.15	138.60
1979:4	17.56	46,738.01	26.98	131.30
1980:1	23.35	40,783.03	46.24	122.20
1980:2	36.82	40,783.03	52.25	124.10
1980:3	48.04	40,783.03	53.37	121.60
1980:4	43.77	40,783.03	38.56	112.50
1981:1	29.31	40,783.03	37.43	104.60
1981:2	11.44	40,783.03	32.21	108.80
1981:3	5.92	40,783.03	30.38	109.90
1981:4	16.65	40,783.03	29.25	123.30
1982:1	37.29	29,979.59	28.42	122.40
1982:2	77.87	23,174.97	62.92	118.20
1982:3	137.55	23,174.97	132.92	128.60
1982:4	208.34	11,457.52	256.41	123.50
1983:1	242.25	5,052.80	275.10	110.10
1983:2	237.47	5,052.80	276.32	106.10
1983:3	184.93	5,052.80	257.59	117.10
1983:4	174.90	3,472.22	285.14	112.70
1984:1	222.64	1,980.67	426.77	106.40
1984:2	352.18	571.62	956.97	103.30
1984:3	670.02	322.69	999.58	103.90
1984:4	1,384.56	157.68	1,854.25	107.10
1985:1	3,465.04	54.33	6,831.39	100.80

(continued)

Table 5.4 (continued)

Year/quarter	M₁	Exchange rate (U.S. dollar)	Price index	Industrial production
1985:2	4,576.99	17.46	6,715.83	101.40
1985:3	9,973.36	9.75	20,072.41	101.90
1985:4	7,614.56	0.80	10,507.25	96.00
1986:1	2,504.65	0.51	2,697.18	87.70
1986:2	1,289.45	0.53	1,083.46	86.00
1986:3	249.85	0.52	183.03	90.40
1986:4	114.76	0.52	84.65	90.30
1987:1	90.89	0.51	22.69	90.00
1987:2	70.66	0.49	16.11	62.10
1987:3	59.42	0.48	10.16	95.50
1987:4	42.49	0.47	10.62	98.00
1988:1	27.23	0.45	8.09	92.90
1988:2	30.41	0.43	13.46	0.00
1988:3	25.43	0.42	20.93	0.00
1988:4	36.36	0.41	21.05	0.00
1989:1	35.87	0.40	21.30	0.00
1989:2	26.14	0.39	13.86	0.00
1989:3	16.61	0.36	10.28	0.00
1989:4	2.36	0.34	15.37	0.00
1990:1	6.78	0.33	16.73	94.80
1990:2	13.23	0.32	17.26	99.40
1990:3	32.91	0.31	17.78	113.40
1990:4	35.54	0.30	17.40	113.80

Source: International Monetary Fund (IMF), *International Financial Statistics* (various issues).

four-months adjustment rule, which was replaced in May 1985 with monthly indexation of wages. From May to August 1985, the annual inflation rate reached 60,000 percent.[51]

In addition to runaway inflation, output levels declined dramatically. By 1985, the level of industrial production was about 70 percent below the 1978 levels (see Table 5.4), and GDP was almost 20 percent lower than in 1982.

It was in the midst of these dangerous economic conditions and unprecedented inflation that in August 1985 newly inaugurated President Paz Estenssoro introduced his New Economic Policy (NEP) through Supreme Decree 21060.[52] The NEP's goals were, first, to stabilize prices, and second, to put the economy back on the recovery track. The NEP included two sets of measures for ending hyperinflation: one set was aimed at stabilizing prices immediately and the other was designed to bring about long-term economic stability through structural reforms.

The short-term provisions, designed to stabilize prices quickly, included two important components. First, the government immediately cut its deficit by substantially increasing prices of state-produced products. The government began charging prices for these products that were at least equal to their world prices. The most important price increase was a 500 percent price hike for oil and its derivative products. It must be remembered that Bolivia is self-sufficient in oil and that even before the price increase the oil industry was a profitable enterprise for the government. The oil price increase thus was not an attempt at getting "the price right," but was a form of taxation. In three months, the "gasoline tax" increased government revenues by about 5.5 percent of GDP.[53] On the expenditure side, the government checked its expenses by freezing the wages of public sector employees and abolishing a great many welfare and social programs.

Second, the government used the exchange rate as the nominal anchor for achieving price stability. By 1985, the U.S. dollar had replaced the peso as the medium for the store of value and the unit of account.[54] Despite the existence of informal wage indexation, financial instruments were not indexed as they were in, for example, Brazil. As a result, the U.S. dollar was used as the only effective and liquid financial hedge against inflation and the rapid loss in the purchasing power of the domestic currency. Since the economy was widely "dollarized," it was possible to bring down the inflation rate immediately and drastically by stabilizing the peso. The government practically eliminated the parallel market premium on the dollar by devaluing the exchange rate from the official 75,000 pesos to the dollar to the black market rate of 1,000,000.[55] The black market premium on the dollar, which had reached 1,500 percent in August vanished by September.

This drastic devaluation resulted in a significant current account deficit as the current account deficit–GDP ratio increased from 6 percent in 1985 to 10 percent in 1986. This problem was to a large extent due to a 50 percent deterioration in the trade balance as imports increased by 12 percent and exports declined by 15 percent. The deterioration in the current account, however, did not translate into balance-of-payments difficulties because a $190 million payment from Argentina for gas purchases and a resumption of foreign capital inflows, especially from banks and multilateral agencies, strengthened the capital account. Moreover, the Bolivian government suspended servicing its foreign debt at a saving of $330 million in 1985. After returning to the negotiation table to restructure its foreign debt, Bolivia reduced its foreign obligations by repurchasing $265 million of its $677 million foreign debt at 11 cents per dollar using credit extended to it by the international community.[56]

The NEP's long-term stabilization prescription included five measures. First, the government cut the budget deficit by abolishing subsidy programs. Second, the government reformed the external sector by liberalizing

Figure 5.2 **Quarterly Inflation Rates in Bolivia, 1984:1–1986:4**

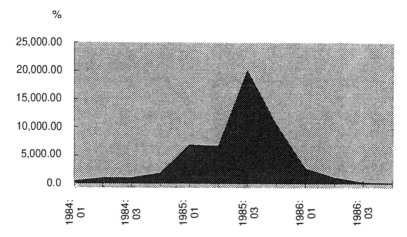

trade and capital movement, abolishing the fixed exchange rate system, unifying the foreign exchange market, and removing exchange rate controls. Third,
the government streamlined the public sector by decentralizing control over
state enterprises and through gradual privatization. Fourth, the government
reformed the banking system and deregulated domestic capital markets.[57] Fifth,
the government overhauled the tax structure by simplifying the outmoded and
inefficient system that mostly relied on income taxes. The new system recognized that there was widespread evasion of income taxes and thus levied taxes
on consumption and wealth. As a result, government tax revenues rose to about
9 percent of GDP in 1987 from only 2 percent in 1984.[58]

   These measures proved exceptionally successful in ending Bolivian hyperinflation (see Figure 5.2). The remarkable Bolivian experience with inflation and stabilization can be captured by two statistics: in the first nine
months of 1985 the monthly inflation rate averaged 60 percent; in the
following twenty-seven months (until the end of 1987) the monthly inflation rate was barely over 3 percent. Stabilization in Bolivia was thus
achieved through an orthodox program that carefully blended short-term
measures designed to halt inflation immediately with structural reforms
intended for ensuring long-term price stability.[59]

   But before deciding to use the Bolivian experience as a blueprint for
achieving stabilization elsewhere in Latin America, we need to discuss a
number of important caveats. First, the peculiarities of the Bolivian economy,
such as its small size, make stabilization programs in that country more manageable (see introduction).

Second, the Bolivian NEP benefited from a certain degree of political repression. Labor union leaders who opposed the stabilization measures were arrested and some were sent to internment camps. The government used many undemocratic means, such as imposing states of siege, to make it clear that it would not tolerate opposition to its NEP.[60]

Third, Bolivia's suspension of payments on its international debt did not bring the wrath of the international financial community upon the country. To the contrary, between 1986 and 1988 the IMF provided Bolivia with about 187 million SDRs (Special Drawing Rights) in loans and credit. The international financial community agreed that Bolivia could not pay back its foreign obligations without jeopardizing economic stability and eventually wrote off the Bolivian debt. Bolivia was later allowed to buy back half of its debt at 11 percent of its face value using money granted by foreign governments, and rescheduled its remaining debt on attractive terms. This unusual show of understanding on the part of the Paris Club, the IMF, and international bankers was due to the fact that the Bolivian debt problem was finally accurately diagnosed as a solvency problem and that the magnitude of the Bolivian debt constituted only a very small portion of the international banking community's portfolio.

Finally, despite restoring economic stability, the NEP and the long-term structural adjustments it introduced have not resulted in economic growth. The NEP's draconian measures taxed the rate of economic growth especially heavily in the 1985–86 period. As can be seen from Table 5.5, in 1985 and 1986 real GDP per capita dropped by 3 and 5.5 percent, respectively. Table 5.5 also shows that for the 1985–92 period the Bolivian real GDP per capita declined by an annual average of 0.62 percent. As the ninth anniversary of the NEP approaches, the Bolivian economy remains in doldrums, undermining the success of the Bolivian New Economic Plan.

Conclusion

By considering the experiences of Argentina and Bolivia with (hyper)inflation and stabilization, we have shown that in both countries external shocks and fiscal mismanagement combined to bring about the inflationary episodes of the 1980s. Moreover, both countries achieved stabilization through a two-pronged strategy that used a nominal anchor to bring about immediate price stability and introduced significant structural reforms to maintain low inflation in the long run. In both countries, the exchange rate was the nominal anchor of choice and structural reforms were based on neoliberal prescriptions designed to bring about sound public finance and to free trade.

Table 5.5

Real GDP, Population, GDP Per Capita, and Change in GDP Per Capita for Bolivia, 1985–92

Year	GDP in 1985 pesos (millions)	Population (millions)	Per capita GDP	Change in GDP per capita
1985	2,867	6.4	445.88	−2.97
1986	2,784	6.6	421.18	−5.54
1987	2,868	6.8	421.76	0.14
1988	2,953	7.0	422.46	0.17
1989	3,036	7.2	422.25	−0.05
1990	3,159	7.4	426.89	1.10
1991	3,303	7.6	434.03	1.67
1992	3,417	7.8	436.40	0.54

Sources: IMF, *International Financial Statistics Yearbook*, 1991, and *International Financial Statistics* (May 1994).

In Argentina, as in Brazil, the failure of orthodox policies of the 1970s and early 1980s and the diagnosis of inflation as an inertial phenomenon led to the adoption of a series of heterodox anti-inflation plans in the second half of the 1980s. A closer look at the stabilization policies of 1985–90 shows that heterodox measures created widespread disequilibrium and failed because fiscal deficits were not brought under control. In the face of persistent fiscal imbalances, the government resorted to money creation, which fueled inflation. Argentina finally brought its inflation problem under control by adopting the Cavallo Plan, which employed essentially orthodox tools to restore the country's internal and external balances.

The Bolivian experience shows that the same type of coordinated blending of short-term (nominal anchor) and long-term (orthodox) measures can end hyperinflation. The success of the Bolivian experience in ending inflation is to be evaluated in the context of heavy output cost of achieving stabilization. The harsh medicine administered to the Bolivian economy for achieving price stability brought with it considerable losses in terms of real income per capita.

It must be remembered that the Bolivian approach to stabilization may not be universally applicable for three important reasons. First, the Bolivian economy is much simpler than the economies of Brazil, Mexico, and Argentina. The Bolivian labor force consists of less than 1.7 million people, of which 50 percent work in the agricultural sector. More workers work for the metallurgy factories in the Brazilian city of São Paulo than work in the entire industrial and mining sectors of Bolivia. The relative simplicity of the Bolivian economy makes the design and the administration of stabilization policies there much less complicated than in larger countries of Latin America. Second, the Bolivian stabilization plan benefited from the heavy hand of the state. The 1985 stabilization program included antilabor provisions that were put into effect despite labor discontent. The workers bore the burden of stabilization as the government suppressed wages, prohibited strikes, and arrested union leaders. The nascent democracies of Brazil and Argentina, which had recently provided for free expression of social discontent, could ill afford a stabilization policy with similar antidemocratic components. Third, it has been argued that orthodox policies succeeded in Bolivia because the formal and informal indexation mechanisms that propagated inflation in Brazil and Argentina and gave inflation its inertial nature were absent.[61] But the inertial characteristic of inflation is not necessarily dependent upon the existence of widespread indexation. For example, if economic agents are backward looking in forming their expectations, as in the adaptive expectation model, today's inflation can propagate into the future without indexation. Similarly, in Eckstein's inflation model the core rate of inflation is based on the workers' and the firms' expectations of future inflation rates and persists independent of formal indexation.

The Argentine and Bolivian experiences demonstrate that even in the presence of pronounced inertia, the use of the exchange rate as the nominal stabilization anchor in conjunction with sound public finance can put an end to chronic and hyperinflation. But the art of moving from stabilization to economic growth was not practiced with equal eloquence in both countries.

6

Empirical Analysis of Inflation: Evidence from Error-Correction Modeling and VAR Models

Introduction

As discussed in chapter 2, high inflation has long been a distinct feature of the Brazilian economy. With the exception of 1953, since 1947 the Brazilian annual inflation rate has always been in the two- to four-digit range despite a score of stabilization attempts to bring about lasting price stability.[1] As Brazilian inflation has persisted, so has the controversy over its causes. From this controversy, two main explanations for Brazilian inflation have emerged: one, advanced by the monetarist camp, identifies excess money creation as the root cause of inflation while the other, structuralist in its origins, emphasizes cost-push factors and the inertial nature of inflation (see chapter 1). More recently, some scholars have argued that exchange rate devaluations, caused by balance-of-payments pressures, are also important determinants of the Brazilian inflation.

The purpose of this chapter is to explore the dynamics of Brazilian inflation using recently developed econometric techniques. In particular, econometric analysis is used to address two questions central to understanding the nature of inflation in Brazil and other Latin American countries. First, the impact of money and the exchange rate variables on inflation is examined by using cointegration and error-correction (CI-EC) models. In particular, the CI-EC framework is employed to evaluate the long-term behavior of inflation, money, and exchange rate and to examine how short-term adjustments in the inflation variable are made in response to long-term equilibrium requirements.

Second, we analyze the strength of the inertial component of inflation by using vector autoregressive (VAR) and structural VAR (SVAR) models. In particular, we ask to what extent a shock to important macroeconomic variables, including inflation, has a lasting effect on the inflation variable.

The results of the CI-EC analysis show that disequilibrium conditions in the foreign exchange market and in the monetary sector significantly affect the behavior of the inflation variable, although the important role of the structural elements cannot be overlooked. The evidence from VAR and SVAR analysis suggests that the persistence of inflation in Brazil has been greatly exaggerated.

The plan of this chapter is as follows. In the first section, a structural model for Brazilian inflation is introduced. This model is then used in conjunction with error correction and cointegration analysis to examine the underlying causes of Brazilian inflation. In the second section, we analyze the stationary nature of variables used in our study of Brazilian inflation. We do so to safeguard against the possibility of drawing erroneous conclusions based on spurious relations. In the third section, CI-EC analysis is used to examine how deviations from long-term equilibrium conditions in the monetary sector and the foreign exchange market affect the inflation variable. In the fourth section, vector autoregressive (VAR) and structural vector autoregressive (SVAR) models are used to confirm general conclusions drawn from simultaneous equation–CI-EC system estimation. The VAR and SVAR models are also used to examine the dynamic interaction between model variables by analyzing the response of the inflation variable to various shocks in the economy. The conclusion section summarizes and evaluates our findings.

The Model

The Price Equation

We start by modeling the aggregate price level at time t (P_t) as a linear homogeneous function of the exogenously determined price level in the agricultural sector at time t ($P_{A,t}$) and the price level in the industrial sector ($P_{I,t}$):[2]

$$P_t = P_{A,t}^\alpha \, P_{I,t}^\beta \ . \tag{6.1}$$

By adopting a simple markup rule for price formation in the industrial sector, we obtain a tractable way of modeling industrial sector prices based on unit input costs:

$$P_{I,t} = k.ULC_t.UKC_t \qquad (6.2)$$

where ULC and UKC represent unit labor and unit capital costs, respectively, and k is the markup factor.[3] Equation 6.2 gives the industrial sector inflation as a function of increases in input prices and a constant markup and assumes that firms pass on to consumers any increase in their production costs. This type of price formation modeling is consistent with the neostructuralist view that the dominance of oligopolies and widespread market imperfections make markup pricing practices the norm in the industrial sector.[4] Furthermore, it demonstrates that wage indexation directly affects the general price level through an increase of the unit labor cost and industrial prices.[5] Indexing wages to the inflation rate results in:

$$ULC_t = W_t = (1 + Q_t + \pi_t)W_{t-1} \qquad (6.3)$$

where Q_t shows the change in labor productivity and π_t is the inflation rate at time t. By using the time derivative of the Cambridge version of the Equation of Exchange, we obtain a simple proxy for the inflation rate variable in 6.3:

$$\pi_t = \dot{M}_t - \dot{Y}_t \qquad (6.4)$$

where M is the nominal money supply and π_t is the real gross domestic product (GDP), and the dots above the variables show time derivatives.[6] Equation 6.4 is a simple explanation of inflation that holds money creation in excess of output growth as the root cause of inflation. From 6.4 and 6.3, under the assumption that the change in labor productivity is constant over the period under consideration,[7] we obtain the following wage equation:

$$W_t = (1 + \dot{M}_t - \dot{Y}_t)W_{t-1}. \qquad (6.5)$$

Next we consider the factors that determine unit capital cost. Because imported intermediate capital goods play an important role in the production process in Brazil, we write the unit capital cost as a homogeneous function of the domestic price of imported goods and the rate of interest:

$$UKC = R^{\delta}(E.P_w)^{\lambda} \qquad (6.6)$$

where R is the interest rate, P_w is the price of imported goods and E is the domestic price of a unit of foreign currency (the exchange rate). By substituting 6.5 and 6.6 into 6.2, and substituting the resulting equation in 6.1 we obtain a price equation of the form:

$$P_t = P_{A,t} \{k \, [(1 + \dot{M}_t - \dot{Y}_t) \, W_{t-1}][RX_t^8(E_t P_{w,t})^\lambda] \}^B \tag{6.7}$$

According to Equation 6.7, the overall price level in the economy is determined by the money supply, agricultural prices, the markup factor, lagged wages, the interest rate, the exchange rate and the price of imported products. The model given by Equation 6.7 is essentially a monetarist model, but it also allows for structural factors and inflation inertia.[8] The usefulness of 6.7 for empirical analysis is enhanced by considering its logarithmic transformation:

$$P_t = \alpha_0 + \alpha_1 P_{A,t} + \alpha_2 m_t + \alpha_3 y_t + \alpha_4 w_{t-1} + \alpha_5 r_t P_{w,t} + \varepsilon_t \tag{6.8}$$

where lowercase letters denote logarithmic transformation.

The Money Demand Equation

In this subsection we introduce a simple money demand equation, which is later estimated using multivariate cointegration. Since the important contribution of Cardoso (1983), various studies have reported different functional forms and have drawn different conclusions regarding the functional form for Brazilian money demand. Cardoso (1983) specified a money demand function that included a Koyck-adjustment mechanism, income, inflation, and short-term interest rates. She concluded that the inflation rate variable was insignificant in determining the demand for real cash balances. This unexpected result was soon challenged by Darrat (1985) and Gerlach and Nadal di Simone (1985), who criticized the model specification and the econometric approach chosen by Cardoso. Darrat objected to the use of the Koyck lag structure and instead employed the Almon distributed lag process. Using Cardoso's sample for the 1966–79 period, Darrat concluded that this modification made all variables—including the inflation rate variable—significant. Darrat also showed that the exclusion of the inflation rate variable from the model resulted in an unstable money demand function. Gerlach and Nadal di Simone employed an autoregressive distributed lag model to show that Cardoso's results were not robust and that both the inflation rate and the nominal interest rate variables were significant determinants of the demand for real balances. Rossi (1989) extended Cardoso's study into the 1980s and tested for structural changes. By including a lagged dependent variable in the money demand specification, Rossi concluded that the inflation rate was significant. Calomiris and Domowitz (1989) accurately observed that because of financial innovations in the inflation-prone economy of Brazil, it is not sufficient to use the expected interest rate as the sole measure of the opportunity cost of holding money. Instead, they employed the rate of indexation, the yield on bill of exchange, and T-bill rates in addition to the expected inflation rate variable to improve the measurement of the opportunity cost of holding cash balances.

In general, studies of money demand function postulate a relationship between the demand for real balances (M^d), real income (Y), and an array of variables (Z) that measure the opportunity cost of holding money:

$$M^d = f(Y, Z) .$$ (6.9).

A number of questions about the functional form of f and the choice of variables need to be addressed. First, some have argued in favor of a logarithm-linear function for the money demand equation where all variables except the interest rate enter in the logarithm form. Fair (1987), for example, stresses that scaling problems may result in situations where a logarithmic transformation of the interest rate variable translates into large and exaggerated changes relative to other variables in the model. To safeguard against this potential problem, some researchers have used the interest rate variable in levels.[9] In the case of Brazil, however, where quarterly and sometimes even monthly interest rates vary in the two-digit range, the scaling problem is not troublesome and a logarithm-logarithm model can be adopted in accordance with the Baumol–Tobin theoretical framework.

Second, researchers still debate the choice of variables that constitutes Z, the opportunity cost of holding cash balances. Normally, nominal interest rates and the expected rate of inflation are used to capture this cost. Because high and persistent inflation has resulted in a shortening of the time horizons for most nominal contracts, here we use the three-month Treasury Bill (OTN) rates as a measure of the long-term interest rate in the money demand function. The exchange rate variable is another strong candidate for measuring the opportunity cost of holding cash balances because black market dollars, which provided an alternative to holdings in cruzeiros, were widely available to Brazilians.[10]

Another question relates to the choice of the appropriate monetary aggregates. In this study the narrow definition of money (M_1) is used for two reasons. First, all previous studies in this area have used this definition of money and for consistency choosing M_1 seemed appropriate. Second, as pointed out by Batten and Thornton (1983) for the U.S. data and Rossi (1989) for the Brazilian data, the use of a broader definition of money requires explanatory variables that capture the behavior of components as diverse as currency and time deposits. These variables are not the usual variables used in a common specification of the money demand function.

As a result of the above factors, a general model for the logarithm of demand for real balances (m) can be written as:

$$m^d = f(y_t, r_t, e_t, \pi_t^e) \tag{6.10}$$

where y, r and e are logarithms of real income, three-month T-bill, and cruzeiro/dollar exchange rates, respectively, and π^e is the expected inflation rate. For estimation purposes, we express Equation 6.10 in the following form:

$$m^d = \beta_0 + \beta_1 y_t + \beta_2 r_t + \beta_3 e_t + \beta_4 \pi^e + \upsilon_t \ . \tag{6.11}$$

The Exchange Rate Equation

From the 1930s until recently, the Brazilian authorities seldom allowed the forces of the market alone to determine the exchange rate. Instead, a crawling peg exchange rate regime, which periodically lagged behind inflation and resulted in repeated overvaluations, was adopted. Chronic episodes of overvaluation led to recurring balance-of-payments pressures and large devaluations. In general, Brazil kept its currency overvalued to support its import substitution objectives and to fight inflation. But the resulting currency market disequilibriums contributed to higher inflation through the expectations mechanism: as the domestic currency became overvalued, in anticipation of an eventual devaluation, a portfolio shift away from domestic currency occurred. This, in turn, resulted in a drop in seigniorage, which forced the government to increase the money supply.

To examine the impact of disequilibrium in the foreign exchange market on the inflation rate variable, we begin by considering a narrow definition of the purchasing power parity so that the exchange rate equates relative prices of traded goods in two countries:

$$E = \sigma \frac{P_T}{P_T^*} = \sigma \frac{\alpha P}{\alpha^* P^*} \tag{6.12}$$

where starred variables define a foreign country's variables, $\sigma(\neq 1)$ is a constant, and α relates the traded goods prices to the overall price level in each country. By assuming that $\alpha = \alpha^*$ and dividing and multiplying both sides of Equation 6.12 by the nominal quantity of money M and M^*, and by taking advantage of Equation 6.10, we obtain an equation for the exchange rate variable based on the domestic and foreign money supply and demand for cash balances[11]:

$$E_t = h(\frac{p_t}{p_t^*}, \frac{M_t}{M_t^*}, \frac{y_t}{y_t^*}, \frac{r_t}{r_t^*}) \, . \tag{6.13}$$

For estimation purposes, we can write equation 6.13 as:

$$e_t = \gamma_0 + \gamma_1 \frac{p_t}{p_t^*} + \gamma_2 \frac{m_t}{m_t^*} + \gamma_3 \frac{y_t}{y_t^*} + \gamma_4 \frac{r_t}{r_t^*} + \varepsilon_t \, . \tag{6.14}$$

The Data and Testing for Stationarity

In this chapter, quarterly data for the period 1975:1–1985:4 are used for estimating models of Brazilian inflation.[12] Prior to using the data, we analyze the dynamics of each series for evidence of nonstationarity. It is well known that overlooking the nonstationary nature of variables results in unreliable conclusions based on spurious relationships instead of "real" relationships (see Granger and Newbold 1974). Moreover, in regressions with nonstationary series important statistics have asymptotic distributions that are different from those associated with stationary series. In particular, as the sample size increases, the regression coefficients do not converge and conventional statistics such as R^2, Durbin-Watson, and t-tests become unreliable (see Phillips 1986). It is thus crucial to examine the dynamic nature of variables in the model. Essentially, a variable is stationary if it has a finite and nonzero spectrum at all frequencies. A stationary series is said to be integrated of order zero, or $I(0)$. A series that needs to be differenced d times to achieve stationarity is said to be integrated of order d, or $I(d)$. In general, most variables in economics and business are $I(1)$ variables, which means they are nonstationary in levels but are stationary in first differences.

We first determine the order of integration of ten variables of logarithm of nominal money supply (m), the logarithm of real money supply (m), the logarithm of the price level (P), the rate of inflation (π), logarithm of real gross domestic product (y), logarithm of nominal wages (w), logarithm of the exchange rate (e), logarithm of the price of imported goods (p_w), logarithm of an index for agricultural prices (p_A), and logarithm of the interest rate (r). A modified version of the Dickey–Fuller (1979, 1981) test as proposed by Phillips and Perron (1988) was employed to test the order of integration for each of these variables. The test results for the lag length 4 are summarized in Table 6.1. These results were not sensitive to changes in lag lengths. Both the t-test and the k-test show that the null hypothesis of unit root cannot be

Table 6.1

Perron-Phillips Tests for Unit Root with No Trend and Lag = 4[a]

Variable	t-test for H_0: Unit root	k-test for H_0: Unit root
1. m	11.98	45.26
2. p	88.15	15.33
3. w	7.56	1.59
4. e	1.20	2.05
5. pw	−1.30	−2.10
6. p_A	−2.03	−7.65
7. m^d	−1.49	−6.39
8. π	−2.21	−4.66
9. y	−2.25	−5.61
10. r	−0.91	−1.49
11. Δm	−2.51	−27.71
12. $\Delta \pi$	−9.09	−35.51
13. Δy	−8.66	−35.51
14. Δr	−7.60	−22.45
15. Δw	−6.98	−65.54
16. Δe	−6.36	−44.34
17. Δp_w	−5.55	−39.64
18. Δp_A	−6.12	−40.44
	Critical 5% t-value = −2.93	Critical 5% k-value = −13.3
	Critical 1% t-value = −3.58	Critical 1% t-value = −18.9

[a]Calculations were performed using RATS 4.0.

rejected for any of the ten variables and hence all variables are diagnosed as being nonstationary in levels. Nominal money and prices are found to be integrated of order 2 while inflation and real money are $I(1)$. Based on the t-test, the real money variable appears marginally nonstationary, but even at the 1 percent level of significance the k-test provides strong evidence in favor of the hypothesis that the money variable is integrated of order 1, $I(1)$. In summary, nominal money and prices are $I(2)$ and the first differences of inflation, real money, wages, exchange rate, income, interest rate, and import and agricultural prices are all stationary. We thus conclude that all these variables are integrated of order 1: they achieve stationarity after first differencing.[13]

Cointegration and Error-Correction Modeling

Analysis of Cointegration Relations and Long-Run Dynamics

In this subsection we examine cointegration relations for models defined by Equations 6.8, 6.11, and 6.14. This enables us to identify the long run behavior of inflation, money, and exchange rate variables and use the error correction terms obtained from cointegration analysis as long-term constraints that affect the short-term behavior of inflation. We can thereby establish to what extent monetary and exchange rate disequilibrium conditions affect the evolution of the inflation rate variable.

We begin by examining the structural inflation equation given by 6.8. Table 6.1 shows that with the exception of nominal money and prices, all variables in the structural models are integrated of order 1. Since all variables are of the same order of integration, it is possible to proceed with cointegration analysis.[14] For our purposes, a brief overview of some important concepts suffices. The general point of departure is a vector autoregressive (VAR) model of order k:

$$X_t = \sum_{i=1}^{k} A_i X_{t-i} + BD_t + \varepsilon_t \qquad (6.15)$$

where X is a $p \times 1$ vector of model variables; ε is a set of zero mean, independently distributed Gaussian error terms with covariance matrix Ω, D is a vector that includes the intercept term and dummy variables; and A and B are parameter matrices. This model can be expressed in first differences (Δ) as:

$$\Delta X_t = \Phi X_{t-1} + \sum_{i=1}^{k-1} \Gamma_i \Delta X_{t-i} + BD_t + \varepsilon_t \qquad (6.16)$$

where $\Gamma_i = -(A_{i+1} + \ldots + A_k)$ for $i = 1, \ldots, k-1$ and $\Phi = (\sum_{i=1}^{k} A_i) - I$. The rank of the Φ matrix helps us determine the nature of the variables under consideration. If Φ is of rank zero, then all variables in X are integrated of order 1 and estimation based on first differences alone would suffice. If Φ is a full rank matrix, then all variables are stationary and estimation based on the level of variables can be conducted. If Φ's rank is greater than zero but Φ is not a full rank matrix, then while variables in X are nonstationary, one or more linear combinations of them may be stationary. If such a linear combination exists, the variables in X are cointegrated and p by r matrices α and β can be found such that $\Phi = \alpha'\beta$. The vector $\beta'X$ captures the stationary, long-run equilibrium relation among model variables and the weight matrix shows the speed of adjustment from short-term disequilibrium toward the equilibrium state. An examination of the number of cointegration vectors (r) reveals the number of long-term relations among model variables. In general, for a time series vector of order k, ($k-1$) independent cointegrating vectors can exist. Overestimating the number of cointegrating

Table 6.2

Eigenvalues, Maximal Eigenvalue Statistics, and Eigenvalue Trace Statistics for Cointegration Analysis of Inflation Equation

υ	Eigenvalues	Maximal Eigenvalue statistscs[a]	Eigenvalue trace statistics[a]
1	0.035	1.473	1.473
2	0.085	3.626	5.099
3	0.341	17.120	22.219
4	0.449	24.415	46.635
5	0.605	38.060	54.694
6	0.815	69.121[b]	153.816[b]
7	0.864	81.771[b]	235.587[b]

Notes:
[a]Testing H_0: Number of unit roots $\geq \upsilon$. Rejecting this hypothesis implies the existence of at least 8–υ cointegrating vectors.
[b]Significant at the 5 percent level.

vectors results in unreliable statistical inference since the test statistics will not have their standard distribution while underestimating r results in the exclusion of relevant error correction components.[15] The approach adopted here for determining the number of cointegrating vectors is the maximum likelihood method of Johansen (1988) and Johansen and Juselius (1990). In particular, trace and maximum eigenvalue procedures are used to test various hypotheses about the number of unit roots in the model.[16]

Eigenvalues for Φ and the relevant test statistics for the inflation function are given in Table 6.2, arranged from the one closest to the unit circle (the smallest and most nonstationary) to the one furthest away from the unit circle (the largest and most stationary). At the 5 percent level of significance, the null hypothesis is that there are at least five unit roots in the model, implying that there are at least two cointegrating relations among model variables. As we will see in the next section, one of these relationships is the cointegration of the money, income, interest rate, and exchange rate variables.

By employing an unrestricted autoregressive distributed lag of order 3[17] with variables defined by Equation 6.8, we estimate a long-run model for the inflation variable. The estimation results are given in Table 6.3 with important diagnostic statistics appearing below the table. None of these statistics is significant at the 5 percent level of significance and thus it can be concluded that the unrestricted VAR(3) model results in normally distributed, homoscedastic, and white-noise error terms. By dividing the sums of lag polynomials in the last column of Table 6.3 by the sum for the polynomial for money, we can obtain the long-term inflation function as:

$$\pi_t = 1.025m_t + 0.344w_t - 0.03e_t + 0.576r_t + 0.579p_{t,A} + 0.789p_{t,W} - 2.171y_t$$
$$\quad\;\;(0.43)\quad\;\,(0.11)\quad\;\;(0.08)\quad\;(0.15)\quad\;(0.19)\quad\quad(0.32)\quad\quad(0.78)$$

$$(6.17)$$

where numbers in parentheses are estimated standard deviations of coefficients. Figure 6.1 shows the long-term behavior of the Brazilian inflation rate for the period under consideration and the inflation rate estimated by Equation 6.17. From this graph and important test statistics reported in Table 6.3 it can be concluded that our model does an adequate job explaining the long-run behavior of the Brazilian inflation rate. The model variables behave as expected with money, wages, interest rates, import, and agricultural prices having significant and positive impacts on the inflation rate variable. Income and exchange rate variables have a negative impact with the exchange rate variable being the only insignificant variable in the model. The upshot of these results is that the variables singled out by the monetarist and the structuralist camps as causing inflation indeed contributed to Brazilian inflation for the period under consideration, while the exchange rate variable did not have a direct and significant impact on the long-run behavior of the inflation variable.

Next we examine the long-run behavior of the money demand function given by Equation 6.10. An autoregressive AR model of order 3 was chosen for generating a proxy for the expected rate of inflation variable because it outperformed all other AR models according to the Hannan and Quinn (1979) information criterion (HQC) and Schwarz's (1978) Bayesian information criterion (BIC) and passed Box and Jenkins (1970) diagnostic checks of model adequacy. This model of expectations formation confirms Leiderman's (1981) choice of an AR(3) process as an adequate model for inflation expectations in Brazil and amounts to assuming that economic agents forecast the next period's inflation by optimally using available information on the present and the preceding two periods' inflation rates. Eigenvalues for Φ and the relevant test statistics for the money demand function are given in Table 6.4, arranged from the one closest to the unit circle to the one furthest away from the unit circle. At the 5 percent level of significance, the only null hypothesis that can be rejected is the hypothesis that there are at least five unit roots in the model. The rejection of this hypothesis implies that there is at least one cointegrating relation among model variables. The evidence, however, does not seem to support the existence of two or more cointegrating relations. Having concluded that

Figure 6.1 Actual and Estimated Rates of Inflation in Brazil: Long-Term Dynamics of Inflation

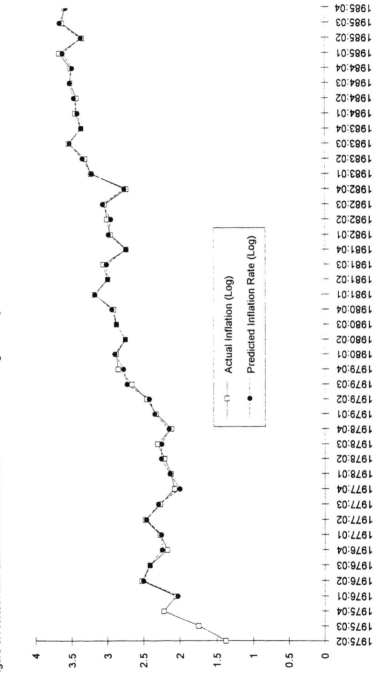

Table 6.3

General Autoregressive Distributed Lag Model for Prices, Agricultural Prices, Money, Wages, Interest Rate, Exchange Rate, and Imports Prices

Variation/lag	0	1	2	3	ε
p	−1.00	−0.10	0.47	−0.46	−1.09
S.E.	0.00	0.32	0.24	0.15	0.35
p_A	0.46	0.00	0.66	−0.49	0.63
S.E.	0.18	0.22	0.30	0.21	0.19
m	−0.30	−0.72	4.28	−2.14	1.11
S.E.	0.29	0.61	0.99	1.01	0.46
y	2.23	−2.92	−2.24	0.58	−2.36
S.E.	0.61	0.83	0.87	0.66	1.03
w	−0.20	−0.36	0.79	0.15	0.37
S.E.	0.39	0.42	0.33	0.32	0.09
r	0.89	0.57	0.14	−0.97	0.63
S.E.	0.29	0.33	0.26	0.20	0.21
e	−0.04	0.08	−0.04	−0.03	−0.03
S.E.	0.07	0.09	0.11	0.09	0.08
p_W	2.52	0.71	−0.55	−1.81	0.86
S.E.	0.66	0.60	0.66	0.64	0.49

Notes:
$R^2 = 0.99$; Jarque and Bera (1980) test for normality = 0.24; Schwarz Information Criterion (BIC) = −5.96; Hannan-Quinn Criterion (HQC) = −6.67.

Table 6.4

Eigenvalues, Maximal Eigenvalue Statistics, and Eigenvalue Trace Statistics for Cointegration Analysis of Money Demand Function

υ	Eigenvalues	Maximal Eigenvalue statistics[a]	Eigenvalue trace statistics[a]
1	0.001	0.075	0.075
2	0.149	6.303	6.378
3	0.177	7.604	13.984
4	0.496	26.762	40.741
5	0.762	56.031[b]	96.777[b]

Notes:
[a]Testing H_0: Number of unit roots $\geq \upsilon$. Rejecting this hypothesis implies the existence of at least 6-υ cointegrating vectors.
[b]Significant at the 5 percent level.

there is a single long-term relationship that ties the variables in Equation 6.11 together, we now examine the nature of this relationship by considering a general vector autoregressive (VAR) model of order 4 for real money, income, expected inflation rate, and exchange rate. The choice of order 4 was also based on results obtained from the BIC and HQC.[18]

The results for the estimation of unrestricted autoregressive distributed lag of order 4 specification of money demand is given in Table 6.5. Below the table some important statistics for diagnostic checking are given. None of these statistics are significant at the 5 percent level of significance and thus it can be concluded that the unrestricted VAR model results in normally distributed, homoscedastic, and white-noise error terms. By dividing the sums of lag polynomials in the last column of Table 6.5 by the sum for the polynomial for money, we can obtain the long-term money demand function as:

$$m_t^d = 1.2y_t - 0.43\,\pi_t^e - 0.09r_t - 0.06e_t \qquad (6.18)$$
$$(0.34)\quad(0.1)\quad\;\;(0.02)\quad(0.03)$$

where numbers in parentheses are estimated standard deviations of coefficients. From the long-term estimated money demand function given by 6.18, it can be concluded that, as expected, the impact of the expected inflation, interest rate, and exchange rate variables is negative and significant. The income variable has a significant and positive impact on the money variable.

Table 6.6 shows the eigenvalues and other important test statistics obtained from an AR(2) model with a trend dummy for the exchange rate equation based on Equation 6.14.[19] Again the dimension of the VAR model was chosen by using HQC and BIC. The test results support the existence of one cointegrating relation among model variables. Estimation results for the exchange rate equation are summarized in Table 6.7, which gives the following long-run exchange rate model:

$$e_t = -0.593r_t/r_t^* - 0.127y_t/y_t^* + 0.074m_t/m_t^* + 2.346\,p_t/p_t^* - 0.189\,\text{Trend}$$
$$(0.58)\qquad\;\;(0.57)\qquad\;\;(2.80)\qquad\;\;(1.2)\qquad\;\;(0.09)$$
$$(6.19)$$

The price differential variable has the expected sign and is significant. The other variables are insignificant and the coefficient of the interest rate differential variable is not statistically different from zero as predicted by Dornbusch's (1976) sticky price model. This can be explained by the observation that "fluctuations in international capital flows motivated by changing profit prospects or interest rate differentials would a priori seem to be relatively less important" as a determinant of exchange rate in developing

Table 6.5

General Autoregressive Distributed Lag Model for Real Money, Income, Expected Inflation, Interest Rate, and Inflation

Variation/lag	0	1	2	3	4	ε
m	−1.00	0.58	−0.27	0.06	0.27	−0.31
S.E.	0.00	0.20	0.24	0.31	0.25	0.12
y	0.51	0.37	−0.20	0.16	−0.34	0.50
S.E.	0.24	0.46	0.27	0.28	0.25	0.30
π^e	−0.14	−0.01	−0.04	0.05	−0.04	−0.19
S.E.	0.11	0.08	0.06	0.06	0.04	0.10
r	−0.21	0.17	−0.20	0.35	−0.13	−0.02
S.E.	0.15	0.14	0.12	0.11	0.14	0.38
e	−0.06	−0.04	0.11	−0.08	−0.04	−0.01
S.E.	0.08	0.09	0.11	0.09	0.07	0.35

Notes:
$R^2 = 0.99$; Jarque and Bera (1980) test for normality = 0.24; Schwarz Information Criterion (BIC) = −5.96; Hannan-Quinn Criterion (HQC) = −6.67.

Table 6.6

Eigenvalues, Maximal Eigenvalue Statistics, and Eigenvalue Trace Statistics for Cointegration Analysis of Exchange Rate Equation

υ	Eigenvalues	Maximal Eigenvalue statistics[a]	Eigenvalue trace statistics[a]
1	0.011	0.473	0.473
2	0.130	5.721	6.194
3	0.320	15.805	22.000
4	0.443	23.967	45.967
5	0.630	40.751[b]	86.718[b]

Notes:
[a]Testing H_0: Number of unit roots $\geq \upsilon$. Rejecting this hypothesis implies the existence of at least 6-υ cointegrating vectors.
[b]Significant at the 5 percent level.

countries "because of the lower degree of financial integration between domestic and foreign capital markets."[20]

The Error-Correction Model of Inflation

In this subsection we trace the origins of Brazilian inflation to a monetary source and a balance-of-payments source by applying some recently devel-

Table 6.7

General Autoregressive Distributed Lag Model for Exchange Rate, Price Differential, Money Differential, Income Differential, and Interest Rate Differential

Variation/lag	0	1	2	ε
e_t	−1.00	0.61	−0.01	−0.40
S.E.	0.00	0.18	0.20	0.18
p_t/p_t^* 3.38	−4.40	2.04	0.95	
S.E.	2.59	3.70	2.26	0.75
m_t/m_t^*	−0.66	0.24	0.45	0.03
S.E.	0.59	0.90	0.80	0.46
y_t/y_t^*	−0.99	1.74	−0.80	−0.05
S.E.	1.03	1.28	0.96	0.23
r_t/r_t^*	−0.06	−0.59	0.41	−0.24
S.E.	0.41	0.66	0.46	0.28
Trend	0.08	—	—	0.08
S.E.	0.06	—	—	0.06

Notes:
$F(15, 27) = 739.06 [0.00]$.
DW = 2.06.
$R^2 = 0.996$; Jarque and Bera (1980) test for normality = 0.33; Schwarz Information Criterion (BIC) = −1.30; Hannan-Quinn Criterion (HQC) = −1.70.

oped econometric techniques to studying the dynamics of Brazilian inflation for the period 1974:1–1985:4. In particular, along the lines suggested by Surrey (1989) and Juselius (1992), by analyzing the monetary and balance-of-payments sources of inflation, a distinction is made among the factors that have shaped the dynamics of Brazilian inflation. The monetary source affects prices in the long-run whenever the change in the quantity of money outpaces the rate of output change. The balance-of-payments source puts pressure on prices when disequilibrium in the external sector forces devaluations, which, through increases in the domestic price of imported products and expectations, cause inflation.

By choosing $k=2$, we estimate an unrestricted first-differenced autoregressive distributed lag of π, on m, y, e, r, w, p_W, p_A, ecm_1, ecm_2, and ecm_3 where ecm's show error-correction terms for the inflation, money, and exchange rate models, respectively. The resulting constrained error correction model (ECM) provides a convenient mechanism for examining the short-term dynamic adjustment process of the system. The simple restrictions and a short lag structure are chosen because, in addition to statistical support provided by BIC and HQC, such a structure allows for speedy adjustment of money to changes in model variables as consistent with the inflationary environment of Brazil. Table 6.8 reports the final estimation results obtained from eliminating all variables that were insignificant at the 5 percent level using the "general-to-specific"[21] approach. The final model was reestimated by the instrumental variable technique and diagnostic tests were performed again. The final error-correction model is given by:

$$\Delta\pi_t = 1.409\ \Delta\ m_t + 0.308\ \Delta e_t - 1.134\ \Delta y_t - 1.872\ \Delta y_{t-1} + 2.246\ \Delta m_{t-1} +$$
$$\quad (0.46) \qquad (0.09) \qquad (0.38) \qquad (0.50) \qquad (0.65)$$

$$0.174\Delta e_{t-2} + 0.685\Delta r_t + 0.001\ p_{A,t-1} + 1.130ecm_1 - 1.716\ ecm_2 - 0.045\ ecm_3$$
$$\quad (0.05) \qquad (0.19) \qquad (0.00) \qquad (0.16) \qquad (0.04) \qquad (0.03)$$
$$\tag{6.20}$$

Test statistics for autoregressive conditional heteroscedasticity (ARCH), residual autocorrelation (Durbin-Watson and AR), and normality (Jarque and Bera) are all insignificant at the 5 percent level, indicating white noise, homoscedastic, normally distributed error terms (see Table 6.8). Figure 6.2 shows that the model presented by Equation 6.20 provides good estimates of changes in the inflation variable.

From an economics perspective, Equation 6.20 indicates that in the short term, inflation is positively influenced by current and lagged changes in money supply, current and lagged exchange rate devaluations, changes in current agricultural prices, and lagged changes in the interest rate. Current and lagged increases in output reduce the rate of inflation. Moreover, short-term inflation adjusts by about 1.7 percent in reaction to a previous disequilibrium condition in the monetary sector (ecm_2) and exchange rate disequilibrium (overvalued currency) will have an inflationary impact. One way of explaining this last result is through the expectations mechanism: as the domestic currency becomes overvalued, there is a portfolio shift away from domestic currency in anticipation of a pending devaluation. This results in a decrease in the size of seigniorage, which, in turn, forces the government to increase the money supply and to feed inflation.

Empirical Analysis of the Inertial Component of Inflation

The purpose of this section is to analyze the persistence of Brazilian inflation. We saw in previous chapters that the view identifying inertia as the most important determinant of Latin American inflation was instrumental in shaping economic policy in the second half of the 1980s. An important question then is to what extent the inflation variable has an inertia attribute. In this section we examine the inertial component of inflation in three ways. First, it is shown that the choice of low-frequency (quarterly) data in a VAR

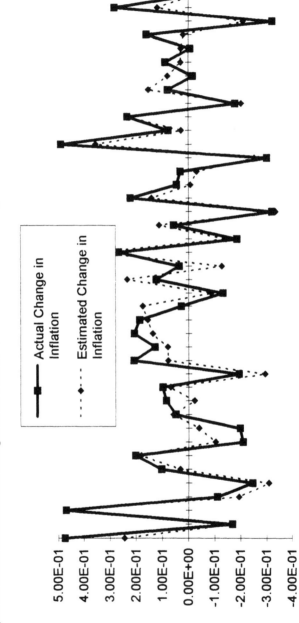

Figure 6.2 Actual and Estimated Changes in the Brazilian Inflation Rate: Short Term Dynamics of Inflation

Table 6.8

The Final Error-Correction Model for Inflation

Variable	Coefficient	Std. error	t-value
Δm_t	1.41	0.46	3.06
Δe_{t-1}	0.31	0.09	3.42
Δy_{t-1}	−1.13	0.38	−2.98
Δy_{t-1}	−1.87	0.50	−3.72
Δm_{t-1}	2.25	0.65	3.48
Δe_{t-2}	0.17	0.05	3.27
Δr_t	0.68	0.19	3.54
$\Delta p_{A, t-1}$	0.00	0.00	2.57
ecm_1	1.13	0.16	7.14
ecm_2	−1.72	0.04	−3.85
ecm_3	−0.04	0.03	−1.34

RSS = 0.23, σ^2 = 0.09; DW = 1.71; Specification $\chi^2 (2)/ 2 = 1.13$; $\chi^2 (11)/11$ testing $\beta = 0$: 10.29; χ^2 Test for Normality : $\chi^2 (2) = 0.93$; ARCH Test - $\chi^2 (3) = 15.22$ with $F(3, 18) = 5.44$.

LM test for serial correlation from lags 1 to 2: $\chi^2(2)/ 2 = 0.51$.
LM test for serial correlation from lags 1 to 3: $\chi^2(3)/ 3 = 0.65$.

model similar to the one used by Novaes (1993) results in pronounced inertia. Second, it is shown that this result is due to inappropriate data transformation and that the use of stationary series results in weak inertia even with low-frequency data. Finally, recognizing the limitations of VAR models, evidence is presented based on structural VAR (SVAR) models to support the conclusion that the inertial component of Brazilian inflation is not strong.

VAR Model with Quarterly Data

Since the influential paper by Sims (1980), vector autoregressive (VAR) models have become increasingly popular for macroeconometric analysis because they introduce few restrictions and treat all variables as endogenous. Consider the following four-variable VAR model for analyzing Brazilian inflation:[22]

$$p_t = \sum_{i=0}^{4} a_{1,i} p_{t-i} + \sum_{i=0}^{4} b_{1,i} m_{t-i} + \sum_{i=0}^{4} c_{1,i} w_{t-i} + \sum_{i=0}^{4} d_{1,i} e_{t-i} + \varepsilon_{1,t} \tag{6.21}$$

$$m_t = \sum_{i=0}^{4} a_{2,i} p_{t-i} + \sum_{i=0}^{4} b_{2,i} m_{t-i} + \sum_{i=0}^{4} c_{2,i} w_{t-1} + \sum_{i=0}^{4} d_{2,i} e_{t-i} + \varepsilon_{2,t} \tag{6.22}$$

$$w_t = \sum_{i=0}^{4} a_{3,i}\, p_{t-i} + \sum_{i=0}^{4} b_{3,i}\, m_{t-i} + \sum_{i=0}^{4} c_{3,i}\, w_{t-1} + \sum_{i=0}^{4} d_{3,i}\, e_{t-i} + \varepsilon_{3,t} \qquad (6.23)$$

$$e_t = \sum_{i=0}^{4} a_{4,i}\, p_{t-i} + \sum_{i=0}^{4} b_{4,i}\, m_{t-i} + \sum_{i=0}^{4} c_{4,i}\, w_{t-i} + \sum_{i=0}^{4} d_{4,i}\, e_{t-i} + \varepsilon_{4,t} \qquad (6.24)$$

where p, m, w, and e denote the price, money, wages, and exchange rate variables, respectively. These equations can be written in a compact form as

$$X_t = A_0 X_t + \sum_{i=0}^{4} A_{t-i} X_{t-i} + V_t \qquad (6.25)$$

where $X_t = (p_t, m_t, w_t, e_t)'$ represents the vector of variables, V_t represents the vector of structural error terms, and A is the coefficients matrix for the VAR system. If the residuals in Equations 6.21 through 6.24 are correlated, the Cholesky decomposition of the residual covariance matrix can be used to orthogonalize the error terms. This results in variable-specific shocks that can be used for examining the impact of an unexpected innovation to one variable on other variables. Because we are interested in analyzing the dynamics of the inflation variable, we write the A_0 matrix in Equation 6.25 as:

$$A_0 = \begin{matrix} 1 & 0 & 0 & 0 \\ \alpha_1 & 1 & 0 & 0 \\ \alpha_2 & \alpha_3 & 1 & 0 \\ \alpha_4 & \alpha_5 & \alpha_6 & 1 \end{matrix} \qquad (6.26)$$

This allows for shocks from all variables in the model to affect the evolution of the inflation variable.

In this study quarterly data for the period 1975:1–1985:4 are used for estimating the VAR model defined by Equations 6.25 and 6.26. We begin by using the inflation rate and the first difference of money supply, exchange rate, and wages. Figures 6.3 through 6.6 show the impact of an unanticipated one-standard deviation shock to each of the model variables on the inflation rate variable. Figure 6.3 shows strong evidence of inertia: a price innovation at time zero has a lasting effect on the evolution of the inflation rate variable. The impact of the initial shock does not dissipate even after twenty-four quarters. Figure 6.4 shows that a positive money innovation has a lasting and large effect on inflation. In response to unanticipated changes in the money supply, the inflation rate increases steadily after the third quarter, not tapering off even after twenty-four quarters.

Figure 6.3 **Inflation Response to Price Innovation Based on VAR**

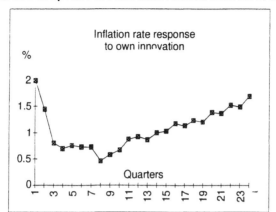

Figure 6.4 **Inflation Response to Money Innovation Based on VAR**

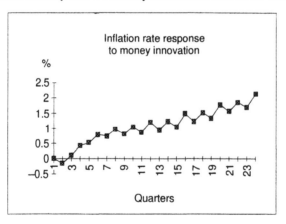

Figure 6.5 exhibits the negligible effect of a positive one-standard deviation wage innovation. Figure 6.6 shows that exchange rate innovation has a positive and considerable impact on the inflation rate variable such that even after twenty-four quarters the initial innovation leads to an increase of close to 1 percent in the rate of inflation.

The above analysis of impulse responses seemingly highlights an important characteristic of Brazilian inflation: the inflationary impact of a shock to any of the four variables that comprise the system lingers on for a long time. This is exactly what is meant by inflation persistence and inertia. But these results are misleading and are due to mishandling of the data.

Figure 6.5 **Inflation Response to Wage Innovation Based on VAR**

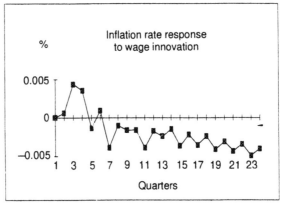

Figure 6.6 **Inflation Response to Exchange Rate Innovation Based on VAR**

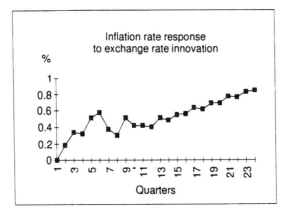

As we saw from test results summarized in Table 6.1 (page 142), the null hypothesis of unit root cannot be rejected for any of variables in our VAR model. But, with the exception of the price and nominal money variables, the first differences of all variables are stationary. The inflation rate achieves stationarity only after first differencing.[23] To avoid spurious results, we use the first difference of the inflation variable and the percentage changes of the other three variables. Using variables that are of the same order of integration results in markedly different conclusions regarding the persistence of Brazilian inflation. Figures 6.7 through 6.10 show that a one-standard deviation shock to system variables has no lasting impact on the evolution of the inflation variable.

Figure 6.7 **Inflation Response to Own Innovation with Only I(0) Variables and VAR Model**

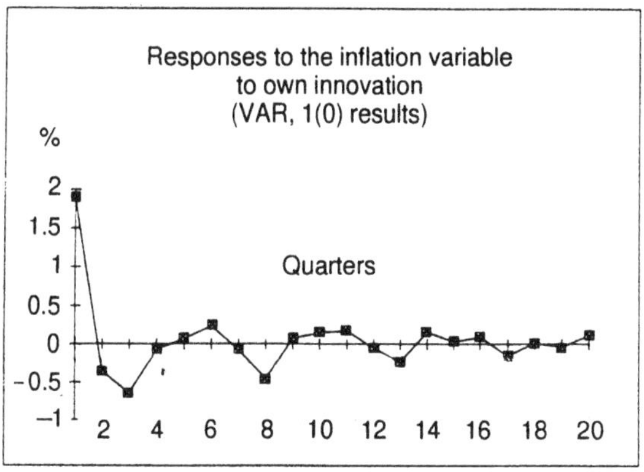

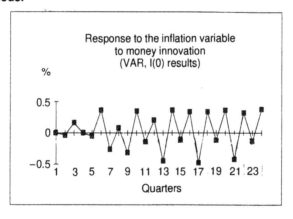

Figure 6.8 **Inflation Response to Money Innovation with Only I(0) Variables and VAR Model**

Results from SVAR Models

Next we show that structural vector autoregressive models lead to a similar conclusion regarding the lack of inflation inertia. It is widely recognized that VAR models rely on atheoretical relationships among economic variables in the system.[24] This atheoretical approach results in two difficulties: first, if the Cholesky decomposition is truly atheoretical, then one cannot speak of structural impacts of different shocks; second, the Cholesky decomposition implies a recursive system of equations while economic theory often requires a simultaneous equation system. Structural VAR (SVAR) models overcome these drawbacks by identifying the shocks based on the hypothesized structural relationships among system variables. Taylor

Figure 6.9 **Inflation Response to Wage Innovation with Only I(0) Variables**

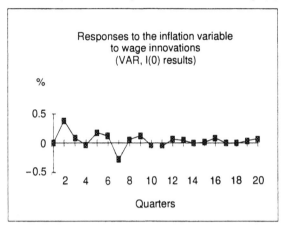

Figure 6.10 **Inflation Response to Exchange Rate Innovation with Only I(0) Variables**

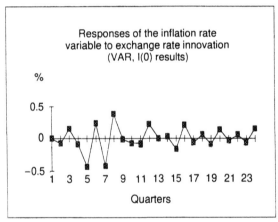

(1986), Sims (1986), Blanchard and Watson (1986), Blanchard (1989), and Keating (1990) use SVAR models for analyzing different aspects of the U.S. economy. Along the same lines, in this section, a four-variable SVAR model for the Brazilian economy is developed and tested.

The identifying restriction imposed on the model is in the form of the relations between innovations of the structural equation (6.25) and reduced-form system of the form:

$$X_t = \sum_{i=1}^{4} (I - A_0)^{-1} A_{t-i} X_{t-i} + U_t \qquad (6.27)$$

where I is the identity matrix. From 6.25 and 6.27 it can be seen that:

$$V_t = A_0 U_t + v_t \ . \tag{6.28}$$

Given the relationships between structural and reduced-form innovations, the following restrictions are imposed on matrix A_0:

$$U^p_t = \alpha_1 U^m_t + \alpha_2 U^w_t + \alpha_3 U^e_t + \varepsilon_{1,t} \tag{6.29}$$

$$U^m_t = \beta_1 U^p_t + \varepsilon_{2,t} \tag{6.30}$$

$$U^w_t = \Upsilon_1 U^p_t + \varepsilon_{3,t} \tag{6.31}$$

$$U^e_t = \delta_1 U^p t + \varepsilon_{4,t} \tag{6.32}$$

The structural system is thus given by Equation 6.25 with the A_0 matrix defined by Equations 6.29 through 6.32. The model contains six parameters and four standard deviations that need to be estimated. Since the variance-covariance matrix of the reduced form has ten useful moments, the system is exactly identified. Equation 6.29 is the price-setting equation that is designed to allow for price innovations to respond to all unexpected shocks in the money, wages, and exchange rate variables, as well as to a price innovation. Equation 6.30 specifies a money rule that allows money innovations to depend on price shocks and money-supply innovations. The wage equation allows for the wage variable to respond to variations in prices as well as wage innovations that reflect changes in wage indexation mechanisms and in bargaining power. Finally, the exchange rate innovations are determined by innovations in the exchange rate and innovations in prices in accordance with purchasing power parity.

The dynamic effects of surprise shocks (innovations) on the inflation rate are illustrated in Figures 6.11 through 6.14, which show the responses of the inflation variable to a one-standard deviation increase in innovations of each variable in the model. Figure 6.11 shows the impact of a positive price innovation over time: a one-standard deviation price innovation increases the rate of inflation by approximately 1.7 percent after one quarter. Thereafter, the impact of this initial shock declines but remains positive and considerable until the fourth quarter. The dynamic pattern of responses of the inflation variable to a money innovation are captured in Figure 6.12. The response of the inflation variable to a money supply shock is close to 1 percent after one quarter, but it dissipates quickly. A similar conclusion can be drawn regarding the impact of a wage innovation (Figure 6.13). The negative response of the inflation rate variable to a positive wage innova-

Figure 6.11 **Inflation Response to Own Innovation with Only I(0) Variables and SVAR Model**

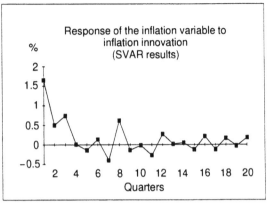

Figure 6.12 **Inflation Response to Money Innovation with Only I(0) Variables and SVAR Model**

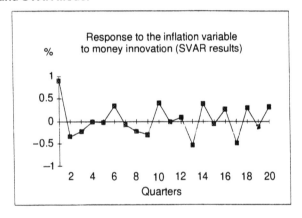

rigidity of wages due to indexation mechanisms that adjusted wages for inflation too slowly. Finally, Figure 6.14 shows that over time a one-standard deviation exchange rate impulse has a relatively weak but positive impact on the inflation rate: in the first quarter, a one-standard deviation shock leads to an increase in price inflation of about 1 percent; thereafter its impact is negligible.

Table 6.9 makes it possible to determine how much of the model's forecast error is caused by surprise movements in each system variable by breaking down the variance of forecast error for the inflation rate. Using these results we can identify the impact of the movements in any one variable in the model on the evolution of inflation rate. It can be seen that

Figure 6.13 **Inflation Response to Wage Innovation with Only I(0) Variables and SVAR Model**

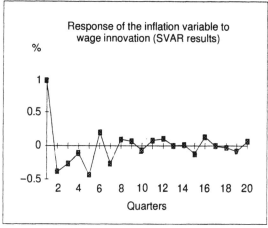

Figure 6.14 **Inflation Response to Exchange Rate Innovation with Only I(0) Variables and SVAR Model**

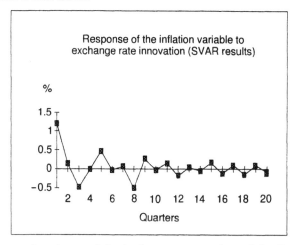

the movements in price explain the largest proportion of the forecast error. As the forecast horizon increases, a greater proportion of the forecast error variance is attributed to nonprice variables. Moreover, the contribution of the money variable increases over time such that in the long run money dominates the wage and exchange rate variables in influencing the evolution of the inflation rate variable.[25]

Next, to isolate the impact of innovations in the growth of p, m, w, and e on the inflation rate, we decompose the historical values of the inflation rate from 1978:1 to 1985:4 into base forecasts and the accumulated effects of

Table 6.9

Composition of Forecast Error Variance for Inflation

Step	Standard error	Inflation	Money	Wage	Exchange rate
1	0.025	100.00	0.000	0.000	0.000
2	0.027	95.647	0.097	0.168	4.097
3	0.028	94.860	0.713	0.675	3.752
4	0.028	94.673	0.711	0.878	3.738
5	0.029	88.637	0.810	5.289	5.263
6	0.030	85.316	3.503	6.170	5.010
7	0.031	80.658	4.621	9.407	5.314
8	0.032	78.677	4.553	11.723	5.047
9	0.032	76.958	6.352	11.462	5.228
10	0.033	75.362	8.293	11.240	5.104
11	0.033	75.104	8.564	11.244	5.088
12	0.034	73.908	9.176	11.908	5.008
13	0.034	71.690	12.113	11.383	4.814
14	0.034	70.328	13.894	11.093	4.686
15	0.034	69.845	14.000	11.455	4.700
16	0.035	68.217	15.342	11.865	4.576
17	0.035	66.068	18.080	11.456	4.396
18	0.036	64.941	19.431	11.303	4.325
19	0.036	64.723	19.555	11.366	4.356
20	0.036	63.443	20.949	11.348	4.261

exogenous shocks on prices, money supply, wages, and exchange rate. The impact of exogenous shocks on inflation is shown in Table 6.10. Two main conclusions can be drawn from the results reported in this table. First, exogenous shocks have played an important role in inflation acceleration. Second, relative to innovations in money, wages, and exchange rate, the unexpected movements in the inflation variable contribute more to the acceleration of inflation.

Conclusion

This chapter offers an elaborate empirical analysis of Brazilian inflation. Clearly, the techniques employed here can serve as useful tools for uncovering the root causes of inflation in other countries and for analyzing the strength of the inertial component of inflation elsewhere. From an examination of long-run and short-run dynamics of Brazilian inflation, using a structural model in conjunction with error correction and cointegration analysis, several general conclusions can be drawn. First, we conclude that for the period under consideration money supply was a key variable in shaping

Table 6.10

Historical Decomposition of Brazilian Inflation, 1978:1–1985:4

Quarter	Projected	Inflation rate	Price	Money	Wages	Exchange rate
1978:1	0.004	0.012	–0.023	0.000	0.011	0.003
1978:2	0.007	0.001	0.038	–0.010	–0.018	–0.012
1978:3	0.009	0.025	–0.021	0.010	–0.008	0.001
1978:4	–0.002	0.002	0.000	–0.010	0.001	–0.010
1979:1	0.020	0.014	0.023	–0.001	–0.005	–0.014
1979:2	0.013	–0.016	–0.015	0.012	0.023	0.009
1979:3	0.024	0.022	–0.037	0.005	0.011	0.023
1979:4	0.026	–0.006	0.020	0.013	–0.003	0.000
1980:1	0.004	0.021	–0.001	–0.019	0.001	0.002
1980:2	–0.019	–0.020	0.002	0.007	0.003	–0.010
1980:3	0.018	0.023	0.009	–0.016	–0.016	0.017
1980:4	0.006	–0.014	0.013	0.006	0.003	–0.002
1981:1	0.047	0.029	–0.005	–0.001	0.001	0.014
1981:2	–0.033	–0.015	–0.009	–0.003	–0.000	–0.005
1981:3	0.010	0.024	–0.003	–0.012	0.000	0.001
1981:4	–0.049	–0.017	–0.006	0.011	–0.029	–0.008
1982:1	0.033	0.029	–0.009	–0.005	0.004	0.014
1982:2	0.008	–0.012	0.030	–0.003	–0.001	–0.007
1982:3	0.006	0.026	0.010	–0.009	–0.016	–0.005
1982:4	–0.050	–0.017	–0.006	–0.017	0.017	–0.022
1983:1	0.081	0.027	0.004	0.025	0.003	0.020
1983:2	0.016	–0.012	–0.005	–0.000	0.012	0.020
1983:3	0.050	0.026	0.006	0.014	–0.001	0.009
1983:4	–0.043	–0.015	–0.003	–0.010	0.004	–0.019
1984:1	0.018	0.026	0.002	0.003	–0.014	0.001
1984:2	–0.004	–0.010	–0.020	–0.001	0.018	0.019
1984:3	0.022	0.026	–0.047	0.020	0.010	0.012
1984:4	–0.001	–0.012	0.026	–0.004	–0.005	–0.006
1985:1	0.043	0.026	0.032	–0.012	0.004	–0.006
1985:2	–0.080	–0.009	–0.001	–0.015	–0.037	–0.019
1985:3	0.070	0.026	0.005	0.023	0.006	0.010
1985:4	–0.001	–0.009	–0.009	0.012	–0.005	0.002

the long-run behavior of Brazilian inflation and disequilibrium conditions in the monetary sector had pronounced short-term impact on the inflation variable. Second, the government's decision to maintain an overvalued currency as a means of fighting inflation brought about higher inflation rates in the short term. We explained this seemingly paradoxical result by observing that expected devaluations will cause citizens to shift away from domestic currency, which, in turn, forces the government to commit the inflationary act of increasing the money supply in an attempt to recover lost revenues due to smaller seigniorage. In the long run, however, the exchange rate variable is not a significant factor in explaining Brazilian inflation. The "balance-of-payments" explanation of inflation thus seems to work only in explaining the short-run behavior of inflation. Third, we found that variables such as wages, agricultural prices, and the price of imported goods, which have long been considered to be important determinants of inflation according to the (neo)structuralists, are significant contributors to Brazilian inflation.

Finally, results from VAR and SVAR analysis show that the dynamics of the Brazilian economy are such that a small positive shock to system variables creates weak inertia without a prolonged effect. This weak persistence of inflation in Brazil markedly differs from the view advanced by the neostructuralists regarding the inertial nature of Brazilian inflation.

7

Conclusions

Why Fight Inflation?

From a close examination of the Latin American experience of the last three decades, we conclude that sustained growth is not likely in an economy plagued with instability and high inflation. For this reason alone (ignoring the social and political consequences of inflation), policymakers should maintain equilibrium in internal and external accounts and fight inflation.

Inflation retards the growth prospects of an economy in four ways. First, high inflation results in high uncertainty about relative prices. Relative price uncertainty, in turn, reduces market efficiency and causes output loss. Second, high inflation brings about increased variability in overall prices and more uncertainty regarding future prices. This uncertainty leads to a shortening of contract lengths, increased indexation, and loss in efficiency as resources are directed away from productive efforts and into speculative activities. Under these circumstances, stagflation may develop as higher inflation corresponds to lower output and higher unemployment.[1]

Third, in their haste to end inflation quickly in order to reap a political profit, governments of developing nations often make the mistake of undermining market forces. The *Tablita* plan in Argentina and the Collor Plan in Brazil provide sobering examples of the dire consequences of government zealousness in fighting inflation through the use of nonmarket forces. Governments too eager to end inflation quickly and without the needed sacrifice cause more harm than good.

Fourth, inflation has significant redistributive effects. In Latin America, where income distributions are among the most unequal in the world, inflation resulted in a redistribution of income from the lower and middle classes to the privileged classes. One important economic ramification of increased income inequality is slower growth. Recent research shows that in a democratic society inequality is harmful for economic growth because it results in policies that tax investment and do not protect property rights.[2] Thus, by creating distributional conflicts, inflation could reduce growth indirectly.

How to Fight Inflation?

We saw that the genesis of the economic instability of the 1980s was the balance-of-payments shocks of the 1970s and 1980s and (with the exception of Chile) the authorities' reluctance to go through needed adjustments because of the economic and political consequences of austerity. Once policymakers had decided to avoid a recession even at the cost of higher inflation, structural peculiarities of Latin American countries gave inflation a self-propelling momentum that did not respond to conventional orthodox stabilization programs.

In Brazil and Argentina, the failure of orthodox stabilization attempts of the late 1970s and the early 1980s opened the way for the neostructuralist alternative to stabilization. The neostructuralists criticized the orthodox policies by pointing to the failure of monetary austerity in ending inflation in Latin America. But blaming the orthodox blueprints for the failure of IMF-sponsored stabilization attempts ignores the fact, repeatedly demonstrated in this book, that the central requirement of establishing fiscal order was not honored by governments that apparently accepted the conditions set by the IMF. As discussed in chapter 1, in the presence of significant and persistent public deficit, tight money does not bring about disinflation.

In addition to the failure of Latin American governments to restore fiscal balance, the IMF's mechanical and unimaginative approach to stabilization in the early 1980s undermined disinflation attempts. Indexation, introduced in Latin America to make living with inflation easier, made fighting it more difficult. Indexation propagated the impact of major shocks to the budget, terms of trade, and exchange rate well into the future. It thus introduced considerable inflation persistence, which interfered with orthodox stabilization attempts. The experiences of the Latin American countries considered in this book show the need for eliminating the inertial component of inflation, a need brushed aside by the IMF. In the presence of a strong inflation inertia, the use of some nominal anchor of stabilization is a prudent policy for achieving stabilization.

While nominal anchors bring down inflation quickly (the easy part), fiscal discipline and monetary adjustment are needed to keep it low (the hard part). The neostructuralist heterodox stabilization attempts of 1985–90 failed because they essentially overemphasized the use of nominal anchors, especially in the form of incomes policy, and did not put enough effort into establishing fiscal balance. The key to effective stabilization is the careful blending of fiscal and monetary austerity with nominal anchors.

Restoring Fiscal Balance

From the Latin American experience we conclude that the requirement for price stability is *semper eadem:* fiscal austerity. Establishing fiscal balance is a difficult process that needs to be approached thoughtfully. It should be remembered that low inflation is not an end in and of itself; rather, it is a means for achieving the long-term growth potential of the economy.

It is in this context that policy to restore fiscal equilibrium should be made: fiscal equilibrium should be achieved in a way least detrimental to economic growth. This requires an intelligent approach to budget management that recognizes the important role developing countries' governments play in their economies. Unfortunately, when it comes to reducing government expenditures there is a tendency not to distinguish between public investment and government consumption.[3] Indeed, reducing government investment is usually the path of least resistance because the alternative, cutting government expenditures on subsidies and social programs, is immediately conspicuous and politically unpopular.

In Latin America, despite structural reforms of the past ten years, the need for public investment in areas that complement private investment persists. Because of the complementary nature of some public investments, across-the-board spending cuts may retard economic growth. Government's active role in supporting and improving the infrastructure, health and social services, and education remains crucial for establishing a dynamic and prospering economy. As we saw in the case of Mexico, the austerity program's fiscal measures cut deeply into the investment pool and contributed to a pronounced economic slowdown. Chile, on the other hand, despite fiscal austerity invested heavily in infrastructure and reaped the benefits of its investment.

A more prudent alternative to controlling fiscal expenditure is reducing or eliminating government subsidies. Public subsidies essentially redistribute income from consumers to producers in an arbitrary way and interfere with market forces by favoring a given producer or industry over others. Moreover, there is no evidence that subsidies have any tangible impact on economic growth of Latin American countries.

Another aspect of the adjustment process aimed at improving government finances is privatization and reforming state enterprises. The breakdown of Latin American economies in the 1980s under the burden of foreign debt had as its collateral effect the weakening of the state as an economic actor. Meanwhile, the forces of Washington consensus pushed hard for a reduced role of the state in the economy as a means of restoring fiscal balance and introducing market efficiency. Privatization suddenly became the buzzword in Latin America as Chile, Bolivia, Argentina, Mexico, and Brazil introduced privatization programs one after another.

The sudden shift in the conventional wisdom regarding the respective roles of the private and public sectors in the development process of Latin American countries was surprising. Only a few years earlier the private sector had been considered unreliable when it came to making the needed investments and taking the necessary risks. By the late 1980s and early 1990s, however, the private sector was perceived as being in a superior position relative to the public sector for undertaking such initiatives. Yet from Chile's experience with the privatization program of the 1970s, we learn that haphazard privatization can prove extremely costly.

While privatization, when aimed at restoring fiscal balance and efficiency, is conducive to stabilization and growth, a number of important consequences of privatization need closer scrutiny. The sale of state enterprises gives the government a one-time revenue shot that helps the government to reduce its debt burden and, in the case of money-losing enterprises, help its cash flow. But since the private sector is naturally most interested in profit-making enterprises, the government is likely to lose a source of future cash flow in return for a lump-sum current payment.[4] It is thus not surprising that the recent evidence from the Brazilian privatization programs of the 1990s points to a negligible fiscal windfall from privatization.[5] The more important and perhaps least tangible aspect of privatization is the signal it sends regarding the government's commitment to the principles of the free market.

The impact of privatization on income distribution is also worthy of attention.[6] Privatization worsens income inequality in two ways. First, it usually results in a nontrivial increase in unemployment, which hurts the lower and middle classes the hardest. Second, privatization spells increased prices for publicly produced goods and services such as transportation services and utilities. Because the lower classes are the prime beneficiaries of these subsidized products, they will be most adversely affected by privatization.

An alternative to privatization is improving the efficiency of state-run enterprises, which are usually inefficient because they do not face competition; when they do, going out of business is not a serious threat due to the government's financial backing. Most state-run companies are bloated with bureaucracy and labor force excesses, as evidenced by state companies that have been privatized and have successfully reduced their workforce while improving their efficiency and return to equity.[7] There seems to be plenty of room for reducing the inefficiencies of state enterprises and making them financially viable ventures for the state.

On the revenue side, it is important to keep tax rates low to encourage economic growth while increasing government revenues. In Latin America this seemingly impossible task can be accomplished by reforming the tax system, which has been burdened by collection inefficiencies and tax evasion. In a recent study, Fishlow and Friedman (1994) show that as the implicit inflation tax increases, so too do incentives for increased tax evasion. Thus, while effective stabilization means an end to seigniorage, its adverse impact on fiscal revenues is lessened by enhanced tax receipts. In addition to ending inflation as a means of reducing tax evasion, better enforcement of the tax code and increased penalties for evaders are needed for augmenting tax revenues.

The Choice of Nominal Anchors

It is well known that an economy can have multiple inflation equilibria points and that, depending on the elasticity of key nominal variables such as the exchange rate and wages to the rate of inflation, a high and stable inflation equilibrium may develop. If an economy is trapped in a stable high inflation equilibrium point, nominal anchors may be used to push it to a stable low inflation equilibrium point.

In Latin America, because of the strong inertial component of inflation, nominal anchors were needed to push the economy from a "meta-stable" to a low and stable inflation point.[8] The use of a fixed exchange rate as the nominal stabilization anchor has become popular in Latin America because it has proved less disruptive than wage and price freezes favored by the neostructuralist school. Bolivia (1985), Mexico (1987), and Argentina (1990) used fiscal adjustment and monetary restraint in addition to an exchange rate anchor to reduce inflation quickly and stabilize the economy. Recently, Brazil (1994) implemented a similar policy mix in the form of the Real Plan to engineer a return to economic stability.

Once fiscal discipline is restored, policymakers decide whether they should use an exchange rate anchor, a monetary growth anchor, or a combination of nominal anchors to force disinflation. The bulk of historical and theoretical evidence points to a preference for the use of the exchange rate anchor over the monetary anchor. Pegging a weak domestic currency to a strong foreign currency gives the domestic money instant credibility (as long as the public believes that government can defend the newly set fixed exchange rate). Because high and persistent inflation results in an exodus from the domestic currency, by fixing the exchange rate the government can engineer renewed confidence in the domestic currency and bridge a return to price stability.

In choosing between the exchange rate and the money supply as the stabilization anchor, considerable attention should be given to the cost associated with each approach. Using a two-period model for a small and open economy, Fischer (1986) shows that under certain conditions exchange rate stabilization results in a less severe recession than monetary stabilization. But recent evidence given by Calvo and Végh (1994) indicates that the choice between exchange rate and money supply as the stabilization anchor is essentially a choice about the timing of recession: the money supply anchor brings about a near-term recession while the exchange rate anchor results in a medium-term recession. When the exchange rate nominal anchor is used, a consumption boom occurs in the immediate aftermath of stabilization to be followed by a later recession.[9]

If the new exchange rate policy is credible, a quick and clear signal is sent to the public regarding government's seriousness in taming inflation. The use of monetary targets, on the other hand, is more elusive and leaves more uncertainty regarding government's objectives.[10] As mentioned above, the success of exchange rate–based stabilization depends on the credibility of the policy.[11] While central bank independence is not a necessary condition for stabilization, it is helpful in isolating monetary policy from fiscal mismanagement and it represents an important step toward establishing credibility (see chapter 1). It is not surprising that in a comparative study of central bank independence, Brazil, Mexico, and Argentina were ranked at the bottom of a group of forty-seven countries in terms of their central banks' independence and at the top of the group in terms of inflation.[12]

If inflation is particularly persistent and the inflationary memory cannot be cleared effectively by using only one nominal anchor, two or more anchors may be used simultaneously. The evidence presented here, however, suggests that the use of multiple nominal anchors may be counterproductive and unnecessary. Empirical evidence from Brazil, long suspected of having the most persistent inflation in the region, showed that the inertial component of inflation is much weaker than previously assumed (see chapter 6). Furthermore, the evidence from Mexican stabilization (chapter 4) demonstrates that the use of multiple anchors could be detrimental to economic growth as the combination of tight money and exchange rate anchors forces the economy into prolonged recession.

From Stabilization to Growth

The Latin American experience of the 1980s ended the neostructuralists' euphoria of achieving stabilization without any output or employment costs.

The fiscal austerity needed for stabilizing the economy translates into significant reductions in government expenditure, and the austerity program's wage squeeze reduces consumer demand. Moreover, during the stabilization period, high interest rates are adopted as a means of fighting capital exodus and inflation and reducing demand. High interest rates and uncertainty about the economy result in further declines in private investment and consumption.

Because successful stabilization entails a substantial reduction in demand, it is associated with short-term economic slowdown. During the 1980s, significant declines in private and public investments combined with a substantial capital outflow to bring about a dramatic reduction in investment and economic retardation. The investment–GDP ratio for Latin American countries dropped from an annual average of 23 percent in 1970s to 17 percent in 1980s, while the overall investment levels declined by more than 3 percent per year during the 1980s. The resumption of capital inflows of the 1990s has been only marginally beneficial because much of the new capital has been attracted to the equity markets (see, for example, chapter 4) with dubious impacts on economic growth.

Investment is the key to growth, but stabilization does not automatically result in a rise in increased investment. The IMF and Washington consensus believe that market-oriented structural adjustments are sufficient for restoring growth. In the short run, the government could encourage private investment by implementing supply-side tax policies. In the long run, it can foster increased productivity and investment by investing in primary and secondary education and human development programs.

Despite short-term tax incentives, the private sector may be reluctant to commit sufficient investment in the face of lackluster domestic demand. If exchange rates are set competitively, then it is possible for the export sector, operating on the basis of comparative advantage, to push the economy out of its recessionary doldrums. But because the exchange rate is usually used as the nominal stabilization anchor, and it is often overvalued, the export sector may not be able to generate sufficient current account surpluses to lead an economic recovery. In the absence of a strong domestic impetus for growth, foreign resource inflow can play a crucial and constructive role in the transition stage from stabilization to growth. Governments should adopt policies that welcome long term capital inflow in the form of direct foreign investment. For example, they should remove exchange rate uncertainty, relax or eliminate regulations that limit profit repatriation and dictate the maximum share of foreign interest in joint ventures.

Notes

Notes to Introduction

1. Milton Friedman, Arnold Harberger, and the Brazilian economist Alberto Campos are most closely identified with the monetarist approach.
2. See, for example, Bleany (1985).
3. Bresser Pereira (1993, 19).
4. Williamson (1990b, 8–17).
5. Fischer (1990) and the World Bank (1991, 11).
6. World Bank (1991, 5).
7. Taylor (1993, 41).
8. Ibid.
9. For a perspective on structuralism see, for example, Taylor (1981).
10. Juan Noyola Vázquez, Dudley Seers, Hans Singer, and Osvaldo Sunkel, among others, are some of the important early contributors to the structuralist school.
11. For more on the structuralist approach in Latin America, see Arndt (1985), Wachter (1976), and Canavese (1982).
12. Feinberg (1990, 22).
13. See, for example, Sachs (1987b).
14. See Edwards (1993) for further discussion of these issues.
15. See Nunnenkemp (1992) for a discussion.
16. See Diaz-Alejandro (1982) and Frenkel (1986) for perspectives on the performance of orthodox policies in Latin America.
17. See Taylor (1993), Lessard and Williamson (1987), and Das (1986) for a discussion of capital inflow, capital flight, and developing countries.

Notes to Chapter 1

1. See Dornbusch, Sturzenegger, and Wolf (1990).
2. Gordon (1982) argues rather convincingly that since the central characteristic of the so-called rational expectation framework is the degree of price flexibility and not how the expectations are formed, it is misleading to call this approach the "rational expectation approach" because it is possible for economic agents to have rational expectations in a world characterized by inertia. As we will discuss later, one version of the

neostructuralist approach indeed assumes expectations that are rational.

3. In Brazil, the Federal University of Rio de Janeiro, Maria Tavares, and Luiz Belluzzo are most closely associated with the neo-Keynesian approach. For more on their approach, see Tavares and Belluzzo (1984) and Bier et al. (1987).

4. See Beenstock (1980, chapter 3) for more.

5. This is in sharp contrast with the income–expenditure type models, which take the price level as the exogenous variable in the model.

6. Friedman (1974, p. 26).

7. Lucas (1972a, 1972b, 1973), Friedman (1976), and Cukierman (1984).

8. One possible explanation rests on the idea of aggregation. Each employer relies only on his or her own price increases. This aggregates to all employers knowing relevant prices whereas each worker-consumer faces thousands of prices and thus a much more costly process of obtaining information.

9. McCallum (1990, 985) convincingly argues that the monetary authority that has control over the monetary base can technically dominate the fiscal authority. This, however, is not a likely scenario in countries where there is no independent central bank and the treasury determines the money supply.

10. This was the title of the influential Sargent and Wallace (1981) article.

11. McCallum (1990).

12. See ibid. for a review.

13. See Brunner et al. (1980) and Cukierman (1984).

14. Tobin (1972).

15. From "Inflation: To Sacrifice for the Common Good," *Vital Speeches of the Day*, May 1, 1978, reprinted in Colander (1979, 25–32).

16. Arida and Lara Resende (1986, 22).

17. In chapter 5 we consider the experiences of Argentina and Bolivia, where the exchange rate was employed as the stabilizing nominal anchor.

18. Lemgruber (1978, chapter 5) used both annual data (1954–71) and quarterly data (1958:1–1972:2).

19. In a footnote, Lemgruber (1984, 44, fn. 23) acknowledges this problem but claims that the estimates obtained from using two-stage or three-stage least-squares were similar. This is rather surprising especially because in an earlier work (1974), Lemgruber himself offered econometric evidence that suggested the estimates were very sensitive to the choice of the estimation procedure.

20. Parkins (1991) actually takes an imaginative approach to the problem by using an AR(3) model to obtain instrumental variables for jointly determined variables in his model. This is justified by the author by pointing out that using *ad hoc* approaches is widespread in applied econometrics. The estimated results are *visually* compared to ordinary least-squares estimates, and the existence of bias is tested using Wu–Hausman tests. It is not clear how the author estimated each equation and how strongly the simultaneity bias is present in the reported results. What is clear is that even if one accepts the use of the OLS estimation procedure, one still remains highly skeptical of the reported results because of the serious degrees of freedom problem caused by a sample of size 18.

21. This issue was first addressed by Tobin (1956).

22. For lower inflation rates, however, both methods seem to result in small (a few percentage points of GDP) costs.

23. For a useful classification of the theoretical approaches that establish a relationship between higher inflation and higher variability of relative prices, see Fischer (1981c).

24. These studies include, among others, Blejer (1981, 1983), Bordo (1980), Hercowitz (1981), and Fischer (1981a).

25. Fischer (1981a).

26. See Gray (1976) for the relationship between inflation and optimal contract length.

27. Fischer (1986, 20).

28. Ibid., Blinder and Esaki (1978), and Bach and Stephenson (1974).

29. Cardoso et al. (1992, 3) calculated these ratios from the annual household survey *Pesquisa Nacional de Domicilios* (PNADs).

30. Fischer and Modigliani (1978).

Notes to Chapter 2

1. Simonsen (1984, 21).

2. Baer (1989, 77).

3. This definition of macroeconomic populism is given by Dornbusch and Edwards (1991, 247).

4. The view of the Goulart government presented here differs from the view advanced by Foxley (1980). Foxley brands the Goulart stabilization policies as essentially orthodox: "The policy consisted in limiting monetary expansion, cutting back public investment, and reducing credit available to private sector," and elimination of subsidies on services provided by state enterprises (896). The available data, however, do not support such a view.

5. See Skidmore (1976) for more on Goulart's economic policies.

6. See Baer et al. (1989) for more on this point.

7. For a study of macroeconomic populism in Latin America see Dornbusch and Edwards (1991).

8. Baer (1979, 169).

9. Syvrud (1974, 133–34). Still, correction was not entirely based on market forces; instead, it was a case of "correction by decrees."

10. This smart characterization of the Brazilian inflation was first used by Fishlow (1974).

11. See Fishlow (1974) and Baer (1979, chapter 8).

12. For a complete discussion of indexation rules in Brazil under military governments, see Simonsen (1984).

13. Fishlow (1974, 266).

14. For a discussion of anti-inflation policies of the 1964–69 period, see Simonsen (1970).

15. See Baer (1979), Skidmore (1976), and Syvrud (1974).

16. See Lopes (1977) and Cline (1981) for more.

17. See Hirschman (1981) for the social and political aspects of inflation.

18. Baer (1987).

19. Investment in developing countries was perceived as safe because, as Walter Wriston, then the chairman of Citicorp, put it, "countries do not go bankrupt."

20. This figure ($70,957 million) is for Brazil's total debt in 1980. Of this total, $57,431 million was long-term debt. (Source: *World Debt Tables: 1990–91*, Washington D.C.: The World Bank).

21. Bresser Pereira (1990, 504, fn.) distinguishes between populist-developmentist economic policy and populist-distributivist policy by stating that "populism can be distributive when it has its origins to the left, or developmentist, when its origin is in the right. Its results are not much different in terms of internal and external adjustments."

22. *Conjuntura Econômica* (September 1992: 25).

23. Werneck (1987), cited in Baer (1989, Table 6.16, 129).

24. Baer (1989, 128).

25. For more on the IMF policies in Brazil, see *Forum Gazeta Mercantil* (1983).

26. Calculated as the percentage change in the real money supply (M_1) from the first quarter to the fourth quarter of 1983.

27. Sarney (1988).

28. This plan froze the prices of products produced by state firms and by some major oligopolies.

29. For a good overview of the March 1985–February 1986 stabilization attempts, see Modiano (1988b).

30. Faria (1988, 51).

31. See, for example, Bresser Pereira and Nakano (1984) and Arida and Lara Resende (1985) for more on the inertial nature of the Brazilian economy. For detailed analysis, see chapter 1.

32. See Peláez (1986) for a comparative analysis of the Cruzado and the Austral plans.

33. The first Brazilian money was the real, which is better known as its plural réis. In 1942 the real was replaced by the cruzeiro at the rate of 1,000 to 1. In 1967 the military government cut three zeros off the cruzeiro. In February 1986, the cruzado replaced the cruzeiro at the rate 1,000 to 1. On January 15, 1989, the Summer Plan's cruzado novo replaced the cruzado at the rate 1,000 to 1. In March 1990, the Collor Plan reintroduced the cruzeiro, which replaced the cruzado novo at the 1:1 exchange. In July 1994, the Brazilian government introduced the real.

34. This replaced the commonly practiced quarterly and the official biannual adjustments of wages for inflation.

35. Baer (1989, 167).

36. Sayad (1988, 11).

37. Bresser Pereira (1987).

38. Marques (1988, 122).

39. Ibid., p. 121.

40. The budget deficit calculated from *International Financial Statistics*, CD-ROM, March 1992; for inflation rates see Table 2.4, p. 54.

41. In 1992, the government promised that starting in 1993 it would begin paying back the public for its "investment" in the National Development Fund.

42. Baer (1989, 185)

43. Ibid., 186.

44. See, for example, Modiano (1988b) and Barbosa and Simonsen (1989) for a perspective on the magnitude of the plan design.

45. Baer (1989, 173).

46. From a personal interview with Bresser Pereira.

47. Calculated from *Conjuntura Econômica* (November 1989).

48. Hyperinflation is defined here as a monthly inflation rate in excess of 50 percent, as in the classic work of Philip Cagan (1956).

49. In particular, the government paid an average effective monthly interest rate of −0.68 percent. See Brandão and de Faro (1990, 244)

50. Sargent and Wallace (1981) have shown the unpleasant consequences of high interest rates in an inflationary environment.

51. See Sargent (1986) and chapter 5 for more.

52. Based on Dornbusch and Simonsen (1988), 457–60.

53. The pre-shock monthly rate of money expansion had reached the 80 percent mark.

54. Júnior (1991, 12).

55. For detailed information on Brazilian tariff rates, see *Tarifa Aduaneira do Brasil*, 1994.

56. Calculated from *Conjuntura Econômica* (May 1992: 74).

57. *Conjuntura Econômica* (August 1991: 327).

58. See de Faro (1991) for more on the Collor Plan II.

59. The so-called *overnight* bank accounts paid interest that was indexed for inflation every twenty-four hours. These accounts were discontinued after February 28, 1992, and replaced by Fundos de Aplicações Financeiros (FAFs). FAFs also pay interest on a daily basis, but the tax levied on the earned interest diminishes as the number of days the funds stay in the account increases.

60. See Cardoso (1994, articles 50–57) for details.

61. With a fixed exchange rate the money supply becomes an endogenous variable.

62. Cash reserves. Balance of payments and liquidity definitions of reserves were slightly higher. See *Boletim do Banco Central do Brasil* (September 1994: 154).

63. Calculated from *Conjuntura Econômica* (December 1994: 6–7).

64. There is also another possible lesson that has not been discussed extensively in the literature: the existence of a vast informal sector—often a direct result of economic failures and distributive injustice—reduces the potential effectiveness of policies that control prices by directly intervening in the "legal" market.

65. Ronci (1992, 44–48).

66. See Moskoff and Nazmi (1992) for more on stabilization and the return to democracy in the former Soviet Union, Argentina, and Brazil.

Notes to Chapter 3

1. For pre-1973 economic conditions see, for example, Corbo (1974) and Larraín and Meller (1991).

2. See Corbo and Solimano (1991) for a detailed analysis of a money overhang for the period under consideration.

3. Edwards (1985, 226).

4. Foxley (1983, chapter 3).

5. These enterprises, seized by the Popular Unity government, had not officially become state-owned and their ownership remained ambiguous.

6. Bitran and Sáez (1994, 332–33).

7. Ibid., 336.

8. Lagos (1992).

9. See Lagos (1992) for more details and an explanation of some other factors that may have contributed to the failure of the PER, such as the lack of credibility associated with the plan.

10. For more on the theoretical aspects, see chapter 1. For more details on the context of the Argentine *Tablita*, see chapter 5.

11. Dornbusch and Edwards (1994, 89).

12. See, for example, Kiguel and Liviatan (1992).

13. Labán and Larraín (1994, 124) observe that for the 1978–81 period approximately 73 percent of capital inflows were used to cover the current account deficit. This high ratio, however, is due to 1981, when almost *all* of capital account surplus was used to offset current account deficit.

14. The real interest rate on foreign obligations would be the actual interest rate adjusted for the expected devaluation rate and expected domestic inflation rate. See Bosworth, Dornbusch, and Labán (1994, 8).

15. Edwards (1985, 236).
16. Marshall and Montt (1988).
17. This is because asset prices are determined based on the expected future price of goods and factor prices. See Corbo and Fischer (1992).
18. The sequencing of stabilization vs. liberalization itself is subject to controversy. See, for example, Edwards (1992), Krueger (1981), Sachs (1987b), and Fischer (1986, 1987).
19. In addition to these factors, Edwards and Cox-Edwards (1991) also mention the lack of democratic channels that made an open and constructive discussion of policy choices impossible.
20. See McKinnon (1982) and Edwards (1992).
21. Programa de Empleo Mínimo.
22. Programa Ocupacional para Jefes de Hogar.
23. Coloma (1987, 219).
24. Calculation based on the use of the price index of exports and the volume index of exports.
25. Central Bank of Chile, *Bulletins and Economic Indicators* (December 1990).
26. Calculated from *Foreign Investment Committee* and Central Bank of Chile data.
27. Hojman (1993, 169).
28. INE, Manufacturers' Census & Foreign Investment Statute, Decree Law 600.
29. See Edwards (1993b) for more on this point.
30. See Corbo and Fischer (1994).
31. See Foreign Investment Committee (1993), Decree Law 600, Title II, Article 4.
32. Hojman (1993, 166).
33. IMF, *International Financial Statistics* (1994: 279).
34. See Calvo, Leiderman, and Reinhart (1994).
35. See Labán and Larraín (1994).

Notes to Chapter 4

1. As we shall see below, until the mid-1980s the state played a key role in the investment process through active participation in socioeconomic and infrastructure projects.
2. Bazdresch and Levy (1991, 223).
3. For a more detailed analysis of the roots of the Mexican economic development of the 1950s and the 1960 and the impact of the end of the Korean War on the Mexican economy, see Hansen (1971).
4. Bazdresch and Levy (1991, 231).
5. For a detailed examination of the means of protection used under ISI to encourage industrialization, see King (1970).
6. See Ramirez (1986) for a discussion about the role of the state in encouraging and financing private investment.
7. See Loser and Kalter (1992) for details.
8. For more on Mexican agriculture and the impact of industrialization policy on agriculture, see Barkin and Zavala (1978) and Barkin (1990).
9. Bazdresch and Levy (1991, 231–32).
10. According to Robert Looney (1978, 44), however, for the period 1940–70 the objectives of the Mexican government included income redistribution, economic development (not only growth), and the enhancement of the country's socioeconomic yardsticks.
11. Gribomont and Rimez (1977, 786–87).
12. Aspe and Beristain (1984, 26).

13. See Bazdresch and Levy (1991, 239, fn).

14. Buffie (1990, 419–20).

15. See Cypher (1990) for a discussion of the role of the state in the Mexican economy.

16. Primary deficit is defined as the difference between noninterest public spending and public revenues.

17. A phrase coined by President José López Portillo (1976–82).

18. El Mallakh et al. (1984, 31).

19. Secretaría de Patrimonio y Fomento Industrial (1979, 23–24).

20. Looney (1985, 234).

21. Bazdresch and Levy (1991, 251).

22. PEMEX president Jorge Díaz Serano was fired over differences in pricing strategy with the president.

23. See Dietz (1990: V–19 and V–20) for more details.

24. United States Government, *Economic Report of the President* (1993: 428).

25. Ramirez (1993).

26. See Gruben, Welch, and Gunther (1994) for more on bank nationalization.

27. See Ramirez (1994) for more on complementarity and substitutability between public and private investment in Mexico.

28. Beristain and Trigueros (1990, 155).

29. Banco de México, *Informe Annual.*

30. Kaufman (1988, 86).

31. Lusting (1992, 29–35). See her Table 2.3 for a comparison of PIRE's targets and actual performance.

32. Mexico's foreign reserves dropped from a surplus of $3.2 billion in 1984 to a deficit of $2.3 billion in 1985.

33. In the aftermath of the 1982 debt crises, Mexico had imposed license requirements on all imports.

34. See Szymczak (1992) for detailed information on the 1985 trade liberalization program. Also see Lusting (1992, 118–119).

35. Weiss (1992, 718–19).

36. Secretaría de Programación y Presupuesto.

37. Kaufman (1988: 90).

38. Sheahan (1991, 27).

39. The 13 percent increase in imports is calculated for the period 1988–90 from U.S. Government, *Economic Report of the President* (1993), 349.

40. See Gregorio, Guidotti, and Végh (1993) for an explanation of the durable goods demand boom in the aftermath of successful stabilization.

41. For an analysis of public sector solvency in 1988, see Werner (1992, 751–72).

42. Sheahan (1991, 28).

43. *New York Times*, July 25, 1989, 25.

44. Calculated from International Monetary Fund, *International Financial Statistics*, CD-Rom Version (1993).

45. Ramirez (1991, 72).

46. See Sheahan (1991) for more details.

47. See Kaufman (1988).

Notes to Chapter 5

1. Martínez de Hoz (1990, 151).

2. During 1975–76 period the average real interest rate was just under –8.5 percent.

3. The reduction was done in two stages: by 1977 the reserve requirement was decreased to 45 percent and then it was reduced again in 1979 to 10 percent. See Beckerman (1991, 69).

4. Martínez de Hoz (1990, 153–54).

5. The theoretical underpinning of the plan can be captured either by the pre-announcement model of Rodríguez (1979) or the coherence model of Rodríguez (1980), and Calvo and Fernández (1980).

6. Theoretically, as the traded goods prices come under pressure, resources shift out of traded goods production and into the nontraded goods sector, but a short-run deviation from PPP is likely because good prices adjust slower than asset prices (exchange rates) (see Frenkel [1981]). McNown and Wallace (1989) show that in the long run the PPP holds in Argentina.

7. Martínez de Hoz (1990, 173).

8. Calculated from CEPAL (1984, 39).

9. See Dornbusch and de Pablo (1990) and their Table 1.

10. Ibid.

11. Di Tella and Braun (1990, 25).

12. This is one of the three factors offered by Fernández (1985) as the reasons for the failure of the plan. The other two factors are the financial crises of 1980 and political problems that undermined the credibility of the plan.

13. Fernández (1985, 886–87).

14. The plan was named after the president of the Central Bank at the time. The economics minister was actually Dagnino Pastore (July–August) followed by Jorge Wehbe (August–December). Cavallo is currently the economics minister of Argentina and the architect of the Menem stabilization plan.

15. Dornbusch (1988a, 202–3).

16. Peláez (1986, 113).

17. Dornbusch and de Pablo (1990, 106).

18. The Shacht Plan in Germany is perhaps the best known modern-day example of heterodox stabilization plans.

19. For more detailed discussion of the Austral Plan, see Canavese and di Tella (1988), Heyman (1987), Machinea and Fanelli (1988), Beckerman (1991), and Kiguel (1991), among others.

20. Kiguel (1991, 972).

21. Peláez (1986, 114).

22. Ibid., 116

23. Ortega (1989, 31).

24. Peláez (1986, 117).

25. Dornbusch and de Pablo (1990, 108).

26. Not all of this was fresh money; it included some refinancing.

27. Kiguel (1991).

28. Machinea and Fanelli (1988).

29. For more on the financial system of Argentina, including the period after the Austral Plan, see Damill (1987).

30. This explanation was first offered by Arida and Lara Resende (1985) and was applied to the Austral Plan by Canavese and di Tella (1988).

31. Beckerman (1991, 74).

32. See Beckerman (1991) for a more detailed analysis including one on the role played by monetary authorities.

33. Canavese (1992, 8).

34. Ibid., 10.

35. The devaluation of the *official* exchange rate was close to 20 percent.

36. Griffith (1992, 18–22).

37. Alves (1990, 12–13)

38. Lora (1987, 213).

39. In the 1980–81 period, Bolivia had to allocate about 60 percent of its total export revenues to servicing its foreign debt.

40. Lora (1987, 213).

41. Kharas and Pinto (1989, 436).

42. This is in accordance with Cagan's model of hyperinflation. See Sachs (1987a, 280).

43. The UDP constituted of the Movimiento de Izquierda Revolucionaria (MIR), the pro-Soviet Partido Comunista de Bolivia (PCB), and Movimiento Nacionalista Revolucionaria de Izquierda (MNRI).

44. Bedregal Gutiérrez (1987, 48).

45. Cole (1987, 59).

46. Morales (1988, 311).

47. Anaya (1987, 187).

48. Mann and Pastor (1989, 170).

49. Morales (1988).

50. Again, we are using Philip Cagan's definition of hyperinflation: a monthly inflation rate exceeding 50 percent.

51. Sachs (1987a, 279).

52. For the complete text of Supreme Decree No. 21060, see Bedregal Gutiérrez (1987, 199–252).

53. Anaya (1987, 194).

54. Sachs (1987a, 281).

55. Pastor (1991, 224).

56. Acqua (1989, 116).

57. Cole (1987, 60–61), and Mann and Pastor (1989, 171–73).

58. Cariaga (1990, 45).

59. Kharas and Pinto (1989) show that coordinating fiscal and exchange rate policies was an important factor in bringing about stabilization in Bolivia.

60. See Conaghan (1994) for details.

61. Morales (1988, 308), and Morales and Sachs (1990, 170–71).

Notes to Chapter 6

1. See chapter 2 for an overview.

2. This is a framework similar to models used by Johnson (1984) and Nazmi (1990).

3. This equation shows the inelasticity of demand in some major Brazilian industries of Brazil due to the lack of competition created by import substitution policies (see chapter 2).

4. See Baer, (1989, 137–40).

5. In Brazil, such feedbacks from wages to inflation worked especially well after the introduction of wage indexation in 1979, which adjusted wages semiannually to overcome the problem of income erosion due to inflation. Prior to 1979 wages were adjusted once a year according to the expected rate of inflation. This practice, however, systematically underestimated the inflation rate and, therefore, systematically decreased real wages and slowed down inflation.

6. See Beenstock (1980, chapter 3) for more.

7. This assumption is made due to a lack of data on labor productivity in Brazil.

8. To see the inertial component of the model, note that Equations 6.7 and 6.8 can give inflation a self-propelling dynamic through wage–price spirals.

9. See Fair (1987, 473) for a numerical example of this problem.

10. For the 1950–73 period, Blejer (1978) reports the significance of the expectation of black market depreciation in money demand function. On the other hand, Dornbusch et al. (1983) and Calomiris and Domowitz (1989) offer strong evidence against the use of the exchange rate as an explanatory variable in the Brazilian money demand function. Moreover, Blejer's choice of an adaptive expectation model proves inadequate for the high inflation post-1974 period, which exhibits an integrated inflation rate variable.

11. See Dornbusch (1976) for more details.

12. While data for the 1986:1–1993:4 period are available, the post-1986 data were excluded because of various wage–price freeze programs implemented in the 1986–90 period. The considerable variability and swings in nominal variables caused by these plans may *prima facie* seem desirable from an econometric perspective, but serious problems arise when formulating a simple model for inflation expectations. Models of expectation formations break down in the presence of unexpected and frequent price freeze and control programs such as the ones implemented in the 1986–90 period. One way out of this dilemma is to assume perfect foresight such that the expected inflation rate equals the actual inflation rate. In the case of Brazil, this common practice is suspect since it requires that economic agents accurately anticipate policy changes as well as the timing and the nature of stabilization policies. Data sources are available from the author upon request.

13. In reality, the data show that prices and money are $I(2)$. The rate of change in prices (the inflation rate) is $I(1)$ and money and prices cointegrate as real money into an $I(1)$ process.

14. A detailed overview of cointegration analysis is provided in Engle and Granger (1991), among others.

15. Hendry (1992).

16. See Johansen and Juselius (1990) for details.

17. The lag length was chosen based on evidence from HQC and SC.

18. In particular, BIC = -5.37, -5.43, and -5.96, while HQC = -5.77, -5.98, and -6.67 for lags 2, 3 and 4, respectively.

19. The United States data are used for finding the interest rates, income, money, and price differential variables. All these variables are found to be $I(1)$, as expected.

20. Black (1981).

21. See Hendry and Richard (1982, 1983) and Hendry (1982).

22. Montiel (1989) used a five-variable VAR model to conclude that exogenous movements (shocks) in money and exchange rate variables "played the dominant roles" in determining the inflation rate in Brazil, and offered evidence against the inertialist view of the Brazilian inflation. Novaes (1993) used the VAR model and innovation analysis to conclude that the inflation variable does not persist for a long period.

23. In reality, the data show that prices and money are $I(2)$. The rate of change in prices (the inflation rate) is $I(1)$ and money and prices cointegrate as real money into an I(1) process. The transformations used by Novaes—the use of percentage changes of P, M, W, and E— will therefore result in bundling together series with different integration orders.

24. See, for example, Leamer (1985), and Cooley and LeRoy (1985), among others.

25. The results reported in Table 6.9 (page 162) are generally in accordance with Novaes's (1993) findings (her Table 7), except that the evidence presented here based on

SVAR models suggests that the exchange rate and wage variables do exert some pressure on prices. Moreover, relative to Novaes's findings, our results show a slightly stronger impact from the price variable in the short run. Novaes's results and our conclusions differ dramatically from the results reported by Montiel (1989) in two key aspects. According to Novaes's and our results, (1) the price variable plays the dominant role in determining the future rate of inflation, and (2) the exchange rate variable does not play an important role. The Montiel results may be considered less reliable because they are drawn from a VAR model with nonstationary variables.

Notes to Chapter 7

1. See Friedman (1977b).
2. Persson and Tabellini (1994).
3. Tanzi (1989).
4. See, for example, Baer and Birch (1992) for a discussion of this and related issues.
5. Pinheiro and Giambiagi (1994).
6. See, for example, van de Walle (1989).
7. Pinheiro and Giambiagi (1994).
8. See Bruno and Fischer (1986).
9. See Calvo and Végh (1993) for a theoretical model.
10. Also see Bruno (1991).
11. See Edwards (1993b) for more on this point.
12. Cukierman (1992).

Bibliography

Acqua, F. 1988. "O programa de ajustamento econômico boliviano." *Conjuntura Econômica* (January: 113–18).

Alesina, A. 1988. "Macroeconomics and Politics." In NBER *Macroeconomics Annual*, ed. Stanley Fischer, 17–25. Cambridge, MA: MIT Press.

———. 1989. "Politics and Business Cycles in Industrial Democracies." *Economic Policy* 8: 58–98.

Alesina, A., and L. Summers. 1993. "Central Bank Independence and Macroeconomic Performance: Some Comparative Evidence." *Journal of Money, Credit and Banking* 25: 151–62.

Alves, J. 1990. *A Argentina Menem, um ano depois*. São Paulo: Banco Martinelli.

Anaya, J.A.M. 1987. "Estabilización y nueva política económica en Bolivia." *El trimestre económico* 54, núm. especial: 179–211.

Arida, M., and A. Lara Resende. 1985. "Inertial Inflation and Monetary Reform." In *Inflation and Indexation: Argentina, Brazil, and Israel*, ed. J. Williamson. Washington, DC: Institute for International Economics, 27–45.

Aspe, P. 1993. *Economic Transformation: The Mexican Way*. Cambridge, MA: MIT Press.

Aspe, P., and J. Beristain. 1984. "The Evolution of Income Distribution Policies during the Post-Revolutionary Period in Mexico." In *The Political Economy of Income Distribution in Mexico*, ed. P. Aspe and P. Sigmund. New York: Holmes and Meier.

Bach, G., and J. Stephenson. 1974. "Inflation and Redistribution of Wealth," *Review of Economics and Statistics* 56: 1–13.

Baer, W. 1967. "The Inflation Controversy in Latin America." *Latin American Research Review* 2 (Spring: 3–25).

———. 1979. *The Brazilian Economy: Its Growth and Development*. 1st ed. Columbus: Grid.

———. 1987. "The Resurgence of Inflation in Brazil, 1974–86." *World Development* 15: 1007–34.

———. 1989. *The Brazilian Economy: Growth and Development*. New York: Praeger.

Baer, W., D. Biller, and C. McDonald. 1989. "Austerity under Different Political Regimes: The Case of Brazil." In *Paying the Costs of Austerity in Latin America*, ed. Howard Handelman and Werner Baer. Boulder, CO: Westview Press, 19–42.

Baer, W., and M. Birch. 1992. "Privatization and the Changing Role of the State in Latin America." *New York University Journal of International Law and Politics* 25: 1–25.

Bailey, M.J. 1956. "The Welfare Cost of Inflationary Finance." *The Journal of Political Economy* 64: 93–110.

Baillie, R., and D. Selover. 1987. "Cointegeration and Models of Exchange Rate Determination." *International Journal of Forecasting* 3: 43–51.

Ball, L. 1990. "Why Does High Inflation Raise Inflation Uncertainty?" Working Paper 3224. Cambridge, MA: National Bureau of Economic Research.

Ball, L., and Cecchetti, S. 1990. "Inflation and Uncertainty at Short and Long Horizons." *Brookings Papers on Economic Activity* I: 215–54.

Barbosa, F.H. 1983. "A inflação brasileira no pós-guerra." Rio de Janeiro: IPEA/INPES.

Barbosa, F.H., and P.D. McNelis. 1990. "Inflation and Inflationary Inertia: Brazil 1964–1985." *The World Bank Economic Review* 3: 339–57.

Barbosa, F.H., and P.L.V. Pereira. 1989. "O insucesso do Plano Cruzado: a evidência empírica da inflação 100% inercial para o Brasil." In *Plano Cruzado: inércia x inépcia*, ed. F.H. Barbosa and M.H. Simonsen. Rio de Janeiro: Globo.

Barbosa, F.H., and M.H. Simonsen, eds. 1989. *Plano Cruzado: inércia x inépcia*. Rio de Janeiro: Globo.

Barkin, D. 1990. *Distorted Development: Mexico in the World Economy*. Boulder, CO: Westview Press.

Barkin, D., and A. Zavala. 1978. *Desarrollo regional y reorganización campesina: la Chontalpa como reflejo del problema agropecuario mexicano*. México, D.F.: Editorial Nueva Imagen.

Barro, R. 1972. "Inflationary Finance and the Welfare Cost of Inflation." *Journal of Political Economy*, 80: 978–1001.

Barro, R.J. 1976. "Rational Expectations and the Role of Monetary Policy." *Journal of Monetary Economics* 2: 1–32.

Barro, R.J., and S. Fischer. 1976. "Recent Developments in Monetary Theory." *Journal of Monetary Economics* 2: 133–67.

Batten, D.S., and D.L. Thornton. 1983. "M_1 or M_2: Which Is the Better Monetary Target?" *Federal Reserve Bank of St. Louis Review* (June/July: 36–42).

Bazdresch, C., and S. Levy. 1991. "Populism and Economic Policy in Mexico." In *The Macroeconomics of Populism in Latin America*, ed. Rudiger Dornbusch and Sebastian Edwards. Chicago: University of Chicago Press.

Beckerman, P. 1991. "Recent Heterodox Stabilization Experience: Argentina, Israel, and Brazil, 1985–1989." *Quarterly Review of Economics and Business* 31, no. 3: 65–94.

Bedregal, G. 1987. *Dialectica de la Hiperinflacion en Bolivia*. La Paz, Bolivia: Liberia Editoral Juventud.

Beenstock, M. 1980. *A Neoclassical Analysis of Macroeconomic Policy*. Cambridge: Cambridge University Press.

Beristain, J., and I. Trigueros. 1990. "The Three Major Debtors: Mexico." In *Latin American Adjustment: How Much Has Happened?* ed. J. Williamson, 154–68. Washington, DC: Institute for International Economics.

Bhalla, S. 1981. "The Transmission of Inflation into Developing Economies." In *World Inflation and the Developing Countries*, ed. William Cline, pp. 52–102. Washington, DC: The Brookings Institution.

Bier, A., L. Paulani, and R. Messenberg. 1987. "O desenvolvimento em Xegue." *Novos Estudos* 19: 153–71.

Bitran, E., and R. Sáez. 1994. "Privatization and Regulation in Chile." In *The Chilean Economy: Policy Lessons and Challenges*, eds. B.P. Bosworth, R. Dornbusch, and R. Labán. Washington, DC: The Brookings Institution.

Black, S. 1981. "The Impact of Changes in the World Economy on Stabilization Policies in the 1970s." In *Economic Stabilization in Developing Countries*, ed. W. Cline and S. Weintraub. Washington, DC: The Brookings Institution.

Blanchard, O. 1989. "The Dynamic Effects of Aggregate Demand and Supply Disturbances." *American Economic Review* 79: 655–73.

Blanchard, O., and M. Watson. 1986. "Are Business Cycles All Alike?" In *The American Business Cycle: Continuity and Change*, R. Gordon, ed.: NBER and University of Chicago Press, pp. 123–56.

Blejer, M.I. 1978. "Black-Market Exchange-Rate Expectations and the Domestic Demand for Money: Some Empirical Results." *Journal of Monetary Economics* 4: 767–73.

———. 1981. "The Dispersion of Relative Commodity Price under Very Rapid Inflation." *Journal of Development Economics* 9: 347–56.

———. 1983. "On the Anatomy of Inflation: The Variability of Relative Commodity Prices in Argentina." *Journal of Money, Credit and Banking* 15: 469–81.

Blejer, M.I., and K. Chu, eds. 1989. *Fiscal Policy, Stabilization and Growth in Developing Countries*. Washington, DC: IMF.

Blinder, A., and H. Esaki. 1978. "Macroeconomic Activity and Income Distribution in the Postwar United States." *Review of Economics and Statistics* 6: 604–9.

Bollerslev, T. 1986. "Generalized Autoregressive Conditional Heteroscedasticity." *Journal of Econometrics* 31: 307–27.

Bomberger, W.A., and G.E. Makinen. 1976. "Inflation, Unemployment, and Expectations in Latin America: Some Simple Tests." *Southern Economic Journal* 43: 112–23.

Bonomo, M., and R. Garcia. 1992. "Indexation, Staggering and Disinflation." Texto para Discussão, 281, Departamento de Economia, PUC-RJ.

Bordo, Michael D. 1980. "The Effects of Monetary Change on Relative Commodity Prices and the Role of Long Term Contracts." *Journal of Political Economy* 88: 1088–1109.

Bosworth, B.P., R. Dornbusch, and R. Labán, eds. 1994. *The Chilean Economy: Policy Lessons and Challenges*. Washington, DC: The Brookings Institution.

Box, G.E.P., and G.M. Jenkins. 1970. *Time Series Analysis, Forecasting and Control*. San Francisco: Holden Day.

Brandão, A.S., and C. de Faro. 1990. "Política fiscal no plano Collor: o transitório e o permanente." In *Plano Collor: avaliações e perspectivas*, ed. Clovis de Faro. Rio de Janeiro: Livros Técnicos e Científicos Editora Ltda.

Bresser Pereira, C.L. 1986. *Economia brasileira: uma introduçao crítica*. São Paulo: Editora Brasiliense.

———. 1987. "Inertial Inflation and the Cruzado Plan." *World Development* 15: 1035–44.

———. 1990. "The Perverse Logic of Stagflation: Debt, Deficit and Inflation in Brazil." *Journal of Post Keynesian Economics* 12: 503–18.

———. 1993. "Economic Reforms and Economic Growth: Efficiency and Politics in Latin America." In *Economic Reforms in New Democracies: A Social-Democratic Approach*, ed. C.L. Bresser Pereira, et al. Cambridge: Cambridge University Press.

Bresser Pereira, C.L., J. M. Maravall, and A. Prezeworski. 1993. *Economic Reforms in New Democracies: A Social-Democratic Approach*. Cambridge: Cambridge University Press.

Bresser Pereira, C.L., and Y. Nakano. 1984. *Inflação e recessao*. São Paulo: Editora Brasiliense.

Brunner, A., and G. Hess. 1993. "Are Higher Levels of Inflation Less Predictable? A State-Dependent Conditional Heteroscedasticity Approach." *Journal of Business and Economic Statistics* 11: 187–97.

Brunner, K., A. Cukierman, and A. Meltzer. 1980. "Stagflation, Persistent Unemployment and the Permanence of Economic Shocks." *Journal of Monetary Economics* 6: 467–492.

Brunner, K., and A.H. Meltzer, eds. 1982. *Carnegie-Rochester Conference Series on Public Policy* 17.

Bruno, M. 1979. "Stabilization and Stagflation in a Semi-Industrialized Economy." In *International Economic Policy, Theory and Evidence*, ed. R. Dornbusch and J. Ezenkel. Baltimore, MD: Johns Hopkins University Press.

———. 1991. "High Inflation and the Nominal Anchors of an Open Economy." *Essays in International Finance*, no. 183. Princeton, NJ: Department of Economics, Princeton University.

———. 1993. *Stabilization and Economic Reform: Therapy by Consensus*. Oxford: Oxford University Press.

Bruno, M., G. di Tella, R. Dornbusch, and S. Fischer, eds. 1988. *Inflation Stabilization: The Experience of Israel, Argentina, Brazil, Bolivia, and Mexico*. Cambridge, MA: MIT Press.

Bruno, M., and S. Fischer. 1986. "The Inflationary Process: Shocks and Accommodation." In *The Israeli Economy: Maturing through Crises*, ed. Y. Ben-Porah. Cambridge, MA: Harvard University Press.

Buffie, E.F. 1990. "Economic Policy and Foreign Debt in Mexico." In *Developing Country Debt and Economic Performance*, vol. 2, ed. J.D. Sachs. Chicago: University of Chicago Press.

Cagan, P. 1956. "The Monetary Dynamics of Hyperinflation." In *Studies in the Quantity Theory of Money*, ed. M. Friedman. Chicago: University of Chicago Press.

Calomiris, C.W., and I. Domowitz. 1989. "Asset Substitution, Money Demand, and the Inflation Process in Brazil." *Journal of Money, Credit and Banking* 21: 78–89.

Calvo, G.A. 1986. "Temporary Stabilization: Predetermined Exchange Rates." *Journal of Political Economy* 94: 383–98.

Calvo, G.A., and R.B. Fernández. 1980. "Pauta cambiaria y deficit fiscal." In *Inflación y estabilidad*, ed. R.B. Fernández and C.A. Rodríguez. Buenos Aires: Macchi.

Calvo, G.A., L. Leiderman, and C. Reinhart. 1994. "The Capital Inflows Problem: Concepts and Issues." *Contemporary Economic Policy* 22: 54–66.

Calvo, G.A., and C. Végh. 1993. "Exchange Rate–Based Stabilization under Imperfect Credibility." In *Open-Economy Macroeconomics*, ed. A. Worgotter and H. Frisch. London: Macmillan.

———. 1994. "Inflation Stabilization and Nominal Anchors." *Contemporary Economic Policy* 12: 35–45.

Canavese, A. 1982. "The Structuralist Explanation of Inflation." *World Development* 10: 523–29.

———. 1985. "Reflexões sobre o dilema entre inflação e crescimento econômico na década de 80." *Pesquisa e planejamento econômico* 15.

———. 1992. "Hyperinflation and Convertibility Based Stabilization in Argentina." Paper presented at Brasil e Argentina—Parceria para os Anos Noventa, Universidade de São Paulo, January 27.

Canavese, A., and G. di Tella. 1988. "Inflation Stabilization or Hyperinflation Avoidance: The Case of the Austral Plan in Argentina, 1985–1987." In *Inflation Stabilization: The Experience of Israel, Argentina, Brazil, Bolivia, and Mexico*, ed. M. Bruno et al., Cambridge, MA: MIT Press.

Canitrot, A. 1981. "Teoría y práctica del liberalismo: política antiinflacionaria y apertura económica en la Argentina 1976–1981." *Desarrollo económico* 21: 131–89.

Cardoso, E.A. 1983. "A Money Demand Equation for Brazil." *Journal of Development Economics* 12, pp. 183–93.

Cardoso, E.A., and A. Fishlow. 1990. "The Macroeconomics of the Brazilian External Debt." In *Developing Country Debt and Economic Performance*, vol. 2, ed. J.D. Sachs, 269–391. Chicago: University of Chicago Press.

Cardoso, E.A., R. Paes de Barros, and A. Urani. 1992. "Inflation and Unemployment as Determinants of Inequality in Brazil: The 1980s." Unpublished manuscript.

Cardoso, F.H. 1994. "Plano Fernando Henrique Cardoso." *Revista de Economia Política* 14: 114–31.

Cariaga, J.L. 1990. "Bolivia." In *Latin American Adjustment: How Much Has Happened?* ed. John Williamson. Washington, DC: Institute for International Economics.

Cavallo, D.F. 1977. "Stagflationary Effects of Monetarist Stabilization Policies." Unpublished Ph.D. dissertation, Harvard University.

CEPAL. 1984. *Establización y liberalización económica en el cono sur*. Santiago, Chile: Naciones Unidas.

Chacel, J., P. Falk, and D. Fleischer, eds. 1988. *Brazil's Economic and Political Future*. Boulder, CO: Westview Press.

Choksi, A.M., and D. Papageorgiou, eds. 1986. *Economic Liberalization in Developing Countries*. New York: Basil Blackwell.

Chow, G. 1966. "On the Long Run and Short Run Demand for Money." *Journal of Political Economy* 74: 111–31.

Cline, W.R. 1981. "Brazil's Aggressive Response to External Shocks." In *World Inflation and the Developing Countries*, ed. William Cline, et al. Washington, DC: The Brookings Institution.

Colander, D., ed. 1979. *Solutions to Inflation*. New York: Harcourt Brace Jovanovich.

Cole, J.H. 1987. *Latin American Inflation: Theoretical Interpretations and Empirical Results*. New York: Praeger.

Coloma, F.C. 1987. "Crear empleo: una tarea urgente." In *Desarrollo económico en democracia*, ed. F. Larraín. Santiago: Ediciones Universidad Católica de Chile.

Conaghan, C.M. 1994. "Reconsidering Jeffrey Sachs and the Bolivian Economic Experience." In *Money Doctors, Foreign Debts, and Economic Reforms in Latin America from the 1890s to the Present*, ed. P.W. Drake. Wilmington, DE: Scholarly Resources.

Contador, C.R. 1977. "Crescimento econômico e o combate à inflação." *Revista Brasileira de Economia* 31.

———. 1982. "Sobre as causas da recente aceleração inflacionária: Comentários." *Pesquisa e Planejamento Econômico* 12: 106–14.

Contador, C.R., and W.A. Santos Filho. 1987. "Pruduto interno bruto trimestral: bases metodológicas e estimativas." *Pesquisa e planejamento econômico* 17:. 711–42.

Cooley, T., and S. LeRoy. 1985. "Atheoretical Macroeconomics: A Critique." *Journal of Monetary Economics* 16: 283–308.

Corbo, V. 1974. *Inflation in Developing Countries*. Amsterdam: North-Holland.

Corbo, V., and S. Fischer. 1994. "Lessons from the Chilean Stabilization and Recovery." In *The Chilean Economy: Policy Lessons and Challenges*, ed. B.P. Bosworth, R. Dornbusch, and R. Labán. Washington, DC: The Brookings Institution.

———. 1992. "Adjustment Programs and Bank Support: Rationale and Main Results." In *Adjustment Lending Revisited*, ed. V. Corbo, S. Fischer, and S. Webb, 7–17. Washington, DC: The World Bank.

Corbo, V., M. Goldstein, and M. Khan, eds. 1987. *Growth Oriented Adjustment Programs*. Washington, DC: IMF and the World Bank.

Corbo, V., and A. Solimano. 1991. "Chile's Experience with Stabilization, Revisited." The World Bank, Working Paper WPS 579, Washington, D.C.

Cukierman, A. 1979. "The Relationship between Relative Prices and General Price

Level: A Suggested Interpretation." *American Economic Review* 69: 444–47.

———. 1982. "Relative Price Variability, Inflation and the Allocative Efficiency of the Price Mechanism." *Journal of Monetary Economics* 9: 131–62.

———. 1984. *Inflation, Stagflation, Relative Prices, and Imperfect Competition.* Cambridge: Cambridge University Press.

———. 1992. *Central Bank Strategy, Credibility, and Independence: Theory and Evidence.* Cambridge, MA: MIT Press.

Cypher, J. 1990. *State and Capital in Mexico: Development Policy since 1940.* Boulder, CO: Westview Press.

Damill, M. 1987. "O sistema argentino após o austral." *Revista de economia política* 7: 66–80.

Darrat, A. 1985. "The Demand for Money in Brazil: Some Further Results." *Journal of Development Economics* 18: 485–91.

de Carvalho, F. 1993. "Strato-Inflation and High Inflation: The Brazilian Experience." *Cambridge Journal of Economics* 17: 63–78.

de Faro, C., ed. 1990. *Plano Collor: avaliações e perspectivas.* Rio de Janeiro: Livros Técnicos e Científicos Editora Ltda.

———, ed. 1991. *Plano Collor II.* Rio de Janeiro: Livros Técnicos e Científicos Editora Ltda.

de Faro, C., and A.S. Brandão. 1990. "Política fiscal no Plano Collor: o transitório e o permanente." In *Plano Collor: avaliações e perspectivas*, ed. C. de Faro.

Dickey, D., and W. Fuller. 1979. "Distribution of the Estimators for Autoregressive Time Series with a Unit Root." *Journal of American Statistical Association* 74: 427–31.

———. 1981. "Likelihood Ratio Statistics for Autoregressive Time Series with a Unit Root." *Econometrica* 49: 1057–72.

Dietz, H.O. 1990. *Mexico: Banco de Datos.* Mexico: Editoral Marsa, S.A.

di Tella, G. 1979. "Price Oscillation, Oligopolistic Behavior and Inflation: The Argentine Case." *World Development* 7: 1043–52.

di Tella, G., and C.R. Braun, eds. 1990. *Argentina: 1946–83: The Economic Ministers Speak.* New York: St. Martin's Press.

Dornbusch, R. 1976. "Expectations and Exchange Rate Dynamics." *Journal of Political Economy* 84: 1161–76.

———. 1986. "Inflation, Exchange Rates and Stabilization." *Essays in International Finance*, no. 165. Princeton, NJ: Department of Economics, Princeton University.

Durnbusch, R. 1987. "Lessons from the German Inflation Experience of the 1920s." In *Macroeconomics and Finance: Essays in Honor of Franco Modigliani*, ed. R. Dornbusch, S. Fischer, and J. Bossons. Cambridge, MA: The MIT Press.

———. 1988a. *Exchange Rates and Inflation.* Cambridge, MA: MIT Press.

———. 1988b. "Mexico: Stabilization, Debt, and Growth." *Economic Policy* 7: 233–81. Reprinted in Dornbusch, *Stabilization, Debt, and Reform*: 325–66.

———. 1993. *Stabilization, Debt, and Reform.* Englewood Cliffs, NJ: Prentice Hall.

Dornbusch, R., D.V. Dantas, C. Pechman, R. de Rezende Rocha, and D. Simoes. 1983. "The Black Market for Dollars in Brazil." *Quarterly Journal of Economics*, pp. 25–40.

Dornbusch, R., and J.C. de Pablo. 1990. "Debt and Macroeconomic Instability in Argentina." In *Developing Country Debt and Economic Performance*, vol. 2, ed. J.D. Sachs. Chicago: University of Chicago Press, 39–155.

Dornbusch, R., and S. Edwards, eds. 1991. *The Macroeconomics of Populism in Latin America.* Chicago: University of Chicago Press.

———. 1994. "Exchange Rate Policy and Trade Strategy." In *The Chilean Economy: Policy Lessons and Challenges*, ed. B.P. Bosworth, R. Dornbusch, and R. Labán. Washington, D.C.: The Brookings Institution.

Dornbusch, R., and M.H. Simonsen. 1988. "Inflation Stabilization: The Role of Incomes Policy and of Monetization." In *Exchange Rates and Inflation*, ed. R. Dornbusch, 439–65. Cambridge, MA: MIT Press.

Dornbusch, R., F. Sturzenegger, and H. Wolf. 1990. "Extreme Inflation: Dynamics and Stabilization." *Brookings Papers on Economic Activity* 2, 1–84.

Drake, P.W., ed. 1994. *Money Doctors, Foreign Debts, and Economic Reforms in Latin America from the 1890s to the Present*. Wilmington, DE: Scholarly Resources.

Driffill, J., G. Mizon, and A. Ulph. 1990. "Costs of Inflation." In *Handbook of Monetary Economics*, ed. B.M. Friedman and F.H. Hahn. New York: Elsevier Science Publishers.

Eckstein, O. 1981. *Core Inflation*. Englewood Cliffs, NJ: Prentice Hall.

Edwards, S. 1985. "Stabilization with Liberalization: An Evaluation of Ten Years of Chile's Experiment with Free Market Policies, 1973–1983." *Economic Development and Cultural Change* 33: 223–54.

———. 1986. "The Order of Liberalization of the Current and Capital Accounts of the Balance of Payments." In *Economic Liberalization in Developing Countries*, ed. A.M. Choksi and D. Papageorgiou. New York: Basil Blackwell.

———. 1992. "The Sequencing of Structural Adjustment and Stabilization." Occasional Paper no. 34. San Francisco: International Center for Economic Growth.

———. 1993a. "Openness, Trade Liberalization, and Growth in Developing Countries." *Journal of Economic Literature* 31: 1358–93.

———. 1993b. "Exchange Rates as Nominal Anchors." *Welwirtschaftliches Archiv* 129: 1–32.

Edwards, S., and L. Ahamed, eds. 1986. *Economic Adjustment and Exchange Rates in Developing Countries*. Chicago: The University of Chicago Press.

Edwards, S., and A. Cox-Edwards. 1991. *Monetarism and Liberalization: The Chilean Experiment*. Chicago: University of Chicago Press.

Edwards, S., and F.J. Losada. 1994. "Fixed Exchange Rates, Inflation and Macroeconomic Discipline." National Bureau of Economic Research, NBER Working Paper no. 4661.

El Mallakh, R., O. Noreng, and B.W. Poulson. 1984. *Petroleum and Economic Development: The Cases of Mexico and Norway*. Lexington, MA: Lexington Books.

Engle, R. 1982. "Autoregressive Conditional Heteroskedasticity with Estimates of the Variance of U.K. Inflation." *Econometrica* 50: 987–1008.

———. 1983. "Estimates of the Variance of U.S. Inflation Based upon the ARCH Model." *Journal of Money, Credit and Banking* 15: 286–301.

Engle, R.F., and C.W. Granger. 1991. *Long-Run Economic Relationships: Readings in Cointegration*. Oxford: Oxford University Press.

Epstein, E. 1987. "Recent Stabilization Plans in Argentina, 1973–1986." *World Development* August, vol. 15, 191–1005.

Evans, M. 1991. "Discovering the Link between Inflation Rates and Inflation Uncertainty." *Journal of Money, Credit and Banking* 23:169–84.

Fair, R. 1987. "International Evidence on the Demand for Money." *Review of Economics and Statistics* 69:473–80.

Faria, H.P. 1988. "Macroeconomic Policymaking in a Crisis Environment: Brazil's Cruzado Plan and Beyond." In *Brazil's Economic and Political Future*, ed. J.P. Chacel, et al., pp. 42–59. Boulder, CO: Westview Press.

Feige, E.L., and D.K. Pearce. 1977. "The Substitutability of Money and Near-Monies: A Survey of Time-Series Evidence." *Journal of Economic Literature* 15: 439–69.

Feinberg, R. 1990. "Comment." In *Latin Amnerican Adjustment: How much has Happened*, J. Williamson, ed., Washington, DC: Institute for International Economics.

Fernández, R.B. 1985. "The Expectations Management Approach to Stabilization in Argentina during 1976–82." *World Development* 13: 871–92.

Fernández, R.B., and C.A. Rodríguez, eds. 1980. *Inflación y Estabilidad*. Buenos Aires: Macchi.

Fischer, S. 1977. "Long Term Contracts, Rational Expectations, and the Optimal Money Supply Rule." *Journal of Political Economy* 85: 191–205.

———. 1981a. "Toward an Understanding of the Costs of Inflation, II." In *The Costs and Consequences of Inflation*, ed. K. Brunner and A. Meltzer, vol. 15, *Carnegie-Rochester Conference Series on Public Policy*, 5–41.

———. 1981b. "Relative Shocks, Relative Price Variability, and Inflation." *Brookings Papers on Economic Activity* 2: 381–431.

———. 1986. *Indexing, Inflation, and Economic Policy*, Cambridge, MA: MIT Press.

———. 1987. "Economic Growth and Economic Policy." In *Growth Oriented Adjustment Programs*, ed. V. Corbo, M. Goldstein, and M. Khan. Washington, DC: IMF and the World Bank.

Fischer, S., and F. Modigliani. 1975. "Towards an Understanding of the Real Effects and Costs of Inflation." *Weltwirtschaftliches Archiv* 114: 810–33.

Fishlow, A. 1974. "Indexing Brazilian Style: Inflation without Tears?" *Brookings Papers on Economic Activity* 1: 261–282.

Fishlow, A., and J. Friedman. 1994. "Tax Evasion, Inflation, and Stabilization." *Journal of Development Economics* 43: 105–23.

Foreign Investment Committee. 1993. *Foreign Investment Statute, Decree Law 600*. Santiago: Republic of Chile.

Forum Gazeta Mercantil. 1983. *FMI x Brasil: a Armadilha da recessão*. São Paulo: Gazeta Mercantil.

Foxley, A. 1980. "Stabilization Policies and Stagflation: The Cases of Brazil and Chile." *World Development* 8: 887–912.

———. 1983. *Latin American Experiments in Neo-Conservative Economics*. Berkeley: University of California Press.

Frankel, J. 1979. "On the Mark: A Theory of Floating Exchange Rates Based on Real Interest Differentials." *American Economic Review* 69: 610–22.

Frenkel, J. 1981. "Flexible Exchange Rates, Prices and the Role of 'News': Lessons from the 1970s." *Journal of Political Economy* 89: 665–705.

———. 1982. "The Order of Economic Liberalization: A Comment." *Carnegie-Rochester Conference on Public Policy* 17: 199–201.

Frenkel, R. 1984. "Salários industriales e inflación: el período 1976–1982." *Desarrollo económico* 24.

Friedman, M., ed. 1956. *Studies in the Quantity of Money*. Chicago: University of Chicago Press.

———. 1968. "The Role of Monetary Policy." *American Economic Review* 58: 1–17.

———. 1969. "The Optimum Supply of Money." In *The Optimum Supply of Money and other Essays*, M. Friedman, ed. Chicago: University of Chicago Press.

———. 1974. "Money Correction." In H. Giersch, ed., *Essays on Inflation and Indexation*, pp. 25–61. Washington, DC: American Enterprise Institute for Public Policy Research.

———. 1977a. "Time Perspective in Demand for Money." *Scandinavian Journal of Economics* 4: 397–416.

———. 1977b. "Nobel Lecture: Inflation and Unemployment." *Journal of Political Economy* 85: 451–72.

Gerlach, S., and F. Nadal de Simone. 1985. "A Money Demand Equation for Brazil: Comments and Additional Evidence." *Journal of Development Economics* 18: 493–501.

Gordon, R.J. 1982. "Price Inertia and Policy Ineffectiveness in the United States. 1890–1980." *Journal of Political Economy* 90: 1087–1117.

Goulet, D. 1983. *Mexico: Development Strategies for the Future.* Notre Dame: University of Notre Dame Press.

Granger, C.W.J., and P. Newbold. 1974. "Spurious Regressions in Econometrics." *Journal of Econometrics* 2: 111–20.

Gray, J.A. 1976. "Wage Indexation : A Macroeconomic Approach." *Journal of Monetary Economics* 2: 221–36.

Gregorio, J., P.E. Guidotti, and C.A. Végh. 1993. "Inflation Stabilization and the Consumption of Durable Goods." Working Paper, Research Department, IMF. Washington, DC.

Gribomont, C., and M. Rimez. 1977. "La política económica del gobierno de Luis Echeverría (1970–1976): un primer ensayo de interpretación." *El trimestre económico* 44.

Griffith, V. 1992. "Joining the Club." *Latin Finance*, (March): 8–22.

Grilli, V., D. Masciandaro, and G. Tabellini. 1991. "Political and Monetary Institutions and Public Finance Policies in the Industrial Countries." *Economic Policy* 13: 341–92.

Grossman, G.M., and E. Helpman. "Endogenous Innovation in the Theory of Growth." *Journal of Economic Perspectives* 8: 23–44.

Gruben, W.G., J.H. Welch, and J.W. Gunther. 1994. "U.S. Banks, Competition, and the Mexican Banking System: How Much Will NAFTA Matter?" Research Department Discussion Paper no. 94–10, Federal Reserve Bank of Dallas.

Handelman, H., and W. Baer, eds. 1989. *Paying the Costs of Austerity in Latin America.* Boulder, CO: Westview Press.

Hannan, E.J., and B.G. Quinn. 1979. "The Determination of the Order of an Autoregression." *Journal of Royal Statistical Society* B41:. 190–95.

Hansen, R.D. 1971. *Mexican Economic Development: The Roots of Rapid Growth.* Washington, DC: National Planning Association.

Hanson, J.A. 1980. "The Short Term Relation between Growth and Inflation in Latin America: A Quasi-Rational or Consistent Expectations Approach." *American Economic Review* 70: 972–89.

Harberger, A.C. 1964. "Some Notes on Inflation." In *Inflation and Growth in Latin America*, eds. W. Baer and I. Kerstenetzky, 319–51. Homewood, IL: Irwine.

———. 1982. "The Chilean Economy in the 1970s: Crisis, Stabilization, Liberalization, Reform." *Carnegie-Rochester Conference Series on Public Policy* 17, pp. 115–52.

———. 1986. "A Primer on the Chilean Economy, 1973–1983." In *Economic Liberalization in Developing Countries*, ed. A.M. Choksi and D. Papageorgiou. New York: Basil Blackwell.

Helpman, E., and A. Razin. 1987. "Exchange Rate Management: Intertemporal Tradeoffs." *American Economic Review* 77: 107–23.

Hendry, D.F. 1992. "An Econometric Analysis of TV Advertising Expenditure in the United Kingdom." *Journal of Policy Modeling* 14: 281–311.

Hendry, D.F., and J.F. Richard. 1982. "On the Formulation of Empirical Models in Dynamic Econometrics." *Journal of Econometrics* 20: 3–33.

———. 1983. "The Econometric Analysis of Economic Time Series." *International Statistical Review* 51: 111–63.

Hercowitz, Z. 1981. "Money and Dispersion of Relative Prices." *Journal of Political Economy* 89: 328–56.

Heyman, D. 1987. "The Austral Plan." *American Economic Review* 77, no. 2: 284–87.

Hirschman, A.O. 1981. "The Social and Political Matrix of Inflation: Elaborations on the Latin American Experience." In *Essays in Trespassing: Economics to Politics and Beyond*. Cambridge: Cambridge University Press.

Hojman, D. 1993. *Chile: The Political Economy of Development and Democracy in the 1990s*. Pittsburgh: University of Pittsburgh Press.

Ize, A., and J. Salas. 1985. "Prices and Output in the Mexican Economy: Empirical Testing of Alternative Hypotheses." *Journal of Development Economics* 17: 175–99.

Jackson, D., H. Turner, and F. Wilkinson. 1972. *Do Trade Unions Cause Inflation?* Cambridge: Cambridge University Press.

Jarque, C.M., and A. Bera. 1980. "Efficient Tests for Normality, Homoscedasticity and Serial Independence of Regression Residuals." *Economic Letters* 6: 255–59.

Johansen, S. 1988. "Statistical Analysis of Cointegration Vectors." *Journal of Economic Dynamics and Control* 12: 231–54.

Johansen, S., and K. Juselius. 1990. "Maximum Likelihood Estimation and Inference on Cointegration with Application to the Demand for Money." *Oxford Bulletin of Economics and Statistics* 52: 169–210.

Johnson, O., 1984. "On Growth and Inflation in Developing Countries." *International Monetary Fund Staff Paper* 31: 636–60.

Jones, L.E., and R.E. Manuelli. 1993. "Growth and the Effects of Inflation." National Bureau of Economic Research, NBER Working Paper no. 4523.

Júnior, A. 1991. "Moeda indexada e o governo Collor." In *Plano Collor II*, ed. Clovis de Faro. Rio de Janeiro: Livros Técnicos e Científicos Editora Ltda.

Juselius, K. 1992. "Domestic and Foreign Effects on Prices in an Open Economy: The Case of Denmark." *Journal of Policy Modeling* 14: 401–28.

Kaufman, R.R. 1988. *The Politics of Debt in Argentina, Brazil, and Mexico: Economic Stabilization in the 1980s*. Berkeley, CA: Institute of International Studies.

Keating, J. 1990. "Identifying VAR Models under Rational Expectations." *Journal of Monetary Economics* 25: 453–76.

Keynes, J. 1936. *The General Theory of Employment, Interest and Money*. Reprinted in 1964. New York: Harcourt Brace Jovanovich.

Kharas, H. and B. Pinto. 1989. "Exchange Rate Rules, Black Market Premia and Fiscal Deficits: The Bolivian Hyperinflation." *Review of Economic Studies* 56: 435–47.

Kiguel, M.A. 1991. "Inflation in Argentina: Stop and Go since the Austral Plan." *World Development* 19: 969–86.

Kiguel, M., and L. Liviatan. 1987. "Inflationary Rigidities and Orthodox Stabilization Policies." *World Bank Economic Review* 2: 273–98.

———. 1992. "The Business Cycle Associated with Exchange Rate–Based Stabilization." *World Bank Economic Review* 6:. 279–305.

King, T. 1970. *Mexico: Industrialization and Trade Policies since 1940*. London: Oxford University Press.

Krueger, A. 1981. "Interactions between Inflation and Trade Regime Objectives in Stabilization Programs." In *Economic Stabilization in Developing Countries*, ed. W.R. Cline and S. Weintraub. Washington, DC: The Brookings Institution.

Labán, R., and B.F. Larraín. 1994. "The Chilean Experience with Capital Mobility." In *The Chilean Economy: Policy Lessons and Challenges*, ed. B.P. Bosworth, R. Dornbusch, and R. Labán. Washington, DC: The Brookings Institution.

Lagos, L.F. 1992. "Estabilización en Chile: 1975–1980." In *El modelo chileno*, ed. Daniel Wisecarver. Santiago: Instituto de Economía de la PUC de Chile and CINDE.

Laidler, D.E.W. 1985. *The Demand for Money*. 3d ed. New York: Harper and Row.

Lara Resende, A., and F. Lopes. 1981. "Sobre as causas da recente aceleração inflacionária." *Pesquisa e Planejamento Econômico* 11: 599–616.

Larraín, B.F., ed. 1987. *Desarrollo económico en democracia.* Santiago: Ediciones Universidad Católica de Chile.

Larraín, B.F., and P. Meller. 1991. "The Socialist-Populist Chilean Experience: 1970–1973." In *The Macroeconomics of Populism in Latin America,* ed. R. Dornbusch and S. Edwards. Chicago: University of Chicago Press.

Leamer, E. 1985. "Vector Autoregressive for Casual Inference?" In *Understanding Monetary Regimes,* ed. K. Brunner and A. Meltzer. Amsterdam: North-Holland.

Leiderman, L. 1981. "The Demand for Money under Rational Expectations of Inflation: FIML Estimates for Brazil." *International Economic Review* 22: 679–89.

Lemgruber, A.C. 1974. "Inflação: o modelo da realimentação e o modelo da aceleração." *Revista Brasileira de Economia* 28.

———. 1978. *Inflação, moeda e modelos macroeconômicos: o caso do Brasil.* Rio do Janiero: Fundação Getúlio Vargas.

———. 1984. "Real Output-Inflation Trade-Offs, Monetary Growth and Rational Expectations in Brazil, 1950/79." *Brazilian Economic Studies,* no. 8. Rio de Janeiro: IPEA/INPES.

Leontief, W. 1936. "The Fundamental Assumption of Mr. Keynes' Monetary Theory of Unemployment." *Quarterly Journal of Economics* 60: 193.

Liviatan, N. 1986. "Inflation and Stabilization in Israel—Conceptual Issues and Interpretation of Developments." International Monetary Fund: WP/86/10.

Looney, R.E. 1978. *Mexico's Economy: A Policy with Forecasts to 1990.* Boulder, CO: Westview Press.

———. 1985. *Economic Policymaking in Mexico: Factors underlying the 1982 Crisis.* Durham, NC: Duke University Press.

Lopes, F. 1977. "Problemas do controle da inflaçao." In *Brasil: dilema da política econômica,* ed. Dionísio Carneiro. Rio de Janeiro: Editora Campus.

———. 1983. "A crise do endividamento externo: alguns números e suas conseqüências." In *Dívida externa, recessão e ajuste estrutural: o Brasil diante da crise,* ed. Persi Arida. Rio de Janeiro: Paz e Terra.

———. 1984. "Inflation and the Level of Economic Activity in Brazil: An Econometric Study." *Brazilian Economic Review* 8: 225–50.

———. 1986. *O choque heterodoxo: combate à inflação e reforma monetária.* Rio de Janeiro: Editora Campus.

Lora, T.E. 1987. "Una nota sobre la hiperinflación boliviana." *El trimestre económico* 54, núm. especial (septiembre): 213–19.

Loser, C., and E. Kalter, eds. 1992. "Mexico: The Strategy to Achieve Sustained Economic Growth." Occasional Paper No. 99. Washington, D.C.: International Monetary Fund.

Lucas, R.E. 1972a. "Expectations and Neutrality of Money." *Journal of Economic Theory* 4: 103–24.

———. 1972b. "Econometric Testing of Natural Rate Hypothesis." In *The Econometrics of Price Determination,* ed. O. Eckstein. Washington, DC: Board of Governors of the Federal Reserve System.

———. 1973. "Some International Evidence of Output-Inflation Tradeoffs." *American Economic Review* 70: 1005–14.

———. 1977. "Understanding Business Cycles." In *Stabilization of the Domestic and International Economy,* ed. K. Brunner and A.H. Meltzer, Carnegie-Mellon Conference in Public Policy. Amsterdam: North-Holland.

———. 1993. "On the Welfare Cost of Inflation." Working Paper. The University of Chicago.

Lusting, N. 1992. *Mexico: The Remaking of an Economy.* Washington, DC: The Brookings Institution.

McCallum, B. 1990. "Inflation: Theory and Evidence." In *Handbook of Monetary Economics*, ed. B.M. Friedman and F.H. Hahn. New York: Elsevier Science Publishers.

Machinea, J.L., and J.M. Fanelli. 1988. "Stopping Hyperinflation: The Case of the Austral Plan in Argentina: 1985–87." In *Inflation Stabilization: The Experience of Israel, Argentina, Brazil, Bolivia, and Mexico*, ed. M. Bruno, et al. Cambridge, MA: MIT Press.

McKinnon, R.I. 1982. "The Order of Economic Liberalization: Lessons from Chile and Argentina." *Carnegie-Rochester Conference Series on Public Policy* 17, 159–86.

McNown, R., and M. Wallace. 1989. "National Price Levels, Purchasing Power Parity, and Cointegration: A Test for Four High Inflation Economies." *Journal of International Money and Finance* 8: 533–45.

Mann, A.J., and M. Pastor, Jr. 1989. "Orthodox and Heterodox Stabilization Policies in Bolivia and Peru: 1985–1988." *Journal of Interamerican Studies* 31: 163–92.

Marques, M.S.B. 1988. "O Plano Cruzado: teoria e prática." *Revista de economia política* 8, no. 3 (julho/aetembro): 101–30.

Marshall, J., and F. Montt. 1988. "Privatisation in Chile." In *Privatisation in Less Developed Countries*, ed. P. Cook and C. Kirkpatrick. New York: St. Martin's Press, pp. 281–307.

Martínez de Hoz, J.A. 1990. "José Alfredo Martínez de Hoz." *Argentina: 1946–83: The Economic Ministers Speak*, ed. G. di Tella and C.R. Braun. New York: St. Martin's Press.

Maxfield, S. 1990. *Governing Capital: International Finance and Mexican Politics.* Ithaca, NY: Cornell University Press.

Miller, V.J. 1992. "Inflation Uncertainty and the Disappearance of Financial Markets: The Mexican Example." *Journal of Economic Development* 17, no. 1: 131–52.

Modiano, E. 1983. "A dinâmica de salários e preços na economia brasileira: 1966/81." *Pesquisa e planejamento econômico* 13: 39–68.

———. 1985. "Salários, preços e câmbio: os multiplicadores dos choques numa economia indexada." *Pesquisa e planejamento econômico* 15: 1–32.

———. 1988a. "The Cruzado First Attempts: The Brazilian Stabilization Program of February 1986." In *Inflation Stabilization: The Experience of Israel, Argentina, Brazil, Bolivia and Mexico*, ed. M. Bruno, et al. Cambridge, MA: MIT Press.

———. 1988b. *Inflação: inércia e conflito.* Rio de Janeiro: Editora Campus.

Montiel, P. 1989. "Empirical Analysis of High-Inflation Episodes in Argentina, Brazil and Israel." *IMF Staff Papers*, vol. 36.

Morales, J.A. 1988. "Inflation Stabilization in Bolivia." In *Inflation Stabilization: The Experience of Argentina, Brazil, Bolivia and Mexico*, ed. M. Bruno, et al. Cambridge, MA: MIT Press.

Morales, J.A., and J.D. Sachs. 1990. "Bolivia's Economy Crisis." In *Developing Country Debt and Economic Performance*, vol. 2, ed. J.D. Sachs, Chicago: University of Chicago Press.

Moskoff, W., and N. Nazmi. 1992. "Stabilization in the Former Soviet Union: Lessons from Argentina and Brazil." *Comparative Economic Studies* 34, no. 2: 67–81.

Mullineaux, D. 1980. "Unemployment, Industrial Production, and Inflation Uncertainty in the United States." *Review of Economics and Statistics* 62, no. 2: 163–69.

Mussa, M., 1977. "The Welfare Cost of Inflation and the Role of Money as a Unit of Account." *Journal of Money, Credit, and Banking* 9: 276–86.

Muth, J. 1960. "Optimal Properties of Exponentially Weighted Forecasts." *Journal of the American Statistical Association* 55, pp. 299–306.

Nazmi, N. 1990. "Brazilian Inflation Revisited: Another Look at Internal and External Factors." The World Conference of the Econometric Society, Barcelona, Spain.

————. 1993. "Money, Exchange Rates, and Prices: Evidence from SVAR Models." The Latin American Econometrics Society Meetings, Tucumán, Argentina.

Novaes, A.D. 1993. "Revisiting the Inertial Inflation Hypothesis for Brazil." *Journal of Development Economics* 42: 89–110.

Nugent, J., and C. Glezakos. 1982. "Phillips Curves in Developing Countries: The Latin American Case." *Economic Development and Cultural Change*, vol. 30, no. 2, 321–34.

Okun, A.M. 1975. "Inflation: Its Mechanics and Welfare Costs." *Brookings Papers on Economic Analysis* 2: 435–98.

Olivera, J. 1967. "Money, Prices and Fiscal Lags: A Note on the Dynamics of Inflation." *Banca Nazionale del Lavoro, Quarterly Review*, no. 88.

Onis, Z., and S. Osmucur. 1990. "Exchange Rates, Inflation and Money Supply in Turkey." *Journal of Development Economics* 32: 133–54.

Ortega, A.O.E. 1989. *O plano de estabilização heterodoxo: a experiência comparada de Argentina, Brasil e Peru*. Rio de Janeiro: BNDES.

Pack, H. 1994. "Endogenous Growth Theory: Intellectual Appeal and Empirical Shortcomings." *Journal of Economic Perspectives* 8: 55–72.

Parkin, V. 1991. *Chronic Inflation in an Industrializing Economy: The Brazilian Experience*. Cambridge: Cambridge University Press.

Pastor, M. 1991. "Bolivia: Hyperinflation, Stabilization, and Beyond." *Journal of Development Studies* 27: 211–37.

Patinkin, D. 1965. *Money, Interest, and Prices: An Integration of Monetary and Value Theory*. New York: Harper and Row.

Pazos, F. 1972. *Chronic Inflation in Latin America*. New York: Praeger.

Peláez, C.M. 1986. *O cruzado e o austral: análise das reformas monetárias do Brasil e da Argentina*. São Paulo: Editora Atlas.

Perry, G. 1980. "Inflation in Theory and Practice." *Brookings Papers on Economic Activity* 1: 207–41.

Persson, T., and G. Tabellini. 1994. "Is Inequality Harmful to Growth?" *American Economic Review* 84: 600–621.

Phillips, P. 1986, "Understanding Spurious Regressions in Econometrics." *Journal of Econometrics*, 33, 311–40.

Phillips, P.C.B., and P. Perron. 1988. "Testing for a Unit Root in Time Series Regression." *Biometrica* 75: 335–46.

Pinheiro, A.C., and F. Giambiagi. 1994. "Brazilian Privatization in the 1990s." *World Development* 22: 737–53.

Ramirez, M.D. 1986. *Development Banking in Mexico: The Case of the Nacional Financeira, S.A.* New York: Praeger.

————. 1991. "The Impact of Austerity in Latin America, 1983–89: A Critical Assessment." *Comparative Economic Studies* 33: 57–102.

————. 1993. "Stabilization and Trade Reform in Mexico: 1983–1989." *Journal of Developing Areas* 24, no. 2: 173.

————. 1994. "Public and Private Investment in Mexico, 1950–90: An Empirical Analysis." *Southern Economic Journal* 61: 1–17.

Rodríguez, C.A. 1979. "El plan argentino de estabilización del 20 de diciembre." Documento de Trabajo, CEMA.

————. 1980. "Algunas consideraciones teóricas sobre la establidad de reglas alternativas de política cambiaria." Documento de Trabajo, CEMA.

Romer, P.M. "The Origins of Endogenous Growth." *Journal of Economic Perspectives* 8: 3–22.

Ronci, M. 1992. "Uma constituição monetária para o Brasil." *Conjuntura econômica* 46, no. 9: 44–48.

Rossi, J.W. 1989. "The Demand for Money in Brazil: What Happened in the 1980s?" *Journal of Development Economics* 31: 357–67.

Rotemberg, J. J. 1983. "Supply Shocks, Sticky Prices, and Monetary Policy." *Journal of Money, Credit and Banking* 15: 489–98.

Sachs, J.D. 1987a. "The Bolivian Hyperinflation and Stabilization." *American Economic Review* 77: 279–83.

————. 1987b. "Trade and Exchange Rate Policies in Growth-Oriented Adjustment Programs." In *Growth Oriented Adjustment Programs*, eds. V. Corbo, M. Goldstein, and M. Khan. Washington, DC: IMF and the World Bank.

————, ed. 1990. *Developing Country Debt and Economic Performance*, vol. 2. Chicago: University of Chicago Press.

Sargent, T.J. 1986. *Rational Expectations and Inflation*. New York: Harper and Row.

Sargent, T.J., and N. Wallace. 1981. "Some Unpleasant Monetarist Arithmetic." Federal Reserve Bank of Minneapolis, *Quarterly Review*, vol. 5 (Fall): 1–17.

Sarney, J. 1988. "Brazil: A President's Story." In *Brazil's Economic and Political Future*, ed. J. Chacel, et al., 97–106. Boulder, CO: Westview Press.

Sayad, J. 1988. "Brazil's Economic Stabilization Plan: An Analysis." In *Brazil's Economic and Political Future*, ed. J. Chacel, et al., 9–16. Boulder, CO: Westview Press.

Schwarz, G. 1978. "Estimating the Dimension of Model." *Annals of Statistics* 6: 461–64.

Scymczak, P. 1992. "International Trade and Investment Liberalization: Mexico's Experience and Prospects." In *The Strategy to Achieve Sustained Economic Growth*, ed. C. Loser and E. Kalter. Washington, DC: IMF.

Secretaría de Patrimonio y Fomento Industrial. 1979. *Plan nacional de desarrollo industrial, 1979–1982*. Mexico City: SPFI.

Sheahan, J. 1991. *Conflict and Change in Mexican Economic Strategy: Implications for Mexico and for Latin America*. San Diego: Center for U.S.-Mexican Studies.

Sheshinski, E., and Y. Weiss. 1977. "Inflation and the Cost of Price Adjustment." *Review of Economic Studies* 44: 287–303.

Sidrauski, M. 1967a. "Rational Choice and Patterns of Growth in a Monetary Economy." *American Economic Review* 57: 534–44.

————. 1967b. "Inflation and Economic Growth." *Journal of Political Economy* 75: 796–810.

Simonsen, M.H. 1970. *Inflação: gradualismo & tratamento de choque*. Rio de Janeiro: APEC Editôra S.A.

————. 1983. "Indexation: Current Theory and the Brazilian Experience." In *Inflation, Debt, and Indexation*, ed. R. Dornbusch and M.H. Simonsen. Cambridge, MA: MIT Press.

————. 1984. "Inflation and Anti-Inflationary Policies in Brazil." *Brazilian Economic Studies* 8: 1–35.

————. 1988. "Inércia inflacionária e inflação inercial." ANPEC no. 122. Also in *Plano Cruzado: inércia x inépcia*, ed. F.H. Barbosa and M.H. Simonsen. Rio de Janeiro: Globo.

Simonsen, M.H., and R.P. Cysne. 1989. *Macroeconomia*. Rio de Janeiro: Ao Livro Técnico.

Sims, C. 1980. "Macroeconomics and Reality." *American Economic Review* 48: 1–49.

————. 1986. "Are Forecasting Models Usable for Policy Analysis?" Federal Reserve Bank of Minneapolis, *Quarterly Review* (Winter): 2–16.

Skidmore, T. 1976. *Brasil de Getúlio a Castelo*. Rio de Janeiro: Editora Paz e Terra.

Surrey, M.J. 1989. "Money, Commodity Prices and Inflation: Some Simple Tests." *Oxford Bulletin of Economics and Statistics* 51: 219–38.

Svensson, L.E.O. 1993. "The Simplest Test of Inflation Target Credibility." National Bureau of Economic Research, NBER Working Paper no. 4604.

———. 1994. "Fixed Exchange Rates as a Means to Price Stability: What Have We Learned." *European Economic Review* 38: 447–68.

Syvrud, D. 1974. *Foundations of Brazilian Economic Growth*, Stanford, CA: Hoover Institute Press.

Tanzi, V. 1989. "Fiscal Policy, Stabilization, and Growth." In *Fiscal Policy, Stabilization and Growth in Developing Countries*, ed. M. Blejer and K. Chu. Washington, DC: IMF.

Tavares, M., and L. Belluzzo. 1984. "Uma reflexão sobre a natureza da inflação contemporânea." Texto Para Discussão, 65. Rio de Janeiro: IEI/UFRJ.

Taylor, J.B. 1979. "Staggered Wage Setting in a Macro Model." *American Economic Review (Papers and Proceedings)* 69: 108–13.

———. 1980. "Aggregate Dynamics and Staggered Contracts." *Journal of Political Economy* 88: 1–23.

———. 1986. "Improvements in Macroeconomic Stability: The Role of Wages and Prices." In *The American Business Cycle*, vol. 3, ed. R. Gordon. pp. 43–51. Chicago: University of Chicago Press.

Taylor, L. 1983. *Structuralist Macroeconomics: Applicable Models for the Third World*. New York: Basic Books.

———. 1993, "Stabilization, Adjustment, and Reform." In *The Rocky Road to Reform: Adjustment, Income Distribution, and Growth in the Developing World*, L. Taylor, ed. Cambridge, MA: The MIT Press.

Teichman, J.A. 1988. *Policymaking in Mexico: From Boom to Crisis*. Boston: Allen and Unwin.

Tobin, J. 1965. "Money and Economic Growth." *Econometrica* 33: 671–84.

———. 1972. "Inflation and Unemployment." *American Economic Review* 62:1–18.

———. 1976. *Inflation Control as Policy Priority*. New Haven: Yale University Press.

———. 1981. "Diagnosing Inflation: A Taxonomy." In *Development in an Inflationary World*, ed. M.J. Flandez and A. Razin. New York: Academic Press.

Triches, D. 1992. "Demanda por moeda no Brasil e a casualidade entre as variáveis monetárias e a taxa de inflação: 1972–87." Dissertação de Mestrado. Rio de Janeiro: 16— Prêmio BNDES de Economia.

van de Walle, N. 1989. "Privatization in Developing Countries: A Review of the Issues." *World Development* 17: 601–615.

van Wijnbergen, S. 1982. "Stagflationary Effects of Monetary Stabilization Policies: A Quantitative Analysis of South Korea." *Journal of Development Economics* 10: 133–69.

———. 1983. "Credit Policy, Inflation and Growth in a Financially Repressed Economy." *Journal of Development Economics* 13: 45–64.

Wachter, S. 1976. *Latin American Inflation*. Lexington, MA: Lexington Books.

Weiss, J. "Variability of Inflation in Brazil, 1974–1982." *Journal of Economic Development* 14, 1.

———. 1992. "Trade Liberalization in Mexico in the 1980s: Concepts, Measures and Short Run Effects." *Weltwirtschaftliches Archiv* 128: 711–26.

Welch, J. 1989. "Variability of Inflation in Brazil, 1974–1982." *Journal of Economic Development* 14, 1.

———. 1991. "Rational Inflation and Real Internal Debt Bubbles in Argentina and Brazil?" Federal Reserve Bank of Dallas, Research Department.

Werneck, R.F. 1987. *Empresas estatáis e política macroeconômica*. Rio de Janeiro: Editora Campus.

Werner, M. 1992. "La solvencia del sector público: el caso de México en 1988." *El trimestre económico* 59, no. 236: 751–72.

Williamson, J., ed. 1985. *Inflation and Indexation: Argentina, Brazil, and Israel.* Washington, DC: Institute for International Economics.

———, ed. 1990a. *Latin American Adjustment: How Much Has Happened?* Washington, DC: Institute for International Economics.

———. 1990b. "What Washington Means by Policy Reform." In *Latin American Adjustment: How Much Has Happened?*, ed. J. Williamson.

Wisecarver, D., ed. 1992. *El modelo chileno.* Santiago: Instituto de Economía de la Pontificia Universidad Católica de Chile and Centro Internacional Para el Desarrollo Económico.

World Bank. 1979. *Chile: An Economy in Transition.* Washington, DC: The International Bank for Reconstruction and Development.

Yeager, L. 1981. *Experiences with Stopping Inflation.* Washington, DC: American Enterprise Institute for Public Policy Research.

Yoshino, J.A. 1991. "Money and Banking Regulation: The Social Costs of Inflation." Working Paper, The University of Chicago.

Yoshino, J., and L.M. Lopes. 1990. "Liquidez bloqueada: superávits aos 18 meses!" *Informações, Fipe*, no. 118 (março/abril): 7–9.

Zedillo, E. 1987. "Mexico." In *Capital Flight and Third World Debt*, ed. D.R. Lessard and J. Williamson. Washington, DC: Institute for International Economics.

Index

A

adaptive expectations model, 19, 134
Aléman, Roberto, 116
Alfonsín, Raul, 117, 122
Allende, Salvador, 72
ARCH model, 33
Argentina, 11, 12, 132, 133, 134,
    166, 168, 169
  Austral plan, 48, 117–119, 126
  balance of payments, 115
  BIR, 115
  BONEX, 123
  and Brady plan, 125
  Bunge y Born, 122
  Cavallo plan, 65, 123–126, 133
  capital account, 115, 116
  central bank, 115, 122
  Convertibility plan, see Cavallo
    plan
  cost-push factors, 119
  deficit-GDP ratio, 115, 116,
    122
  devaluation, 115, 122
  dollarization, 122
  Economic Emergency Law, 123

Argentina (continued)
  exchange rate, 115,116, 117, 122,
    123
  export sector, 114, 116
  fiscal deficit, 115, 117, 118
  foreign reserves, 115, 122
  hyperinflation, 121
  and IMF, 117, 118, 122
  indexation, 117, 123
  inflation, 117–119, 122–123
  Law of Convertibility, 123
  military regime, 113
  monetary base, 115
  monetary policy, 122
  nominal anchor, 116, 123
  overvaluation, 115
  Primavera plan, 121
  private sector foreign debt, 115,
    116
  privatization, 125
  reserves, 122
  Spring plan, 121
  Tablita plan, 113–116, 165
  VAT, 117
  wages, 117, 118, 122, 123
Australito, 119

Arida, Persio, 48
Aylwin, Patricio, 85

B

Bacha, Edmar, 48, 65
balance of payments. *See specific countries*
balance of trade, 9, *See also specific countries*
Baumol-Tobin model, 139
Bolivia, 11, 12, 112, 126, 168, 169
  balance of payments, 126
  current account, 130
  devaluation, 127
  economic growth, 132
  exchange rate, 130
  export sector, 127
  external shocks, 126
  foreign debt, 126
  gasoline tax, 130
  and IMF, 132
  inflation, 127
  and Mexican moratorium, 126
  mineral and hydrocarbon products, 126
  New Economic Policy, 129–132
  nominal anchor, 130
  orthodox policies, 127
  public deficit, 126, 127, 129
  seigniorage, 126
  structural reform in, 131
  tax reform, 131
  terms of trade, 126
  UDP, 126
Brady plan, 105, 125
Branco, Castelo, 40

Brazil, 11, 12, 14, 126, 132, 133, 134, 166, 168, 169
  abertura, 44
  Bresser plan, 38
  balance of payments, 44, 46, 50, 135, 140
  budget deficit, 41, 59, 62
  Collor plan, 37, 38, 55–64, 165
  Collor plan II, 38
  consumtion boom, 66
  cost of inflation in, 34–36
  Cruzado plan, 38, 47–52, 53, 65
  Cruzado plan II, 38, 50
  econometric models of inflation, 28–30, 143–162
  exchange rate, 14, 50
  foreign capital inflow, 44, 66
  income redistribution, 39
  indexation, 36, 41, 48, 63, 38
  inflation in, 15, 22–23, 34, 39, 135, 136, 163
  inflation expectation in, 145
  and IMF, 44, 46
  and Mexican moratorium, 46
  military regimes' economic policies in, 39–47
  and oil shocks, 42–44
  Phillips curve in, 28–29
  populist-developmentist policies, 43
  price freezes, 49–53, 56, 58
  Programa de Açãoes Econômica do Governo, PAEG, 40
  Real plan, 64–68
  Second National Development Plan, 42
  social pact, 46
  Summer plan, 38, 53–54
  terms of trade, 14

Brazil *(continued)*
  Third National Development Plan,
    44
  URV (Real Unit of Value), 65
Brazilian Miracle, 41–42
Bresser Pereira, Luiz, 52–53
Bresser plan, 38
Bretten Woods, 42
Büchi, Hernán, 79
budget constraint, 20
Bulhões, Octavio, 40

C

Campos, Roberto, 40
capital flight, 9. *See also specific*
    countries
Cardoso, Fernando Henrique, 64–65
Cauas, Jorge, 73
Cavallo, Domingo, 116, 123, 124
Cavallo plan, 65, 123–126, 133
Central Bank, 21. *See also specific*
    countries
Chile, 10, 11–12, 167, 168
  capital account, 78–79
  capital inflow, 76–77, 85
  central bank, independence of, 84
  consumption boom, 76
  copper prices, 78
  and corrective inflation, 72
  economic crises, 1981–84, 77–79
  economic miracle, 75–77
  exchange rate, 80, 84, 85
  export sector, 80–84
  forestry, 81
  foreign capital, 85
  foreign debt, 78
  foreign investment, 85
  external balance, 74

Chile *(continued)*
  indexation, 75
  infrastructure investment, 82–83
  interest rates, 85
  labor cost, 83–84
  and laissez faire economics, 78
  macroeconomic populism in, 71
  mining sector, 80–81
  military dictatorship in, 71
  oil shock and, 74
  privatization, 74, 79–80
  Program for Economic
    Recuperation, PRE, 73
  public sector deficit, 72
  popular capitalism, 79
  Popular Unity government, 72
  sequencing of external accounts
    opening, 78–79
  Tablita plan, 75–77
  tax reform, 72
  timing of external accounts
    opening, 79
chronic inflation, 13
  defined, 14
cointegration, 12, 135–136, 143–144
Collor, Fernando, 54–55, 64
Collor plan, 37, 38, 55–64, 165
Collor plan II, 38
Convertibility plan, *see* Cavallo plan
CORFO, 74
costs of inflation, 30–36
credibility, 20
Cruzado plan, 38, 47–52, 53, 65
Cruzado plan II, 38, 50

D

de la Madrid, Miguel, 100, 103, 104
de Hoz, Martínez, 115, 116

deregulation, 5, 71, 77, 79, 86, 122
Dornelles, Francisco, 47–48

E

Echeverría, Luis Alvárez, 90–91
ECLA, *see* United Nations
    Economic Commission on Latin
    America
Economic Emergency Law, 123
economic reform, 7, 8, 113
Equation of Exchange, 16, 137
error correction, 12, 135–136
exchange rate anchor, 9, 10, 66, 68,
    71, 75, 76, 79, 103, 105, 107,
    111, 112, 116, 122, 123, 124,
    130, 169–170. *See also specific
    countries. See also nominal
    anchors.*
exchange rate uncertainty, 171
expectations, 9, 16, 18–20, 21, 25,
    52, 58, 97, 113, 114, 134, 140,
    145, 150, 151
    adaptive, 19, 134
    rational, 19, 20, 27

F

Figueiredo, João Baptista, 43
fiscal deficit, 9, 16, 21, 25, 91, 102,
    105, 113, 116, 118, 121, 122,
    129, 133
    and foreign resources, 11, 21–22
fiscal balance, 5, 8, 10, 117, 167
fiscal equilibrium, 7, 65, 75, 100,
    119, 166–168
fiscal policy, 5, 15, 20–22, 27, 28,
    37, 40, 42, 43, 46, 47, 52, 69,
    84, 85, 91, 116. *See also
    specific countries.*

fiscal reform, 38, 65, 73–75, 102,
    117, 129–130
Fisher Equation, 16
foreign reserves, 22, 42, 53, 66, 76,
    85, 97
Franco, Itamar, 64
free rider (externality), 8
FRS, 63
Funaro, Dilson, 48, 50

G

GATT (General Agreement on
    Trade and Tariffs), 99, 102
Geisel, Ernesto, 42
German hyperinflation, 23
German stabilization program, 57
Goulart, João, 39–40

H

homogeneity postulate, 17
hyperinflation, 11, 30, 38, 121
    in Bolivia, 112, 126, 127, 129, 131,
        133
    in Brazil, 55
    defined, 14
    in Germany, 23
    in Hungary, 57
    in Latin America, 14

I

International Monetary Fund (IMF),
    5, 11, 44, 46, 91, 97, 98, 99, 100,
    102,112, 117, 118, 122, 132, 166.
    See also specific countries.
import substitution industrialization
    (ISI), 6–7

IOF, 58
income distribution, 165, 168. *See also specific countries.*
incomes policies, 15
independent monetary authority, 21
indexation
  of wages, 9, 14
inertial inflation, 134
  and hyperinflation, 14
  and fights for shares, 20
inflation, 13–17, 19–28, 37. *See also specific countries.*
  causes of, 16
  chronic, 13–14
  cointegration analysis of, 142–148
  costs of, 16, 30–36
  defined, 13
  effects, 37
  and efficiency loss, 37
  empirical evidence, 28–30
  error correction model of, 149–151
  estimation of inertial component of, 151–162
  forecast error variance for, 160–162
  gradualist approach to, 41
  and income distribution, 34–35, 37, 111
  inertia, 8, 14, 25–28, 117
  monetarist view of, 17
  neoclassical model of, 14
  neostructuralist model of, 14
  neostructuralist view of, 23
  and price uncertainty, 32–33
  SVAR model for, 157–162
  and time horizon of contracts, 139
  VAR model for, 151–156
  variability, 33
  wealth redistribution, 35

inflation stabilization
  gradualist approach, 41
  orthodox approach, 5
  output cost, 15, 18–19
  and structural idiosyncrasies, 9, 48
informaton asymmetry, 18
integration order, 141
investment-GDP ratio, 171

K

Keynes, John M., 17, 25
Keynesian economics, 5, 71

L

labor productivity, 137
Lara Resende, Andre, 27, 48, 65
LIBOR, 98, 105
long run dynamics, 142–143
Lopes, Francisco, 48

M

macroeconomic populism
  in Brazil, 40
  in Chile, 71
  in Mexico, 87, 169
market imperfections, 6
mark up factor, 135–136
Medici, Emilio, 42
Menem, Carlos, 122
Mexican miracle, 87
Mexican moratorium, 46, 126
Mexico, 10, 126, 133, 167, 168
  balance of payments, 107
  and the Brady plan, 105
  capital account, 103

Mexico *(continued)*
  current account, 92
  debt-equity swap, 105
  devaluation, 95, 97, 100
  dollarization, 100
  and Dutch disease, 92
  economic crises, 1982–87, 92–100
  Economic Soldarity Pact, 100, 102,
    103, 105
  education, 89, 90, 110
  exchange rate, 105, 111
  foreign debt, 91, 93
  foriegn investment, 107
  foriegn reserves, 97
  and GATT, 99, 102
  health, 89, 90
  human capital, 89, 90
  import license requirements, 88
  import substitution, 88–89
  import tariffs, 102
  and IMF, 91, 97, 98, 99, 100, 102
  income distribution, 89
  indexation, 97
  inertial inflation, 97
  inflation rate, 1954–70, 88
  monetary policy, 107
  and NAFTA, 107
  oil prices, 97, 99
  oil reserves, 91
  oil shock, 91
  Pact for Stability and Economic
    Growth (PSG), 105
  and the Paris Club,.97
  petrolium exports, 92
  PIRE, 97
  PRI, 108
  and protectionism, 89
  primary deficit, 105
  private investment,.98

Mexico *(continued)*
  private sector in, 88
  privatization, 105
  public deficit, 97, 102, 104,
    105
  public investment, 98
  public sector, 90, 100, 102
  public sector borrowing
    requirement, 97, 102
  and the Reagan administration,
    100
  social programs, 109–110
  social security, 90
  shock therapy, 97
  stabilizing development in, 88–
    89
  stock market, 100, 107
  structural problems, 88
  terms of trade, 103
  trade liberalization, 103
  wages, 108–109, 110
  and the World Bank, 97
money demand, 138–139
monetary policy
  and real variables, 20
  independence of, 21

N

NAFTA (North American Free
    Trade Agreement), 107
neo-Keynesian, 15
neoliberalism, 6
neostructuralism, 23–28
Neto, Delfim, 43, 44, 47
neutrality postulate, 18–19
Neves, Tancredo, 47
New Economic Policy, 129–132
Nicaragua, 14

nominal anchors, 9, 27, 71, 75, 76, 87, 102, 103, 105, 107, 111, 112, 116, 123, 130, 132, 133, 134, 166, 167, 169–170. *See also exchange rate anchor.*

O

Olivera-Tanzi effect, 118, 127
OPEC, 94–95
OTN, 139

P

Paris Club, 97, 132
Pastore, José, 116
Peron, Isabel, 113
Peru, 14
Phillips curve, 18, 19, 28–29
Pinochet, Augusto, 72
PEMEX, 94–95
PMDP, 47–48
Popular Unity government, 72
Portillo, López, 92, 97
price uncertainty, 32–33, 34, 36
PRI, 98
Primavera plan, 121
privatization, 7, 11, 168. *See also specific countries.*
   in Argentina, 125
   in Chile, 168
   and Collor plan, 58–59
production bottlenecks, 6
Programa de Açãoes Econômica do Governo, PAEG, 40
Program for Economic Recuperation, PRE, 73
property rights, 5
protectionism, 12, 170, 171
purchasing power parity, 22

R

rational bubbles, 20, 23
rational expectations, 19
Real plan, 64–68
reform programs, 6. *See also specific countries.*

S

Salinas, Carlos de Gortari, 105
São Paulo, 133
Sarney, José, 47, 53
Sayad, João, 47–48, 49
seigniorage, 126
sequencing
   stabilization and adjustment, 6, 8
   trade and capital accounts opening, 71, 78–79
   and timing of opening external accounts, 79
Sigaut, Lorenzo, 116
Simonsen, Mário, 43, 47, 65
simultaneity bias, 29
South Korea, 43
Spring plan, 121
stabilization. *See also specific countries*
   hetrodox approach, 11
   mixed policies, 11
   monetarist view, 17
   orthodox approach, 6, 11
   "social-democratic" approach to 14
stabilization and economic growth, 17, 19, 133, 170–171
stabilization and fiscal balance, 8
state
   as coordinator, 8

state *(continued)*
  enterprises, 49, 51
  the role of, 5, 6, 8, 11, 12
stationary series, 141
strato-inflation, 26
structural VAR models (SVAR),
  136, 164
structuralist view, 11
Summer plan, 38, 53–54

T

Tablita plan
  in Chile, 75–77
  in Argentina, 113–116,
  165
Tlateloco massacre, 90
two-gap model, 12

U

unit roots, 144, 145
United Nations Economic
  Commission for Latin America
  (ECLA),7, 11

V

vector autoregressive models
  (VAR), 136, 143, 144, 148,
  164

W

wage equation, 137
wage indexation, 9, 14. *See also*
  specific countries
wages, 117, 118, 122, 123
Washington consensus, 5, 171

About the Author

Nader Nazmi received his M.S. and Ph.D. from the University of Illinois in Urbana-Champaign. He has been the recipient of various awards and research grants, including a Fulbright-Hayes fellowship. He has been a visiting scholar at the Center for Research on Economic Development at the University of Michigan and is an associate professor at Lake Forest College. He has published extensively in various journals and is a frequent traveler to Latin America.

For Product Safety Concerns and Information please contact our EU
representative GPSR@taylorandfrancis.com
Taylor & Francis Verlag GmbH, Kaufingerstraße 24, 80331 München, Germany

www.ingramcontent.com/pod-product-compliance
Ingram Content Group UK Ltd.
Pitfield, Milton Keynes, MK11 3LW, UK
UKHW020941180425
457613UK00019B/499